LOOKING
FOR THE
LIGHT

Marion Post Wolcott, on assignment in Vermont, 1940

LOOKING

FOR THE

LIGHT

THE HIDDEN LIFE
AND ART OF
MARION
POST
WOLCOTT

PAUL
HENDRICKSON

ALFRED A. KNOPF NEW YORK 1992

OWING TO LIMITATIONS OF SPACE, ALL ACKNOWLEDGMENTS

OF PERMISSION TO REPRINT PREVIOUSLY PUBLISHED

MATERIAL WILL BE FOUND AT THE END OF THE BOOK.

GRATEFUL ACKNOWLEDGMENT IS MADE TO THE ESTATE OF MARION POST WOLCOTT

FOR USE OF HER PHOTOGRAPHS.

LIBRARY OF CONGRESS CATALOGING-IN-PUBLICATION DATA

HENDRICKSON, PAUL.

LOOKING FOR THE LIGHT : THE HIDDEN LIFE AND ART OF MARION POST

WOLCOTT / PAUL HENDRICKSON. — IST ED.

P.   CM.

ISBN 0-394-57729-9

I. WOLCOTT, MARION POST, 1910–1990.   2. PHOTOGRAPHERS—UNITED

STATES—BIOGRAPHY.   I. TITLE.

TR140.W64H46   1992

770'.92—DC20

[B]   91-24658 CIP

MANUFACTURED IN THE UNITED STATES OF AMERICA

FIRST EDITION

For Ceil, who has Marion's strength all over again

I believe our minds have music that can lead us through the tangle to the lost stone of a friend.

—RICHARD HUGO

"December 24 and George McBride Is Dead"

CONTENTS

ACKNOWLEDGMENTS

A BOOK, LIKE A LIFE, has surprises. This book was conceived as a short-term substitute project. That was several years and three drafts and two editors ago. Numerous individuals and several institutions have my deep gratitude. I am indebted to the Lyndhurst Foundation in Chattanooga for providing general financial support on writing projects with no interference. I am grateful to the Washington *Post*—especially Ben Bradlee, Leonard Downie, Bob Kaiser, and Mary Hadar—for permitting me to take leaves of absence from my job as a staff writer. I am particularly thankful to six people: Jonathan Segal, a senior editor at Knopf and a new/old friend who climbed into the saddle of a story that seemed in danger of faltering and then booted the nag home with skill and wit and professionalism; Jay Lovinger, assistant managing editor at *LIFE* magazine, who, in another editorial incarnation, took part in the original discussions of the story and didn't cease believing in it; Jay Acton, my agent of twelve years, who never pushed or intimated hurry up please it's time; Beverly Brannan, curator of photography in the prints and photographs division of the Library of Congress, who, in addition to being a fine neighbor on Capitol Hill for many years, taught me much about documentary photography and also shared contacts; Robert Coles, a long-time mentor and friend and literary inspiration; and Howard Kohn, a fellow writer who read the book in several forms and kept telling me not to quit on it. Among others at Knopf, my thanks go to Iris Weinstein, Andrew Hughes, Carol Devine Carson, Chip Kidd, Melvin Rosenthal, and Ida

Giragossian; in a world of increasingly shoddy workmanship, Knopf's production values are a marvel.

I owe two families on opposite coasts—Marion Post Wolcott's and my own—more than I can express in this space; in different ways they risked a lot, put up with a lot. But more than anybody else, I owe Marion herself. My sorrow is she didn't live long enough to read this story and tell me to my teeth what she thought of it. Maybe she's reading it in another place.

NOTE ON ILLUSTRATIONS

For the most part I have tried to stick to Marion Post Wolcott's original captions and/or titles. Often she compiled caption material quickly, from the road, but then sometimes, many months afterward, when she was back in the home office, she would study her notes and change the wording, although usually not in significant ways. And in later years, it was not uncommon for her to adopt shorthand names for some of her favorite photographs—"Biscuit Lady" or "Picnic" or "The Hepcats' Jalopy." In some cases here I've included those briefer titles. Occasionally the date or locale of an image proved to be wrong; I made the correction whenever I spotted the mistake.

"I've been going out into the 'back woods' with the county school superintendent. We borrowed an old car the first day—had to be pulled out of a creek by a mule, then later hauled out of the sand & finally had a flat miles from everything & no jack! Tore down fencepost & while our driver (a young kid who is the son of the school janitor) tried to prop the car up I was down on my belly in the creek bed piling rocks under it. But we finally got it fixed. We had to do some walking too, so that when we got back late I was one tired girl.

"Next trip we decided to take my car, after having no luck trying to rent or borrow a high truck. We did amazingly well over the worst and most dangerous roads & creek beds I've ever seen. Got a long way with it—only bent the running board a little & ruined one tire (which was almost worn out anyway) over a bad place in what is called a bridge. We took to mule back which is not *too* bad, & finally someone met us with a horse, so we rode over a tiny trail over a mountain just after dark. Two of us on little mountain pony, picking his way over & around rocks & up the steepest places. A mule that was tied to a fence we were passing got mean when our horse came close to him & hauled off & kicked Mrs. Turner (the sch. Supt.) on the foot. It was too narrow to avoid the damn animal."

—From a letter written by Marion Post Wolcott,

September 19, 1940

*Up the south fork of the Kentucky River, Breathitt
County, Kentucky, September 1940*

PROLOGUE

THE MORNING CALIFORNIA SUN IS streaming in over her left shoulder, making her thin gray hair shine a little, gleam, like old pewter newly polished. "Look here," Marion Post Wolcott says, bringing out some drugstore-developed 3 × 5 color snapshots. They're a little out of focus and perfectly ordinary in composition, the kind you might shoot on a picnic with the family Instamatic. But she seems so proud anyway. "I just took these things through the windshield when we were coming back from Albuquerque a few weeks ago. Lee [her husband] was driving. I guess I was wondering if I could still click the shutter, if I could still see light anymore. I mean, all these years I've seen things and not really photographed them. Or didn't bother to. Or didn't want to. Oh, maybe my cameras were in the back of a closet, or I didn't know where they were at all, or didn't have any film just then, or had told myself that the film in the camera was too old, just like you are, Marion, forget it, it's too late. But anyway, on this recent trip, just the two of us coming back through the desert, with Lee driving and me pointing the camera out the window, I decided to try. And what do you know, I found out I could still click the shutter at nearly the right moment."

An infirm woman is smiling, beaming in fact, almost as if no one else were in the room. There doesn't seem such a shimmer of weariness about her suddenly. "I discovered I could still see light through a lens. And it was wonderful."

T H I S   I S   A   S T O R Y about an artist who stopped, who let go of that gifted, magical thing inside her until it was too late and the gift was lost. And yet in spite of this fact she was able to make her survival a grace, not just a dour necessity. The letting go was due to many things, not the least of which was the burden of being human, of being fearful. I would like to tell you about the long life of Marion Post Wolcott, and of the extraordinary body of work she did accomplish, in just three years, a body of work I believe will outlast this century and probably the next one, too. But before I can do that I need to relate a briefer story about myself.

For a long while in trying to come to terms with the story of Marion Post Wolcott, which essentially is about the choices that get made in our lives wittingly and half-wittingly and sometimes with almost no wit at all, I had resisted involving myself. But I see now that's not really possible.

Almost exactly four years ago, as I am putting this down, I began slipping beyond anything I had ever known or could seem to prevent into a small pool of despair. I am not sure any longer that I was in actual danger of doing something physically harmful to myself, but I do know I was desperate enough to be fantasizing such thoughts, letting them gently wash over me, like warm surf, and this is a terrible thing to say for a man who is much in love with his wife and two small sons. But it's true. My sense of hopelessness had arisen over my inability to move forward (or so it seemed to me) as much as one micron on a big-money and high-visibility book project I had been working on, with everything I had in me, for six days a week for better than two years. Suddenly I had run out of time and imagination and will and money—at least I thought I had. Perhaps I wouldn't have felt so finished and frightened had I the least something to show. I had nothing, or practically nothing. I had begun to feel myself lightheaded, I had begun to feel myself paranoid, I had begun to feel myself strangely returned to the place where I had started out. The project had become a hateful house of mirrors for me, and I had no idea how to escape it. I felt, in fact, I could work for the rest of my life and still not succeed. I remember reciting endlessly to myself a line that I think comes from Hemingway: "If we win here, we win everywhere, and if we lose here, we lose everywhere." I was losing horribly. I also found myself beginning to do curious, almost somnambulistic things—such as the morning when instead of working I tape-recorded, and then played over and over, a portion of a book review from the *New York Times*. I recorded it onto a cassette on my writing table. It was a review of the collected letters of Joseph Conrad, and this was the part I seemed so interested in, reading it aloud into the machine in a grave speaking voice:

> Every writer knows that melodramatic expressions of despair about the progress of composition can become a kind of fetish, relied on to ward off the onset of a genuinely catastrophic blockage. But in Conrad's case, despair seems to have been the condition for writing anything at all—a state of affairs he did his best to exacerbate by making it a practice to borrow money from publishers against books he had not yet written. "I sit down for eight hours every day—and the sitting down is all," he complains in an utterly characteristic letter to the critic Edward Garnett. "In the course of that working day of eight hours I write three sentences which I erase before leaving the table in despair. . . . I assure you—speaking soberly and on my word of honor—that sometimes it takes all my resolution and power of self control to refrain from butting my head against the wall. . . . I would be thankful to be able to write anything, anything, any trash, any rotten thing—something to earn dishonestly and by false pretenses the payment promised by a fool."

I think I played that passage about twenty times before I had all the commas memorized. If Conrad could feel despair like that, I thought, why not someone as puny as me? My wife brought lunch down to me that day, and I slapped off the machine when I heard her coming. "How's it going?" she said. "Fine," I said. She knew about my turmoil, of course, but I don't think she knew the goiterlike proportions to which it had grown. When she went back upstairs to take care of our squalling, healthy two-and-a-half-year-old, I put the tape on again, wondering if I was smiling weirdly, like Jack Nicholson in the movie version of *The Shining*.

One cruddy winter afternoon in the middle of this, I let go of any pretense I had of trying to accomplish something, any piece of trash for payment, and instead walked over to the Library of Congress, where I thought I might read a magazine, or stare at one of the useless stacks of research notes I had accumulated, or maybe just kill the rest of the day by taking the visitors' tour of the library's main reading room. (I had only been in the Library of Congress about 200 times in the previous year and had a stack pass and a study shelf to boot.) I did none of these things, but instead began walking around in the gift shop on the ground floor of the main building. Before long I was looking at some black-and-white reproduction prints and post cards and photo-text books by some of the old Farm Security Administration documentary photographers, whose work, during the middle and late years of the Depression, I have known about and loved and been comforted by for almost all of my adult life. These old FSA images of ordinary, enduring Americans have always seemed most meaningful to me in my own times of stress. Indeed, they have always seemed to epitomize for me the truth of what the great latter-day Swiss-American photographer Robert Frank called "the humanity of the moment." When I look at the struggle coming up out of these pictures, I feel somehow as if I'm combing through my own and the country's ancestral attic with Woody Guthrie and John Steinbeck and maybe the Andrews Sisters and the Great Gildersleeve, too, all of us lingering here and there to laugh but more often cry.

So I began gazing that day at several of Walker Evans's sharecropper portraits from the summer of 1936 in Hale County, Alabama, when he and the haunted Southern writer James Agee were working on what would eventually become *Let Us Now Praise Famous Men*. I looked again at Dorothea Lange's iconographic "Migrant Mother" photograph from Nipomo, California; at her "Tractored Out" shot of Childress County, Texas; at her "Woman of the High Plains," in which that bony, stricken, and nameless Panhandle woman has one hand clutched at her throat and the other at her forehead, as if feeling for a fever, as she tells the photographer: "If you die, you're dead—that's all."

And then a little later that day I saw a photograph by Marion Post Wolcott.

Marion Post Wolcott, I said. Why don't I know this name? I thought I had heard of all of the FSA photographers. I felt I vaguely knew the picture in my hand, however. It was titled "Snowy Night, Woodstock, Vermont, 1940" and I think it must have been reaching out that afternoon, through those several dozen other FSA post cards and photo-text books and suitable-for-framing reproduction prints and all those other quite familiar and less familiar FSA names in the Library of Congress archives—Lange, Evans, Ben Shahn, Arthur Rothstein, Russell Lee, Carl Mydans, John Vachon, Gordon Parks, John Collier, Jack Delano—to speak just to me, perhaps a little in the way the angel Clarence suddenly reached out and plucked the desperate Jimmy Stewart, a.k.a. George Bailey, from the

icy deep in Frank Capra's *It's a Wonderful Life.* Maybe that sounds highfa-
lutin, melodramatic, Conradian, aggrandizing. Maybe it sounds like a
small contrivance, the writer's neat hook for his story. It's also exactly what
I continue to feel: saved, or something close to it.

   "Snowy Night, Woodstock, Vermont, 1940" is a picture of a sleeping
clapboard town piled deep and white. The street lamp in the foreground
has a kind of extraterrestrial glow about it, as if visions are momentarily
to appear. The snowbanks along the sidewalks seem like bulky human
forms covered with blankets. There is something almost transcendently
peaceful about the photograph, and I stared at it for a long time that
afternoon before I went on to another picture by Marion Post Wolcott. It

Snowy Night, Woodstock, Vermont, 1940

Man reading LIFE *magazine behind his car in trailer
park, Sarasota, Florida, 1941*

was captioned "Man reading *LIFE* magazine behind his car in trailer
park, Sarasota, Florida, 1941." A contented seventyish figure with silvery
hair and a long pipe and argyle socks and a pair of flimsy wire-rim reading glasses is sitting in a striped canvas beach chair paging through Henry
Luce's famous photo magazine. The light in the picture is stunning—I
wanted to reach out and riffle the old guy's hair. But more than the beauty
of the light, the man in the picture reminded me instantly of my own
"Pop," which is what we used to call my maternal grandfather, Bernie
Kyne, who wintered with "Nonna" in Florida trailer parks in the thirties
and forties, driving down from Greene County, Ohio, once the year's

farming was done. I'd bet anything my pop also sat on a balmy Gulf Coast evening beside his Chevy in argyle socks and a wooden beach chair reading *LIFE* magazine and that he also would have been glad to let an attractive lady photographer working for FDR's New Deal snap his portrait:

You betcha, honey, go ahead and set it on up, pretty big camera you got yourself there, you say you load it with that sheet film, Lordy, that camera's big as a bowling ball, hope I don't crack the thing in two on you, hahaha, you mean you been driving around the country all by your lonesome just taking pictures like this, well, I'll be.

My pop has been dead a long time, but for an instant I had him back.

I came on another Post Wolcott picture that day. The caption said: "Migrant family from Missouri, Belle Glade, Florida, 1939." There are three women in the photograph—a mother and her daughters. There is a man in the foreground, possibly the husband, but he is squatting on his haunches, with his head hung down toward the dirt, as if he doesn't wish the photographer, and the world, to see his face. And you can't. But it is the woman in the picture I could almost not take my eyes off that afternoon. She is wearing a denim apron over a one-piece floral-print dress and she is standing with her angular back against the trunk of a Florida palm. Her gaze, right into the camera, is flat and unbroken; her hand is cocked defiantly on her hip; her straight dark hair is falling straight down on either side of her hard generational face. The woman in the photograph looks so sad, angry, beat-up, and undefeated all at once. How old was she when the picture was taken, I wondered: thirty, thirty-five? What was her name? How long did she live? She couldn't be alive now, could she? Was she a worker in the citrus packing houses, and was the work filthy? Were her children defecating into lard cans, were they sleeping in lean-tos rigged from burlap and corrugated tin? Was her family insulating itself from the January frosts with the rotogravure sections of the Palm Beach *Daily News*? I kept staring at the picture, emotion climbing in my throat. Suddenly I had an almost overwhelming desire to try and locate her. The picture had a second caption, too. It read, and I was certain it must be a quote from the mother, "We ain't never lived like hogs before, but we sure does now."

What sort of gift, not just for photography but for life, would you have to have to get pictures like these, I wondered. "Why haven't I seen these

Migrant family from Missouri, Belle Glade, Florida, 1939. "We ain't never lived like hogs before, but we sure does now."

pictures before?" I think I said out loud. "Who the hell is Marion Post Wolcott?"

I tried to find out something about her immediately, but no one in the gift shop could help me. So I walked across the street and into the Prints and Photographs Division of the library, where the several hundred thousand FSA pictures and original negatives and copy negatives and dust-coated near-duplicates—the greatest photographic document ever assembled in the history of this nation, probably any nation—are stored. The seventy-odd-thousand prints from the collection, mounted on pieces of gray cardboard, with their pen-and-ink captions on the back, are there in row after row of maroon metal filing cabinets.

"I would like to see anything at all you have that's written down about the life of Marion Post Wolcott," I said to the first reference assistant I could corner.

"Well, we have very little," he said, cheerful, helpful. "She's mentioned here and there in books about the Depression, in the basic bibliographies and photo encyclopedias and histories, but, you see, people don't nearly know her in the way they know some of the other FSAers."

"Why not?" I said. "Her work is incredible."

"Well, for one thing she came into the project fairly late, about 1938, and only worked a couple years. And then she stopped. As far as I know, she never took any more pictures the rest of her life. Maybe she did, but I never saw any. The world forgets about you, doesn't it? The magic isn't used, the magic goes. A lot of the others went on to have later careers in photography. Most of them kept in it one way or another. Seems as if your Marion Wolcott went into hiding or something. She's something, though, isn't she?"

"But I don't understand how she could have just stopped like that," I said.

"Beats me, Jack," he said. "She stopped. I guess you'd have to ask her. I think she's still alive. Somewhere out in California. You could probably find her. Very old now. Not too well, I've heard. Been sick a long time, I think. Most all the others are long gone or pretty recently gone. Wolcott's the last great one who's left, I suppose. I think she got married and moved overseas or something. Had kids. Lived on a farm somewhere in Virginia for a long while or something. Maybe it was her husband. I think maybe I've heard that, come to think of it. Married women, never mind married women with children, just didn't run around the country being artists back then, did they? It was the culture, wasn't it? It was the thing between men and women back then, wasn't it? Anyway, the point is she stopped. The point is she disappeared. Vanished, you could say."

"The hell with the culture," I said a little too loudly. "What would she have done with all her . . . her *compulsion* to shoot a picture? How do you cut that off?"

The reference assistant shrugged, suddenly not quite as cheerful as before. Every day of the year cranks and crackpots and kooks come into the Library of Congress with their urgent questions.

For the rest of that day and on into that night, I had a strange, tingling feeling in me. It wasn't a feeling of uplift or ease of my pain, exactly. And yet there was an odd leavening in me all the same. It had to do with a question I had never before even considered, amidst all my other troubles: Was it possible that thirty or forty years hence, the pain I was going to feel, the awful pain of regret and guilt and self-recrimination for having quit too early on something promising, could turn out to be worse, far worse, than any tears of near-suicidal frustration I was currently shedding?

My God, it was an amazing and terrifying thought. . . .

Well, in time I did meet Marion Post Wolcott and her husband, Lee Wolcott, in their pleasant hillside home on Pedregosa Street in Santa Barbara. Marion was in her late seventies when we met, and her memory was both good and not so good. She and Lee had been married almost half a century then. Over the next several years, as she steadily declined, I found myself going back to California, and then back again, and then back half a dozen times beyond that. Always she and her husband accepted me, as friend and inquisitor and quasi-biographer, always they answered my questions to the extent they felt they could. They certainly didn't tell me everything. What Marion mostly wanted to talk about was her three brief years on the FSA road. It was as if all the rest—everything before, everything after—she preferred to keep a kind of shroud around, even though, under tugging, that shroud sometimes came off. What I eventually learned about Marion and her husband—and I might say learned humbly—was that almost nothing was as I had originally thought. Or at least nothing was quite that simple. It seldom is.

At length, too, I found myself traveling to some of the places where a brilliant photographer had frozen time in a box five decades before. I don't really know why I so felt a need to search out these Bardstowns and Brattleboros and Bessemers. Perhaps I sensed from the start in some vague indefinable way that I would never be able to get all the answers to my questions in California, but that there might be other kinds of answers waiting inside the documentary histories of these old gelatin silver-prints: things to help me find my way, understand not just the life of this remarkable woman, but maybe even things about myself.

And maybe I just wanted to go.

FRAME ONE

TIME IN A BOX

The aperture of a camera forms a two-way portal through which both subject and viewer peer into another time. The subject, conscious of the permanence of the document, posts forward a memory. The viewer, aligning with the memory at some later date, works to preserve the sight from disintegration. Both are present at both moments; both experience the revelation of being adrift in time, sampling it laterally.

—RICHARD POWERS
Three Farmers on Their Way to a Dance

A Negro going in the Entrance for Negroes at a movie theater, Belzoni, Mississippi, 1939

BELZONI SATURDAYS

SHE NOT ONLY TOOK the pictures, she could sit down and slap out profane, hilarious letters about her adventures. She wrote them by the hundreds, usually late at night from her steam-clanky hotel room or linoleum-queasy tourist cabin, after she'd dined in the tarnished shine of some sad café on Main Street, after she'd made a stab at the loathsome mileage forms and expense reports, after she'd banged on the wall at the singing drunk next door, after she'd reloaded film in the closet with the lights out, after she'd legged into her pj's (tops and bottoms, she didn't like nightgowns) and decided on tomorrow's clothes (basically today's clothes) and draped her rinsed-out nylons and undies around the chipped rim of the porcelain sink in what passed for a bathroom. Taken together now, these old and furiously scrawled dispatches from the thirties road—the bulk of which have survived—add up to their own kind of vivid and ribald and near-instant documentary portrait of the closing years of the Depression. As with so much else in her life, Marion Post Wolcott never knew.

"Jesus Christ, these social workers are fierce, inhuman stupid prigs. I can't call them enough names!" she wrote one sultry night from Memphis. "Jesus Christ and my God and all the Saints! MORE RAIN!" she wrote on an even steamier night from Natchitoches, Louisiana. "OBLIGING JUICY BLIZ-ZARD. TOUGH SLOW GOING. STAYING BRATTLEBORO TONIGHT. FARTHER NORTH TOMORROW," she wired one Currier & Ives afternoon from the Vermont border. Two weeks later, still frozen in, cranky, she had gotten off this note

3

to headquarters: "This last week was so cold I practically took to sleeping in my clothes. Had on so many different layers I couldn't be bothered to get down to skin again. And no Miss Fancypants underwear either. Long, woolly & ugly."

In January 1939, still new to the job, she wrote: "Much of the hunting was just time wasted—miles up awful little roads that must have been for lumbering—no houses, nothing, or a place that wasn't significant, or someone who chased me off.... They just get in their huts or shacks & build a little fire, & close the wooden window & door & hug their arms close to them, waiting till it gets warm again. And they won't let a stranger inside. Often they wouldn't even let me photograph the outside of the house. I tried every different line I could think of. And carried small bribes & food along with me."

Once, in Georgia, she ran over an ugly old hog and nearly busted an axle of her car. ("I'm afraid there's one hog less in that state," she said.) Once, from Kentucky, she wrote: "Several times when I've had the car parked alongside the road and taken pix nearby, a cop or state trooper has come up, watched me, examined the camera and searched through the car, and questioned and looked at all my identification, etc. The bastards can take their own sweet time about it and ask many irrelevant and sometimes personal and slightly impertinent questions too. I've had to visit more than one sheriff's office, & write my signature & go thru the same routine, but the worst of it is the time they consume—just chewing the fat with you, making you drink a Coca-Cola, showing you everything in the place. They haven't anything else to do, & they don't feel like working anyway—it's too hot, and they think you're crazy anyhow."

On July 5, 1939, after she'd been out on her first extended tour for seven straight months and almost without a single break, she had written back to her boss in Washington: "In general, I'm most tired of the strain of continually adjusting to new people, making conversation, getting acquainted, being polite and diplomatic when necessary. In particular I'm sick of people telling me that the cabin or room costs the same for one as it does for two, of listening to people, or the 'call' girl, make love in the adjoining room. Or of hearing everyone's bathroom habits, hangovers, & fights through the ventilator. And even the sight of hotel bedroom furniture, the feel of clean sheets, the nuisance of digging into the bottom of a suitcase, of choosing a restaurant & food to eat."

Pretend for a moment that it's still 1939, three months after the above missive, a Saturday in early fall. A slender woman with hazel eyes and coils of thick dark hair falling neatly to her shoulders has just driven into Belzoni, Mississippi, in a top-down Plymouth Six. (It isn't known if the top was down, though the weather was good that day.) Hitler is reviewing his troops in vanquished Warsaw. The Yankees are devouring the Cincinnati Reds in the World Series. And a twenty-nine-year-old, comely, unknown documentarian in the employ of the federal government is about to get a picture deep in the Delta that one day will hang in the Museum of Modern Art.

Marion Post, whose last name isn't Wolcott yet, has been doing this strange itinerant work for a little over a year now. She is five-foot-seven and has a straight, plain, seminarrow face. She has long skinny elegant fingers and large ears—which are hidden by the coils of hair. On her right cheek is an inch-long bone-white scar; it's quite fetching, actually. When speaking to people, or when reading something aloud to herself, she has a funny way of making her jaw go up, so that her lip stretches high above her slightly crooked teeth, as if she were trying to squint with her mouth. It's very funny, this squint, and you can imagine half the world's current crop of promising young men willing to go over Niagara Falls in a barrel just for a private glimpse of it—well, that's an exaggeration.

No, you wouldn't quite call her ravishing, but something in her projects a pure, wholesome sensuousness. Many years hence, a man who knows her from these times, who has worked with her and traveled with her a bit (he was a regional supervisor for the Department of Agriculture), will explain it this way: "Well, it was as if she was saying to you, 'I'm not in the habit of laying every good-looking man who comes along, but if I were, you'd be the next.'"

She has spent Christmas away, she has spent July 4 away. She has been to Mosquito Crossing and Cheat Neck, to Plum Bayou and Plant City, to New Iberia and Carboro, to Gee's Bend and Gum Pond and Ducktown. (Also some others a bit better known.) She has sustained bedbugs and red bugs and every manner of small-town dope and rural factotum. She has framed Bennie's Grocery (802 West Gwinnett, Sylvania, Georgia), where the neck bones go two pounds for fifteen cents, and she has squeezed off on the Rose Hill Sorghum Mill and the Pocahontas Hay Press, not to dwell on the Big Brown Pea Huller. She has gotten mule auctions in Montgomery and sock salesmen in Savannah and also the window of a pawnshop on Beale Street in Memphis. Once she nearly lost her car fording the Flint River—that was Georgia. Once she nearly lost her marbles dealing with Miss Edith Lowry's Home Missions Board—that was Florida. Once she got socked in the back of the neck with a grapefruit. (The letter detailing the attack is lost.) She has gotten the black muck in her cameras and the black fits in her dreams. Once she got several of her pictures published in *Collier's National Weekly*. They weren't great shots, to tell the truth, and the editors didn't even give her a credit line.

Some people think she's a gypsy (it's the jangly jewelry and the brightly colored scarves), though others suspect she's a Nazi agent with a camera. What she really is is an American beauty, living by her wits in the back of the back of the country. Uncle Sam pays her $95.83, net, every two weeks (the check catches up to her in God-knows-where). Always she is tired, always she feels behind, always she is pushing on to somewhere else. Always she is wondering where the next infestation of Spanish lice is. Sometimes she wastes whole mornings hanging around Railway Express offices for packages of film or contact sheets. Sometimes she travels at night, the flat feel of the giant moonstruck land hanging right at her elbows: out there, jubilant, exhausted, alone. A shooter.

Today, October 7, 1939, the shooter's come to Belzoni.

She arrived in the Delta via Chapel Hill and Memphis. She drove down only several days ago and will be in Mississippi the remainder of this month. In her last letter to the boss, five days previous, her usual witty mix of news and ampersand and outrage, she noted as how "I was held up for a long time in a rural county—couldn't get anyone or any store to change a $10 bill." That was nothing, as the inconveniences go.

Auto tags are on sale in Belzoni. The school cafeteria menus have just been published, as they always have, on the front page of the weekly *Banner*. The public library has gotten in *The Grapes of Wrath* and *The World Goes Smash*. Turner's Drug over on Hayden is selling bus tickets to Vicksburg for a buck apiece; Jack Selden is up from Louisiana visiting kinfolk; Bryan Motor Company wants the citizenry to walk in and inspect the new '40 Ford V-8, with its twenty-two important improvements. And oh yes: the "Cash Nite" drawing at the picture show last evening paid out $400. Pretty sizable sum for a town whose river is levied off. You had to be there to collect your cash. It's a Depression gimmick to fill up seats.

The name of the picture show is the Crescent and it's in the Alexander Building. There's a horse opera on the bill today and it's playing continuously from one o'clock till 9:45. It's called *Feud of the Range,* it's from

Metropolitan Pictures, the running time is fifty-six minutes, and it stars the diminutive, two-fisted, and brick-jawed Bob Steele. It's a "programmer," tailor-made for grind houses just like this one all over the South.

This is market day, as is any Delta Saturday, and so the government lady photog, who climbs on top of buildings and squats in the middle of crowds and leans out a window of the Walthall Hotel to get a peddler working from the back of his flatbed truck, has plenty to frame. It isn't known how many pictures she takes with her Speed Graphic and Rolleiflex and Leica—probably five or six dozen. Several months from now, twenty-five photographs and their negatives will show up in the files of the FSA in Washington as a catalogued record of a day's work in Belzoni. Of these twenty-five, number eighteen in the series will bear the prosaic caption "A Negro going in the Entrance for Negroes at a movie theater, Belzoni, Mississippi, 1939." It's just a second in eternity, a silhouetted and slightly stooped black man in a fedora and blousey coat entering his town's movie house so that he might relieve his spirit and probably his arches while Bob Steele flicks off Winchester fire at bad men. The shooter sees the photograph, frames it in her sensibility, whirls and clicks—or this is how one wishes it to be.

You can't make out the moviegoer's face, but he seems to be turning toward the lady with the box as if to inquire: *"Why, ma'am, would you wish to take a picture of something as ordinary as this, as ordinary as me?"*

Is it too much to say that in an instant of her art, what an artist sees in the growing shadows of a Mississippi Delta town one fall Saturday in 1939—and probably sees as much in her subconscious as in her conscious imagination—are three great swaths of our cultural history: cowboy dreams, racial bigotry, the pot of gold waiting at the end of the rainbow?

ON AN AUGUST FRIDAY EVENING five decades after that picture was snapped, I kissed my wife, boarded a flight at National Airport in Washington, changed planes at Nashville, flew over to Jackson, Mississippi, rented a car with an FM radio, drove out of the gas-vapor lights of the metro area, drove northward on a dark interstate for a nodding-off hour, curved leftward, got on a two-lane, kept going until I could barely talk aloud to myself, found the outskirts of the fast-asleep place I wanted, found a twenty-five-dollar room with algae growing on the walls of the shower stall, turned the air conditioner all the way up, skinned the bed back to the tissue-thin sheets, slept the sleep of the angels, awoke, got dressed, stepped outside, and discovered myself smack in the middle of a swamp-hot Mississippi Delta Saturday morning. The sun hadn't drilled itself halfway to noon yet and the thermometer already read 95. Perfect. I had this idea, you see, that just the early-August Faulknerian heat alone would help me in what I'd come for. The title of Faulkner's great novel *Light in August* doesn't refer to sunlight; it refers to a piece of Southern folklore: Pregnant women need to be "light" by August because the heat in Mississippi then is too intense for anything, especially carrying children.

The town I had awakened in, or at least in striking distance of (the night clerk had said sourly that the room cost the same for one as it did for two, so it didn't matter if I was hiding anybody in the car), is still the seat of law and commerce for Humphreys County. But cotton isn't king in Belzoni anymore. Catfish farming is—that and the making of Jockey underwear. Nowadays the population is a nudge over 3,000. The big rectangular ditches where the "cats" are cultivated, farm fresh to your table, can be seen from almost any roadside in the county. Mississippi produces 90 percent of all U.S. catfish currently, and Belzoni is about smack in the center of it. Hairnetted Belzonians, black and white, side by side, don yellow slickers and face fish by the ton. There must be times when skinning feedlot fish in a freezer-cooled factory amounts to its own kind of Southern hell, if not quite as hellish as going up and down rows of cotton with a burlap bag dragging at your waist.

The first person I had an extended conversation with on my own Belzoni Saturday was Edna Earl Wooton. She was upper-middle-aged and worked in the library and was friendly as pie. Had lived in town practically all her life. Could remember as a little kid taking her "nigger shooter" (piece of rubber inner tube and an old tree branch with a fork in it) and trying to shoot out the glass in the poster box down at the picture show. (Actually, as I soon discovered, the town had two picture shows back then, but the Joy, which I think was down from Fincher Hardware, never did the business the Crescent did. The Crescent got all the big runs, fifty-six-minute range-mellers with Bob Steele notwithstanding.) Edna Earl stared with curiosity at the photograph I had brought along. She had never seen it before, had never heard of the photographer, had never heard of a documentary project of the Farm Security Administration.

"Well, I'll be," she said finally. "Now see there? That poster box is covered with chicken coop wire. That's because we were always shooting the glass out, and finally they gave up and started using chicken wire to cover it. Didn't matter, we still used to reach our fingers in and tear off little souvenir pieces before that mean old manager used to come out and try to shoo us away."

She stared again. "Now, I told you. Somebody has shot out the light bulb hanging down over the poster box." (Odd, as many times as I had studied the picture, I had somehow never noticed a light pole, even though Marion has perfectly captured its shadow.) Edna Earl Wooton stared deeply for a third time. "You want to know something funny? You see that old Dr. Pepper ad over top his head? See the way that shadow is slicing that clock? Ten, two, and four. That's how often you were supposed to take your Dr. Peppers. Now, when you walk over to the Crescent after a bit, you aren't going to see any Dr. Pepper sign. Heck, I'll bet they've painted that darn sign over at least a dozen times. They paint it right over top of the brick. I think the side of the building is beige now, nothing on it, just a big brick wall. But practically every time after we've had a hard rain, that old Dr. Pepper ad, you know, well, it starts to come back through, just a little, underneath all that paint. Yessir, just when the paint begins to dim, it comes right back through."

Pentimento. The things that were will come back, maybe to haunt you. Good for *LIFE*.

Edna Earl told me the proper pronunciation of her town: Bel-zone-ah. She said that Humphreys County was really *Um*-phreys County. She told me about Greasy Row, a now-gone lowlife district of saloons and gambling houses along the curve of the olive-colored Yazoo. Ladies of the night once sold their goods there to bargemen and steamboaters. The Yazoo River, formed by the merger of the equally euphonious Yalobusha and Tallahatchie, used to carry a good deal of commerce into Belzoni. These days fine houses sit along the east bank, with wicker on the porches and with little tables lit with inviting lamps.

I told Edna Earl Wooton goodbye and walked over to the Crescent. Bright orange bulbs were flashing in sequence around the front of the building. A bicycle lay on its side by the front door. The heat rose off the pavement in waves. The old iron light pole, with its green metal hat, was still hanging down over the spot where the poster box once was—and its light was still out. The exterior staircase was still there against the side wall, but the landing at the top was sealed off now. The "Colored Adm. 10¢" sign wasn't visible, and a spindly stepladder wasn't leaning up against that wall, and a silhouetted black man in a fedora and a blousey coat wasn't going upward to a relieving celluloid dream.

There were several white children playing at the base of the stairs. I waved to them, went about seventy-five paces down the street, turned, squinted through an imaginary box. I felt foolish. I came close to the building again, saw that the words "White Men Only" had been taken off the restroom door under the stairs. There was still a slat missing from this door—the same slat that's missing in Marion's picture. I kept thinking it had been kicked out decades ago, that it had been replaced, and that someone was thoughtful enough to kick it out again in time for my visit.

Willard Kaminer, proprietor of the Crescent, was repairing a Coke machine when I walked into the lobby, that and cussing softly to himself. He was banging at the machine with some tool or other. "Got to mash it," he said, without looking at me. He had a ballcap mashed on his head and a cigar mashed in his mouth. I told him I was from up north, but I suppose he had that figured out already. I took out a copy of Marion's photograph and showed it to him.

"Well, I'll be," he said, echoing Edna Earl and my own Pop, suspending the mashing, removing the cigar, peering in. "That is my place, damned if it isn't. Course, I didn't have it then." Then he said, "So who'd you say took it?"

"Her name is Marion Post Wolcott. She was a photographer working in the last years of the Depression. It was a government project, and the assignment was to go around America recording the country just as it was. Somehow it all turned into art. She did this amazing work for a little over three years, and then she just kind of dropped from sight. She's being rediscovered now."

"Well, I'll be," he said again. "She still around?"

"California," I said.

"Probably very old now," he said.

"Pretty old," I said.

"You been to see her?" he said.

"Yep."

"So why'd she stop?" he said.

"It's complicated," I said. "I don't quite have it yet. Maybe I never will."

The Saturday matinee was about to start, and Belzoni's teenagers, most of them black, were piling in. Some were stopping to get popcorn and giant boxes of Milk Duds at a counter managed by Jane Williams, an attractive young black woman who told me she worked weekdays as a secretary at a local computer store. "My parents went up the outside stair every Friday night," she said. Kaminer stood nearby watching his patrons come. Then he said in a lowered voice, out of earshot of his employee, "I'm probably speaking out of turn, but you see the South is still segregated. Socially, they're just not going to mix. If the blacks come, the whites don't want to come. Course, depends on what you're playing, too. We'll have an almost entirely black house today, I'd say. The town's over eighty percent black these days anyway. You could almost say Belzoni blacks have the franchise now. They got the vote, all right. They aren't sitting in the balcony anymore, nope. Good for it."

He kind of cackled at that, then said: "The movie business gets in your blood. Course, I'm kind of disenchanted with it nowadays. It's all percentage. A lot of these pictures don't interest me. Too much violence. You take today. We're playing *Predator*. I probably won't even watch it."

"Who's in it?" I asked.

"Hell, I don't know. You can go out there and look on the marquee."

I did. It wasn't Bob Steele. It was Arnold Schwarzenegger.

I went up to the balcony. It wasn't a balcony anymore but a separate theater with a smaller screen: Belzoni's Cinema Two. The proprietor had dressed up the place with some gold lamé curtains. But he'd kept the red leather bucket seats, which looked as cracked and fine as the seats in old Jaguars. "They've probably been here since day one," he said. "When I bought this place, in eighty, it hadn't been open in a while. Felt kind of good bringing it back to life, you want to know."

He figured to close for the season in September, he said. For one thing, his wife was scheduled for some treatments on her neck at the National Institutes of Health in Washington, D.C., and for another he didn't even live in Belzoni, but commuted up from Jackson every weekend during the summer months. That was too much like work for a man in semiretirement. "Now, back when your lady photographer came through here, you could make some money in this business. You could get a movie for ten dollars from the Memphis Exchange and get it back in three days with no percentage. As I say, it's all percentage now. These damn distributors want fifty percent and you got to give as much as a hundred and fifty up front to boot. Disgusting."

I said goodbye and walked over to Turner's Drug. I stood in the shade and surveyed the sun-dusty streets. The heat was like a hammer. I missed my family. What was I doing here? When Marion Post Wolcott took a picture of Turner's Drug fifty years ago, the place had a striped canvas awning out front. Now there was an aluminum awning shading the building. I read some headlines through the glass in a newspaper vending box. I climbed on a scale. It said "Weight 1¢. Horoscope and Weight 5¢." I put in a nickel. The dial on the machine sang around three times and stopped at my fortune. It read "You are inclined to be jealous and sarcastic, the kind of person who, once crossed, might spend years seeking revenge. Be careful." I didn't like that, so I jumped with both feet on the machine, mashed at it, and, sure enough, it sang around to something else: "You have a tendency which leads you right to the core of things before you have the basic facts. Watch your step."

OUT OF JERSEY

THE PICTURE YOU SEE HERE was taken in a summertime New Jersey backyard about 1916. Marion Post Wolcott would have been six then. That's a furry pet of some kind in her hands, and there may be a rubber band or a thin bracelet around her left wrist, but in any case the whole barefoot package looks cheeky, infectious, disarming. Marion's older sister, Helen, is in this picture, too. She's second from the left—you can barely make her out—standing behind the Booth Tarkington boy in the tie and knickers who's just moved his hand close to Marion's arm, as if he dares touch her for posterity. But Marion is the one clearly hogging the lens. Next to this long-tressed and slightly pigeon-toed child in the suspendered pants and toothy smile, the other three girls in the picture seem positively frumpy.

Marion Post, Bloomfield, New Jersey,

c. 1916 (photographer unknown)

In the background is the large frame Victorian house where the lens hogger lives with her parents and sister and household help. The address is 17 Park Place, Bloomfield, New Jersey.

On the other side of this seventy-odd-year-old print, or at least on the other side of a latter-day copy of it, a shaky septuagenarian hand has written lightly in pencil: "What a silly spoiled-looking phony brat. I bet my mother made the overalls I have on. No other girls I knew wore them. Is that a puppy or a rabbit I've got? That boy next to me was my sister's boyfriend. Till he became mine. Ha."

It's almost as if this old album print, by its unknown taker, existed now to narrate the story line of a child's early order and happiness. But the truth is that within three or four years of the moment it was made—if not sooner—the world of the six-year-old with the furry pet and the count-the-house eyes was breaking from the inside. Literally the inside. Which is the principal point of a sad tale.

SAMPLING LATERALLY:

She's known as "Sis" because she's the kid sister. She's number two in more senses than one, though it won't always be so. (Actually the shift between two competitive siblings seems well advanced by the time of the backyard photograph, although Marion herself has said it didn't really begin until she was in her mid-twenties and had found her creative gift.) Helen, older by three years, possessor of striking light-blue eyes, perhaps a little stiffer in personality, is her father's clear favorite and the first of the two Post girls to show artistic promise and intellectual gifts. (She will always be a whiz with language.) There is something almost eerie about the life of Helen Post, another lost artist, another government documentary photographer, in fact. Eerie in the sense of how many similarities exist between Marion's life and her own, down to the kind of forceful man she married and pictures she took and ways she eventually hid from her confusions once she decided she wanted to find her art again. But let that piece of the riddle hold.

When she was an old, sick woman with a lost mind, Helen Post wrote, with sudden lucidity, on a yellow lined pad: "Two small girls, one with a 3 yr. start, having parental audience well in hand, were bound to sense rivalry. When the acceptance problems had to include long nights and desperate days of the baby's first summer, not knowing if she would be able to live, that her head had been hurt during her delivery—but not very clearly—the to-do which pervaded the household ... gave me good reason to work out my personality needs more on my own than people were aware."

The younger child, her early months in doubt, is born in a Montclair hospital on June 7, 1910. Bloomfield, two towns down from Montclair, smaller and less affluent, is where the Second and Third rivers flow toward the Passaic; where the Oakes Woolen Mills make fine blue flannel uniforms for New York policemen; where the ancient elms in the lovely Revolutionary parade green have come down with cankerworms. Bloomfield, population 17,000, twenty minutes on the streetcar line from Newark, was founded by Presbyterians who'd migrated from Connecticut in the prior century and bought a parallelogram of land from the Indians. In addition to its woolen mills, the town's other claim to industrial fame is the manufacture of Scott's Emulsion of Cod Liver Oil. There is city water in Bloomfield, and houses have hot-air furnaces, and sewer connections are common, and yet the country lingers here. Blacksmiths and tanners are still doing a brisk business. Peddlers knock at back doors, offering to sharpen knives or sell chunks of coal for the overnight grate fires. On Friday nights in Sis's childhood, farmers clop their horse-drawn wagons down Broad on their way to the Saturday morning markets in Newark. Brookdale, a village next door, has some of the largest horseradish farms in the United States. It's still possible in the shank of the twentieth century for a curious cheeky Bloomfield child, with an innate sense of beauty, to collect her chums and walk within fifteen minutes to open fields where there are cows and jacks-in-the-pulpit.

The town lies twenty-odd miles west of New York City, and when a Bloomfieldian wants to go over he catches the D.L.&W. (Delaware, Lackawanna & Western) to Newark and then on to Hoboken, where he can then pick up the ferry or the tubes across the Hudson. He can also go via Jersey City on the Erie line.

The Victorian Gothic house at No. 17 Park has double halls and curved stairways and a summer kitchen in the cellar and a huge sleeping porch with lattice windows on the second floor in the rear. The house directly faces the oblong green.

The aperture of memory; an elderly woman in California is speaking.

"There was this dark reddish barn behind our house. Once Mother took me down there and said, 'Sis, I want to show you this pretty thing.' It was a spider.

I was terrified. I've never gotten over it. Snakes I can do anything with. It's only spiders. When I was on the road for the FSA I used to walk into a cabin with something ready in my hand to hit them with. I used to examine the closets with a flashlight. I suppose it all goes back to that damn red barn behind 17 Park Place."

The head of this nuclear unit of four is Dr. Walter Post, a family physician. He is a distant, conservative, authoritarian, judgmental, and emotionally bound-up man—or at least this is how he will mainly survive in a younger daughter's memory. Other people have other views. Dr. Post is also an adulterer, but few in the town know this. He is a native of Secaucus, where his family has lived and held farms since the seventeenth century. He was born on Christmas Eve, 1877, which means he is thirty-two at the birth of his second and last child. He is a graduate of Homeopathic Medical College and of Flower Hospital in New York City, the latter being where he is said to have met his ludicrously mismatched spouse. He belongs to Westminster Presbyterian Church, on the corner of Seminary and Fremont, though apparently not ardently. In addition to Mountainside Hospital in Montclair (where Sis is born at some risk), Dr. Post is in association with St. Mary's Hospital, Passaic, and the County Homeopathic, East Orange. A homeopath is a physician who believes that, if administered in small doses, "the thing that makes a man ill also cures him." In these years Sis's father has grown interested in the study of heart disease, which must distinguish him a little from the dozen and a half other physicians who practice in Bloomfield and who live—nearly all of them—in the frame-and-flagstone Victorians snuggling up on the several sides of the green. His examining office is a three-room addition built onto the side of his home, a common arrangement.

Dr. Post is known to have started his practice in Bloomfield right after medical school, bicycling to his more distant patients. Then he switched to a horse and buggy. Now he has a fancy touring car and sometimes his elder daughter drives him. Helen is keen on motoring.

A photograph. A well-built round-faced fellow, not tall, with a prominent nose and expensive-looking shoes, is wearing a tam and holding a trench coat and standing on the boardwalk at Atlantic City. It's a medical meeting of some sort and the whole family has gone along. The face beneath the tam is blurred. The trench coat, draped over one arm, is billowing in the breeze, as if he were on a ship, sailing gaily to the Continent.

Post Family, c. 1914. From left,
Helen, Walter, Nan, Marion
(photographer unknown)

Dr. Walter Post,
Atlantic City, c. 1915
(photographer unknown)

"He just couldn't be close to me, hug me. I don't know why.' I've thought and thought, tried to imagine why not. Sometimes it almost seems I never knew him at all. I can't recall one single instance when my father ever gave me what I would call real physical affection. And yet I can start to see now some of the humiliation Daddy must have felt over the scandal in our house and then the divorce from Mother."

Another voice, not Marion's. It belongs to Mildred Stone, Bloomfield historian, lifelong resident, a woman born in the first years of this century: "I can tell you something about him as a doctor, at least. I think I am the last possible person alive in this town who would remember him at all. Our whole family went to him. I can tell you that he was caring, he was skilled. I think of him as a successful professional man of the town. I remember my mother had twins when I was fourteen, and Dr. Post came out to do it. I believe he took out my grandfather's appendix on the kitchen table. I remember his office looked out onto our green and that he had this big row of leather-bound medical books above his desk. I came home from Vassar once—when would this have been? 'twenty-four?—and went to see him and he took down one of those great books and said, 'Let's look up this thing together, Mildred.' I knew almost nothing about his family life. Funny, I can't even remember Mrs. Post. How could the whole shocking business of the divorce have escaped me? But I do remember vividly that he was a good doctor."

He also was a good philanderer, if one defines the word in terms of discretion. Years after the family had broken itself, long after the gossip-soaked 1924–1925 divorce trial, Sis and her mother would learn that her father had carried on secret sexual relationships with several of his patients and even with one of his wife's good friends—and for considerable periods of time. It isn't known whether Dr. Post, respected man of the town, was conducting any of these relationships during the time he was accusing his wife in Essex County Court of cuckolding, humiliating, and betraying him with a boarder beneath his own rafters.

A second photograph. A little girl in a sunsuit with a big ribbon tied in her hair and sand clotted on her knees. How old is she—four, possibly five? She's seated at the seashore beside a small boy in a sailor suit.

"I believe this boy was the son of my father's then mistress, a friend of Mother's. We never knew, of course. It all came out later. All the town knew during

Marion Post and playmate at the
Jersey Shore, c. 1915.
(photographer unknown)

the divorce was Mother's sinful relationship with Cousin Ed. Mother was the
one made to seem the wanton woman, while Daddy was the good victimized
husband, trying to do his work. It still makes me furious. But anyway this cute
boy. He appears in other pix where we were dressed up as bride and groom, out
on the town green. I think his name was Boyd. Dead now, I'm sure."

The mother in this family is Marion Louise Hoyt Post, but everyone
calls her "Nan." She was born on November 13, 1883, which means she is
almost twenty-seven when Sis comes along. (Helen, her first-born, arrived
thirteen months after Nan wed Walter.) Nan is six years younger than her
spouse. The two were joined in a Presbyterian ceremony in Newark on
April 5, 1906. Across the country, the great San Francisco earthquake
struck thirteen days later.

A photograph. A woman with pursed lips and a pince-nez is posed on
a studio tabletop, her exposed forearms propped out beside her. She's
wearing an ankle-length velvety dress and a throat-wrapped lacy blouse.

She looks formidable and erotic at once. There is no date on the picture, but probably it was taken not long after her marriage and before the second child was born.

What kind of person is Nan Post? In a word, unconventional, at least unconventional for this time and town. She likes to garden, she enjoys sewing and designing her own clothes, she has a close friend who's a classical pianist. Nan is a registered nurse by training and sometimes helps out in her husband's medical office. But medicine as such can't hold her. She's idealistic, reform-minded, gabby, a little prickly. She's in love with New York theater. She thinks of herself as admirable, proud, independent, unsubjugated—and mostly she is. She's of the strange opinion that women ought to be able to decide how many children they wish to have. She can be a bit of a bore about the morality of labor unions, about the equality of the races, about the Russian Revolution as the greatest advance for humanity in the last one hundred years. She's too impulsive for her own damn good. She's prone to depressions and anxieties. She likes mannish watches and crepe blouses and crushed hats with long feathers. Her favorite card game is canasta, and she can play it for hours. She is known to have been beautiful in her youth, and the vanity of this may have lingered past its due because in these years—late teens and twenties—Nan has begun to lose her figure just a little. In sum, you might think of this short solid woman with the bobbed hair and erect bosom and too-large nose as a kind of certifiable Bloomfieldian kook, the more so in that she's a physician's wife.

"For instance, she used to design clothes for herself that everybody else would have thought almost risqué. They were something like gypsy clothes. And she would sew things for me that were something like bloomers that were for back-yard play. Which of course Daddy didn't approve of. She once took me to see Isadora Duncan dance. Well, nobody else in the social group my parents were in would have thought of taking their child to the city to see Isadora Duncan. Who the hell was Isadora Duncan? She was exposing me to art. To Daddy, dancing on a stage was something harlots did in burlesque houses. I remember when I was in junior high getting invited to a prom. My father said, 'She cannot wear an evening dress, it's out of the question.' Mother said, 'She will have an evening dress. Maybe it won't be cut quite as low as I personally would like, but she will have an evening dress.'

"Occasionally she used to drag Daddy to the theater—and he'd be dragged

Nan Post, c. 1908
(photographer unknown)

right out, too. *They would call him during the performances, and he'd go. He must have been very grateful. Mother, on the other hand, had all kinds of cultured friends. She had this one male friend who used to take me to art museums in Manhattan. It must have been the Met. I remember seeing the El Grecos. This man was just some friend of Mother's, I don't think there was anything between them.*

   "*I don't know why Mother and Daddy ever would have married. I think she must always have had deep unfulfilled sexual stirrings, which of course would partly explain Cousin Ed. I remember once looking down on Mother and Daddy from the stairway as they were downstairs fighting. He didn't hit her, but he had hold of her wrists and he was shaking her violently and screaming, 'Look here, woman.' It terrified me. I wish my sister Helen were alive. She knew everything about the family. After the divorce, when Mother was in*

Greenwich Village, I remember her telling me Daddy had never once fulfilled her. She meant physically. That hit me hard. There is something star-crossed about my mother's entire life, and I suppose that's part of the reason I've always loved her so deeply. It was the way she always had to struggle with her life. She was a tremendous influence on me. But it was also her values, which she tried never to compromise. Maybe the one compromise was her marriage to Daddy because she told me once it was an arranged marriage, by my mother's mother. She was an awful person, by the way. I hated that woman. My mother was her exact opposite. Of course, she was Daddy's exact opposite, too. But they must have loved each other once, or convinced themselves they did."

Reasie Heard and her husband, Charles, and their young daughter, Edna, are also part of this household. Reasie and Charles are from Anniston, Alabama. Reasie's mother was born a slave. Reasie does the cooking and housekeeping at 17 Park Place while Charles does chores and also chauffeurs Dr. Post on some of his afternoon and evening rounds, which apparently is when some of the secret philandering gets going. Reasie knows how to pick a ripe switch off a backyard tree, though she seldom uses it. She can loop a rope over a maple limb and fork a board onto it and then set you swinging until the ground below scuffs soft as talc. She has wonderful stories in her about the Deep South and she will have something to do—one is certain—with the brilliance and sensitivity of some Southern photographs to be taken by her charge in another decade.

Once, in a fit of anger over some punishment or other, the charge screams something she has heard neighborhood children say: "I don't like you, you nigger!" Reasie is stunned. Nan, overhearing, plucks the ripe switch. It is a lesson Marion Post never forgets.

Reasie Heard loves Sis and Helen as her own, but especially Sis, and has a deep need to protect her from all she sees coming.

What comes, not to hold it back any longer, is in the person of a robust, outgoing, impeccably attired Albany banker named Edwin Hurd. Listen for a moment to the attorney for plaintiff, Essex County Divorce Trial, Docket No. G-65-178, late summer 1924: "One Edwin M. Hurd, connected by marriage with the defendant, became an inmate of the family of the petitioner and defendant at some time prior to 1920 and obtained an ascendency over defendant's affections\ to such an extent as to alienate them completely from the petitioner. Under the dominance of this strong and unscrupulous personality, the defendant's nature seems to have become so saturated with 'broad' and 'modern' notions that fidelity to her obligations and morality as understood and striven for by ordinary people became unimportant and outworn ideas too gross to survive in the high and rarefied atmosphere into which her seducer introduced her. Accordingly, she first announced to her husband that she withdrew from him his marital rights, and then proceeded to do so, still remaining in his house for a period, then leaving it completely, apparently so as to enjoy the society of this Hurd more freely than she could in petitioner's home."

Cousin Ed—everyone in the family calls him this—isn't an actual cousin of Nan Post. Rather it is Hurd's wife and Nan's mother who are blood relations. Cousin Ed is in his late fifties when he arrives in Bloomfield (one thinks of him toodling off the evening trolley, a pasteboard suitcase in his freckled paw), which means he is roughly twenty years Nan's senior. If he comes in the year 1919—the court documents don't pin it down—then Marion is nine. He has arrived in the first place because his bank is relocating him from a regional upstate office to one of its headquarter offices in New York City. It is unclear, and probably immaterial, who first invites him in, Walter or Nan. But this much is clear: He comes as the boarder and leaves as the lover. The change in Ed's status seems to occur over a period of about three years, when the second child in this household is finding puberty.

"I have seen them together on the mountain, I have seen them get on the trolley car," Dr. Post will testify in the prolonged divorce trial, the words seeming to ring almost operatic on the stenographer's page.

"I remember a story—it is so vague—that Daddy was hiding in the bushes and going to kill him, that he had gotten a revolver. I must have been twelve or thirteen and by now the whole thing was in the open. I can believe it, though it also sounds slightly unreal."

What also sounds slightly unreal is how long Nan Post stays on at 17 Park Place after the relationship has come out onto open ground. If court documents are reasonably accurate about time, then Nan remains in the house on the green from the spring of 1922—when the tryst is found out—until Election Day of the following year. That's close to eighteen months. What kind of emotional havoc, on levels hidden and not hidden, might such a year and a half of staying—and, presumably, of illicit loving—have brought to the two children of 17 Park Place? Is it possible such a relationship could be kept secret from two curious children for eighteen months? Why does Nan stay? Is Walter being cuckolded almost in plain view?

The divorce documents do not spell out satisfying answers to any of these questions, but the strong implication is that, yes, the love affair is conducted in the house, in one fashion or another, even after it is discovered. (And how long has it gone on *before* it is discovered? There's no way to know.) From the testimony in the documents, Cousin Ed seems to depart at one point but then apparently reenters to be with his beloved. It should be emphasized, however, that the court papers are greatly prejudiced in Walter's favor. He is the accuser in a suit that goes uncontested, and his sinned-against righteousness leaps out from every page.

"It is gone, exactly what I knew or didn't know. What seems right to me is that I probably didn't know, at least on conscious levels, for a very long while. They did keep it a secret. That's what my mind tells me. I can tell you this with certainty, though: I don't remember Cousin Ed as a menacing or a threatening or intruding force, upsetting my equilibrium. I know anyone might tend to think so. But the fact is he was warm and wonderfully affectionate and had lots of time for me."

Years hence, trying to summon the Other Man back from beyond, Marion Post Wolcott will put in a letter, concerning the period after Nan had left the family and gotten her own place: "[He] was openly affectionate in front of me—told me how wonderful sex in a deep love could be—told me how important it was to a lasting relationship—how fortunate I was to have beauty and grace, & that I had a responsibility to care for & maintain it & realize its value. That it could open doors for me—*but* I needed more than a pretty face & body. . . . I was sure he cared for me & loved me & wanted to teach me about the things he loved."

In photographs Ed Hurd suggests a formal man with much lurking underneath. There are pictures of him with homburgs and a stuck-out chest. He has four grown children and a wife up in Albany named Alice who is in fragile health and is soon going to drop dead over all this. Cousin Ed has tags of poetry in him, he knows about stars and health food, he's a great ocean swimmer who loves diving under the waves and coming up fifty yards later. Summers, he likes leading Post family expeditions (sans the head of the house) to the mountains or seashore. Sometimes, even Dr.

Post's nurse goes along on these outings to Asbury Park or Far Rockaway. Cousin Ed can regale children with what he knows about trees, rocks, flowers, fungi, ferns, almost any kind of bird.

From a letter to Nan, entered as an exhibit in the divorce trial: "But Nannie dear, your soul was struggling for light and some hidden pawn seemed to stay you from letting me go. . . . You need me as I do you. This force is bigger than all else in life even though to go on meant death itself. And with the struggling of your soul, mine too grew to see the wonder of a love that could put courage in one's heart and know no fear." It ends: "My queen. My love, the bravest and most wonderful girl in all the world. I love you. Your Eddie."

According to the legal documents, what prompts Nan's acknowledgment of the secret love affair is Walter's discovery of "a suspicious incident—they were in the dining room before dinner and she was in his arms." (Marion is about to turn twelve when this happens.) The next morning husband and wife motor to nearby Brookdale, park by the side of the road. The truth comes out.

Nan doesn't leave, though. And Walter doesn't demand she go. From court transcripts:

Q. Going back to the time when you first discovered that the defendant was too much under the influence of this Mr. Hurd, what did you do, if anything, to get him out of the house?
A. I tried to show Mrs. Post that his presence was obnoxious to me, that I did not like the atmosphere. They would frequently quarrel—my wife and Mr. Hurd would frequently quarrel and [were] always making up. At those times chiefly, I would say, "Marion, let Ed go. Don't coax him back, let him stay away." They would quarrel and he would pack his bag and go off and stay a couple of days.
Q. Did these quarrels take place in your presence?
A. Yes, sometimes I was directly present. I knew of other quarrels when I was in the house.
Q. Did you ever tell him to leave?
A. No.
Q. Why?
A. To avoid putting the fat in the fire. That is all I know.
Q. Simply that you didn't want to bring on a crisis?

A.   Didn't want to bring on a crisis and didn't want to create an atmosphere of distrust of my wife.

Q.   At that time did you fear that her preference for him was such that she would side with him instead of you?

A.   On matters of slight importance, yes. If matters came to a crisis I did not think she would turn to him instead of me.

Q.   Still, you didn't want to put it to a test by putting him out of the house?

A.   No. That is a hard thing to explain. I felt that Mrs. Post would come to her senses about it. Their frequent quarrels I hoped would bring on a crisis between them.

Q.   Did you ever discuss with Mr. Hurd the effect that his presence was having on your wife?

A.   I did.

Q.   What did you tell him about it?

A.   I told him his influence was leading Mrs. Post from me and asked him to remove it.

Q.   When was that?

A.   That was—after this open confession of hers in May, 1922.

Q.   Well, what did he say?

A.   He said that he would like to step out of the picture if it would not break up Mrs. Post. He feared the mental effect and he wanted to get out, he said, with a clean slate.

The separation, beginning in November 1923, lasts nine months and then a divorce suit is initiated. Dr. Post continues living in the house on the green while Nan is in a four-room apartment two blocks away, at 202 Broad. The children are forced to choose sides, become pawns for affection, as children always become in such circumstances. Sis gravitates toward her mother, while Helen's loyalty is toward her father. But both girls move back and forth between their parents, housed on separate sides of the park, and this, too, seems so bizarre to the town, out of order. Many times Sis is forced to run home from school with her head down so she won't have to face the taunts of her peers. Sometimes Charles Heard comes for her in the doctor's car.

Q.   The oldest child, Helen, is now living with you. Has she been living with you ever since your wife left the house?

A. Yes.
Q. Do you know as a matter of fact why she did not go with her mother?
A. I know that she was not in sympathy with her mother.

And as to the younger child: "When I spoke to her about going with her mother, she said, 'Daddy, I am going because I feel somebody ought to be with Mother,' in a very emotional way, giving me an impression that it was not a choice but she thought that someone ought to live with her mother."

This is almost certainly a skewed interpretation of the facts.

A minister of the gospel, Otto F. Mohn, appears in court as a witness for the plaintiff. He describes how he has tried to get the adulterous woman to come to her senses.

Q. Was there any urging on your part?
A. Absolutely. I tried to make her see that for the sake of her children she ought to be a good wife and mother and leave Ed Hurd absolutely.
Q. What did she say to that urging?
A. She said she could not and wouldn't. What she wanted me to tell her was that she could still live in the home of Walter Post and have Ed Hurd come whenever he pleased. She didn't see why she couldn't live there as a good mother and wife and still have Ed Hurd coming to see her. . . . She said that Walter had never taught her what love was—that she could not live over there in that house—never wanted to go under that roof again. She said, "Walter said he was going to get a divorce. Why doesn't he do it?" I said, "I imagine he would like to have you straighten this thing out and behave yourself, as any man would." She said, "He needn't wait for that because I will never do it." I said, "Marion [Nan's christened name], are you willing to take a divorce from Walter?" She said, "Absolutely, I am waiting for it. I want to be free and he has a right to be free."

Another voice. It belongs to Peg Sinclair Reiter, childhood friend of Sis, next-door neighbor, daughter of the Presbyterian minister: "We lived at 23 Park, right alongside. My clearest memory of this, really my only memory, is when Marion came over to our house, sat down in the living room, and said there was going to be a divorce between her mother and father. My mother and father were there, so it must have been afternoon. What could you say? My father was the highly respected Presbyterian minister, and I have this funny feeling that Marion had a need to tell him and my mother more than me, that she just wanted to get it out. I certainly would have had no experience with the word 'divorce.' The word 'adultery' wouldn't have been in my vocabulary either. I'm sure no one used such a shocking word at the time."

The divorce suit is formally entered in the courts on August 1, 1924, but isn't settled until the following summer. From the evidence of the documents, Nan appears not to have made an appearance. Sis is sent away to camp during the first summer of the divorce. She hates it. In the autumn she is packed off to a boarding school in Chambersburg, Pennsylvania—which she hates even more. She gets a C − in religion at Penn Hall and cries nightly for home as wan figures patrol the halls and her sleep. Years later she'll write in a letter about that school: "Even now I can see & hear that prissy, dull, narrow-minded, frumpy [Bible] teacher—and she was infallible—no questions, no discussions; except her own answers to anyone's curiosity or doubting."

There is only one photograph of Sis from this period, and what is remarkable about the picture is how radically different a semichubby fourteen-year-old looks from the cheeky six-year-old in the 1916 backyard shot. This girl's shoulders are slumped, she has a big bang drooping down in front of her eyes, her clothes are inelegant and hang loose. The picture is snapped in a studio in East Orange.

Sometime in this period Nan Post contracts cancer of the uterus, which only furthers the nasty little town's nasty talk about her. She is burned in the radiation treatments by her careless doctors. But she refuses to take any financial support from Walter other than an initial cash settlement. Ed Hurd continues to love her deeply, but now his own life begins to turn unexpectedly hard. He loses his job at Morgan Guaranty (it's the adulterous, almost incestuous, liaison); two of his four children strike him from their lives; he develops a heart condition. Ed Hurd, always so vigorous, seems suddenly to have grown into an old man. He and Nan are never to marry. Freedom has secret costs.

Initially Nan tries a dressmaking business, but to make a go of that you have to have people come in and purchase your creations—and she is Bloomfield's Hester Prynne. Before the divorce is finalized, Nan relocates to East Orange, and after that she moves into Manhattan, to the Village, where she sits with penny coffees talking socialism at the Romany Marie café on West 8th, a haunt of twenties bohemians that's just around the corner from her cold-water English basement flat. At one point Nan finds the money to travel to the Soviet Union to observe Communism firsthand. It doesn't win her unqualified approval, is the way the trip will later be remembered. At length Nan Post meets Margaret Sanger, champion of reproductive rights, founder of the American birth control movement, pioneer of a decade-old magazine entitled *The Woman Rebel*. The two, who even look alike, discover they have much in common: Both trained as nurses at New York hospitals. Both left nursing to become wives of professional men. Both had moved with their husbands to suburbs. And both were unable to stop the political and social and personal forces pushing up inside them. Sanger had opened the country's first family planning clinic in 1916 (getting arrested for it) and five years later had founded the organization that was to become known as Planned Parenthood. Nan serves as a compiler and interviewer at the Sanger Research Bureau in the New York offices. She helps set up the first Harlem clinic. Later, as a national field worker for the Sanger movement, she travels out into the country, sometimes by car, sometimes by rail, attempting to lay groundwork for local clinics even as her own second daughter would one day travel the backcountry of the hard-used Depression South taking powerful pictures.

From the hated boarding school in Pennsylvania, fifteen-year-old Sis is sent in 1925 to a coeducational progressive institution in Greenwich, Connecticut. It's called Edgewood and is run by two middle-aged spinsters, Miss Marietta Johnson and Miss Euphrosene Langley. One of them had once headed such an experimental school in Mobile, Alabama. Sis's older sister attends Edgewood for a brief time, too. The Edgewood property was built originally by C. W. Post, the cereal king, as a private estate for his daughter Marjorie—it was said to have cost $300,000 in 1905. The great Tudor stone manor house slopes down to the massive vaulted gate house and timbered stable, with its inlaid hand-tiled corridors. There are twenty acres of woods and fields and a brook that winds over rocky falls and under footbridges to a pond, perfect for skating in winter and boating in summer. There are beech and tulip and maple trees on the wide lawns. The Edgewood School is a loosely structured learning environment, deliberately so, with a concentration in crafts and arts. "It offers the joys of creative achievement, instead of the marks and punishments usually employed," says one of the institution's advertisements. "There is no oppressive atmosphere of compulsion." Sis takes up pottery, metalworking, shop. (She may even have picked up a camera.) The wounded child with the shameful secrets seems to rediscover an earlier self at Edgewood. A cheekiness comes back, a natural sensuality returns. In a student publication called *Wild Geese,* written by classmates the year she graduates, 1927, she is described as someone who can "play any position in basketball, draw, write, sing—oh yes—laugh in a manner all her own, *and* preside over a very select hair-cutting establishment." A few lines further down, there seem coded, unwitting revelations amid the standard poking of fun: "She has the unusual habit of holding nightly conversations with herself; chatting gaily on all secretive subjects in her sleep—a charming talent, say her roommates. [She] might be called 'Dissimulating Sis' for the genius she displays in her various ways of evading disagreeable things—we might say homework. Sis can raise the roof, or be as silent as the hour before the dawn."

Dissimulating Sis stays at Edgewood until she's seventeen, falling in and out of adolescent love with several sons of Manhattan magnates, sometimes driving around with them buck-naked through greater Greenwich in their daddies' Packards and Pierce-Arrows. It's just something naughty and exciting to do.

Old woman in California, wagging a finger, though stifling a grin, too: *"You wouldn't put that in, would you?"*

LET TIME TELESCOPE NOW, vault ahead a few years. It's the summer of 1935 and a twenty-five-year-old woman is learning she can trap time in a rectangle—beautifully. Much has happened to the sunny-seeming child from that misleading backyard 1916 album shot. Sis Post has a full, firm, sensuous mouth and a linear face with hair winging out on either side of it. She isn't gorgeous, but in photographs there is something undeniably erotic and formidable and American about her. Scarred, too, you'd probably say, if you were looking close.

She is against all forms of fascism. She is an advocate for progressive education and the rights of black people. The world of art is making her soul breathe. Like her mother, she has come to believe no woman can truly call herself free until she can choose consciously whether she will or will not bear children.

But before getting to 1935, this glimpse of her preceding eight or nine years, between the end of Edgewood and now, because of course all of it is going into the mix of what she is just about to become:

She has taught in a progressive school in Caldwell, New Jersey, and discovered her natural abilities with small children. She has taken classes at the New School for Social Research: child psychology, anthropology, and some modern dance with Ruth St. Denis, a pioneer of dance. She has enrolled at New York University, where there'd been further experimental dance with a woman named Doris Humphrey. Humphrey, like St. Denis, has long been investigating the laws of kinetic rhythm. She is, you might say, pushing the outside of the envelope. She has come to a theory that the action of human dance exists upon an arc, almost a graph, from balance to unbalance, from fall to recovery. And that between that motionlessness of perfect balance and the "chaos" of a complete yield to gravity lay "an arc between two deaths." Both of these pioneers, Humphrey and St. Denis, believe that dance—no, life—should "move after an inner law." Mumbo jumbo? Maybe, but a gifted shooter who doesn't yet know she's a shooter may already be picking up, by the late 1920s, through the discipline of modern dance, some acute camera sensitivities to the intimacies of social interaction.

She has spent a summer at Vassar as an intern in elementary education. She has apprenticed at a private boarding school in Cambridge, Massachusetts. She has lived on and off with her mother in the Village, where she met a painter with a beautiful body who didn't turn out to be the next Leonardo, after all. Nan's child, Sis finds it easy to fall for stray cats and broke artists, and whatever pin money she makes in this period from posing unrobed in Village art classes usually goes right over to these poor creatures, one way or another.

She has taught in a western Massachusetts mill town. It's a school for the children of upper-level mill managers, and she boards on the other side of town with the mill workers themselves. This is her first eye-opening to the poison of class bigotries in America, and the experience will have much influence later on.

She has buried her father. Walter Post dies of a coronary occlusion on April 1, 1932. He would have been fifty-five that December. His surprisingly small obit is on page six of the Bloomfield *Independent Press,* and while it is true that Mountainside Hospital in Montclair passes a *Whereas* resolution in lament of its late colleague, and that neighbors press their condolences on the family, the death nonetheless has the unmistakable aura of a life concluded in tragedy. Dr. Post is waked in the parlor of the house on the green. His two daughters attend, though not Nan. There's no mention in the newspaper obituary of Cousin Ed or of the bad Florida land speculations that have driven a man downward not seven years past his divorce. The burial is in the town cemetery, where Revolutionary soldiers and a former governor lie. The plot costs $180, and the stone picked by the family is quite modest. The children are named beneficiaries of the small estate, and Bloomfield Bank and Trust is named overseer until each daughter reaches twenty-five.

Home for the funeral, staying that first night at the house of one of her father's friends, Sis awakens to find that man, drunk, pawing at her body. This only intensifies her resolve to be shed of the nasty little place. After this visit, she will never see Bloomfield again.

With monies from the estate, twenty-two-year-old Sis next manages two years of study and travel in Europe on the extreme cheap. She tours in France, Germany, Italy, though mostly in Austria. Her sister, Helen, who has studied applied art and earned a degree in ceramics from Alfred University in western New York, has already been to Europe, has come back to America to teach in rural Kentucky, and is about to return to the Continent just as Sis arrives. At first the younger sister goes to Paris, so she can attend the wedding of one of her old Edgewood classmates. Then she goes to Berlin, where she enrolls in a modern gymnastics dance known as *Tanzgymnastik*. But there she comes down with a slight case of pneumonia, and so the Berlin stay ends sooner than expected. But before leaving Germany, the younger sister experiences the Führer at a Nazi rally. He is high above her, and thousands are screaming. The girl from Bloomfield stands far back in the crowd. It's the magnitude of the crowd, the pageantry. The message of hate is terrifying. Within several months Hitler assumes the chancellorship of the country and history alters.

"I suppose this is why Nazism was so real to me. That experience, and what I saw when I got to Austria, made me very antifascist, as well as against all forms of racial intolerance for the rest of my life. So I'd say first it was my mother, the crusading social worker, all her personal pain, that helped shape my leftist-liberal views. And then witnessing Hitler's rise to power. Those two experiences were profound for me."

After a recuperation in the French countryside and on the Mediterranean (this is the spring of thirty-three, and she is serving briefly as a nanny to the children of some wealthy people she knows from back home), Sis lands in Austria, principally Vienna, schizoid imperial city of psychoanalysis and the waltz, of Zionism and Nazism, of Mozart and Beethoven, of Marie Antoinette and Leon Trotsky. Her sister is in Austria now, studying a new concept in photography called "available light," working with Trude Fleischmann, a Viennese portrait photographer. Fleischmann, a muscular, merry little woman who has a bowl haircut and skis like a man, has a studio in the first district, near City Hall, on Ebendorferstrasse. The place is spacious and full of light, and students flock to it, as do artists, musicians, theater types. Trude has established a reputation throughout Austria for fine, soft-focus, photographic portraiture—of a dewy sixteen-year-old Hedy Lamarr, of the architect Adolf Loos; of the Thimig family, who are Austria's Barrymores. She uses a slow-plate camera with glass-plate negatives, and her pictures have a soft, brown, fuzzy tint. The work

Marion and Helen Post, by Trude
Fleischmann, Vienna, c. 1933

isn't documentary, exactly, and in any event few people are using that word. Trude calls her technique "photo-reporting." A critic will later say her pictures contain something of the casual, the "incidental of the snapshot." Trude is taking the older Post sister into orchestra pits to shoot Toscanini conducting rehearsals—this sort of thing. (Later, after she has emigrated to the States, Trude will get Einstein just by going up to his door; will get Eleanor Roosevelt and Lotte Lenya and Sinclair Lewis and numerous others of the famous and beautiful.)

The younger sister is fascinated by the concept of available light and indeed wonders about camera work for herself. But she still thinks her true vocation is working with young children. No matter her love for dance, her love for mingling with artists in Trude's loft, Sis feels Helen is the real artist of the family.

"I can tell you what I remember of Vienna. Those old dark dour apartments with the very high ceilings and big living rooms and the hard leather furniture. They were permanently cold. After you'd lived in Europe for a time you were just grateful if the place didn't have fleas and had some hot water now and then. I remember this absolutely deadly and beautiful city that seemed to be swirling about me toward civil war. For a time I lived with my sister on Rathausstrasse. This was after we had stayed out in the countryside with a peasant family, and I had helped nurse Helen back from illness. When I got to Vienna there were many rich young Americans in Freudian analysis. I never saw the man himself, but he was there, I had a friend who was going to him. I took some child psychology courses at the university. It was very hard for me because I didn't know the language. So I had some of my beaus do the translating, and that wasn't so hard at all. I didn't have a college degree—I had a lot of scattered education but no degree—and I suppose I knew I wasn't going to get one here. Oh, you'd sit in wicker chairs at cafés—everybody did this—and read the paper forever with café mit schlag. Or Gosser Bier. If you weren't attending classes, you were at Trude's, or maybe going to some semiradical student meeting.

"Earlier, out in the countryside, I had seen swastikas burned in the front yards of peasants, crosses torched in grain fields. Again, it was just so damn terrifying to me. It's true I attended some meetings of extreme left-wing student groups. I suppose they were Communist in nature. I think it was a perfectly legitimate idealism. I suppose it was my urge, the urge of any of us, to try and discover alternative political systems. The world seemed in economic ruin and

here was this very real possibility of global war. I remember at night lying
awake and listening to bombing out in the Floridsdorf district of the city. Even-
tually they closed the university—it was the so-called February Revolution—
and then some months later Chancellor Dollfuss was assassinated and then I
and most of the other Americans had to go home. Everything just seemed so
heightened in that period."

Not least, her passion for Eugen. He is twenty years older than Sis, and
he smokes long thin pipes, and he has dark curly hair, and he wears checkered flannel shirts and polka-dot bandannas, and he doesn't work because
life is more important. His family is in the fur business; Eugen is in the
love business. He's happy to teach a kid sister from the states about Viennese ways of lovemaking. Eugen (it's pronounced Oy-gun in German) has
a young son and an ex-wife in Salzburg. Sis and Eugen, who soon move
in together, make love on the floors of a perpetually cold Viennese apartment. They make love in their dreams. They make love on the banks of
cold streams in the Wiener Wald. They go faltboating on the Danube,
they go mountain-walking way up above the tree line, and when they're
not doing any or all of this, they take in the city's art museums. They're as
impecunious as they are erotic.

A photograph. A man and a woman are sitting with their backs turned
to the camera. They are on a picnic in the country—perhaps the forests
around Vienna. The young woman is in a halter top and a bandanna and
is sliding a ripped-off hunk of bread into her lover's mouth.

"I can't say it ever would have worked. Probably it would not have worked.
He was too much older. I know I loved him deeply. I wanted to be in love with
someone, although I wasn't sure I ever wanted to be married. Being in love was
what was more important to me than anything. But it didn't work out. I never
saw Eugen again after I left. I did have a chance to see him once. I was back in
America and wasn't married to Lee yet, or at least don't think I was. Trude
Fleischmann, who had fled the Nazis and set up a studio in New York, called
me and said, 'He wants to see you badly.' For whatever reason, I didn't see him.
And a week later he dropped dead of a heart attack on a New York street. Oh,
there is one other thing for you to understand: Before he was my lover, Eugen
had a relationship with my sister. Helen never quite had the same relationship
with him I did. For one thing, she knew his wife in Salzburg and knew that
this wife still loved Eugen, even though they were divorced. But then I came

into the picture. I'm not really sure how Helen felt about it, even though she had another more serious interest by then. As I've said, it was always very complicated between my sister and me."

The trustee of Walter Post's estate now sends Sis a one-way ticket to America. It's too dangerous over there, she should return immediately. Besides, opines Mr. Ellis of Bloomfield Bank and Trust, he isn't convinced that the cash he's been advancing is being used purely in the pursuit of education. He got that part right.

But something happens just before Sis leaves Vienna, in the torn and sped-up summer of 1934, a small thing at the time, or so it appears. Trude Fleischmann loans the younger sister a midget Rolleiflex, a "four-by-four." It's a twin-lens reflex, meaning you can see what you're shooting. "Try it out," Fleischmann tells her. The camera has an aperture of f2.8, quite fast. The next weekend, in the mountains, Sis, unobserved, fooling around, points and clicks the instrument. Back in Vienna, she gives the film to Fleischmann. A few days later Fleischmann says, out of Helen's earshot, "Sis, I'm amazed at your eye. You should go on with this."

On her way out of the country Sis Post buys her first camera. It's a four-by-four.

Back in America now (the delayed return has come via a two-month stay in Italy, where she takes many pictures with her new camera), in need of funds, Sis hires on as a teacher at the Hessian Hills School in Croton-on-Hudson, New York. Hessian Hills is a progressive institution in a riverside village of lawyers and stockbrokers and artist-intellectuals. Robert Minor, onetime leader of the Communist Party in America, had built a house in Croton in the twenties. John Reed wrote *Ten Days That Shook the World* in Croton. Max Eastman and Isadora Duncan and Edna St. Vincent Millay had lived in Croton. Hessian Hills is off Mt. Airy Road in a section known locally as "Red Hill." The school has a forge, woodcarving classes, dance, a darkroom. It advertises itself as "A little school in the country where boys and girls from 2–12 years may live and grow in a world not only of text books." The students raise sheep and then spin yarn and then dye it with apple bark. Sis, hired to teach the first and second grades, rents a room from one of the two founders of Hessian Hills, Margaret Hatfield Chase. Nearly every morning she is awakened to a glass of grapefruit juice and Margaret's piercing cry, "Come out, Marion, we must do the bear walk." The two—along with any other students or faculty around—then go up and down the corridors, and sometimes the lawns, on all fours, naked as jaybirds, winter or summer. On Thanksgiving Margaret, a strict vegetarian, serves her guests and her boarder ground nuts in the shape of a turkey. In her free time at Hessian Hills, Sis takes pictures. She gets a child playing in a wooden-wheeled cart. She experiments in the dark-room. Hudson River light can be wondrous. From the Croton shore, you can aim your camera west across the river and snap a whole line of whale-humped blue-green hills.

On weekends the progressive teacher drives down to the city and stays with her sister. Helen has taken a cold-water, bathtub-in-the-kitchen rail-road flat at 30 West 47th Street and is trying hard to get photo assignments from magazines. The kid sister purchases a used exposure meter, an old Weston. Helen teaches her how to develop and make good prints in the kitchen sink (with blankets over the windows and towels stuffed in the crack beneath the door). Sis keeps her secondhand Ford together with bailing wire and a gluepot, and she goes out on dates with many men, and she begins to wonder: But what am I really, a teacher or a photographer?

It is sometime in this period—late thirty-four, early thirty-five—that Sis meets and begins socializing with some of the not-yet-legendary actors and directors and playwrights of the Group Theatre: Clifford Odets, Lee Strasberg, Morris Carnovsky, Elia Kazan, Harold Clurman, Stella Adler, Sanford Meisner, Franchot Tone, John Garfield, Irwin Shaw. The Group is sprinkled with leftists and even Party members who are trying to create art for the masses, and this fits right in with where Sis is going. In essence the Group wants to effect a revolution against stardom and capitalism, wants to present a theater that will show the face of America. Method acting derives from the Group. At the moment Sis comes to know them, the Group's players are having some of their greatest successes: *Waiting for Lefty,* for instance, in which highly emotional scenes close with the Communist salute. An outraged mother in *Lefty* says, "Sure, I see it in the papers, how good orange juice is for kids. . . . Betty never saw a grapefruit. I took her to the store last week and she pointed to a stack of grapefruits. 'What's that!' she said."

Elia Kazan, known as "Gadge," is a member of the CP, and so, too, are Odets and Strasberg. Cell meetings are held every Tuesday night in Joe Bromberg's dressing room. Years later, in a book about the Group called *The Fervent Years,* Group founder Harold Clurman will write: ". . . certain observers with an antipathy for the Group accused the organization of inducing neurosis in normal people; others, less severe but no less critical, asserted that the Group attracted the unbalanced. There is much to be said on this score. . . . Any equivalent group—no matter what its purpose or motivation—would necessarily contain within itself certain iconoclastic elements, since such a group arises from some sense of dissatisfaction as well as from positive and constructive impulses. Thus it will attract people under pressure of some kind, troubled, not quite adjusted people, yearners, dreamers, secretly ambitious."

Marion begins taking pictures of the Group backstage, experimenting with available light in their dressing rooms. Then she sells the pictures to the subjects for five dollars apiece. These people like her spunk. At a Group summer retreat near Bridgeport, Connecticut, she gets John Garfield (known then as Julie Garfield) dog-paddling in a lake. He's ring-curled and sexy and has a pipe clenched in his teeth—does he have trunks on? Sis Post doesn't really know it, but she's becoming a kind of canny director of people herself.

Bobby Lewis, Group pioneer: "Oh, hell, everybody was a Communist in one sense or another back then. What I remember about Marion—and I would have thought she's dead, because I haven't heard about her for years—is this rather attractive girl, not beautiful, but quite attractive and charming and, yes, maybe a little ambitious, who just got in among us because she was delightful and enthusiastic and just wanted to be there and liked our ideas and our talk. She wasn't interested in performing, I don't think. I see her vaguely in my mind now linked with Irwin Shaw, though perhaps this was later and one hesitates to say if one doesn't know for sure."

Shaw—three years younger than Sis, heavy Brooklyn accent; brawny shoulders, killer grin, a jock's rolling, balls-of-the-feet gait—is a struggling American playwright who hasn't yet turned into a wealthy potboiler American novelist. He falls for Marion. A few years from now, the two will meet up in some dusty FSA outpost for a discreet cooling of their libidos. Like all Sis's other passions to date, however, this one isn't destined to last.

Her most serious love from the Group is an actor named Walter Coy. He's from Seattle and has daddy-longlegs and loves to go dancing at the Savoy up in Harlem. For a short while Coy and Sis live in a semiratty apartment on West 4th Street in the Village, next door to Julie Garfield and his wife, Robbie. Coy leaves the Group in 1936 to go to Hollywood, where he becomes a minor actor. When he returns a few years later, Sis has moved on to other loves—and the FSA.

Her closest friends from the Group—friends who will remain friends for a lifetime—are Wilhelmina and Tony Kraber. In the fifties, Tony Kraber will get smeared in the Communist witch hunts of the McCarthy hysteria. In a much later decade Willy Kraber, now a widow, will live alone in a fine old Brooklyn brownstone that gleams with the memories of thirties New York. On Willy's walls, down long hallways, will be sepia photographs taken fifty years before by that emergent camera artist Marion Post, photographs of opening night at such productions as *Golden Boy* and *Till the Day I Die.*

Willy Kraber: "I keep thinking about why we came to mean so much to each other. I suppose it was her generosity, first of all. She bought our child Fritzie's first pair of shoes. I just hadn't gotten around to it yet. Marion said one day, 'Willy, Fritzie needs shoes.' Before I knew it she had brought them to our apartment on Jane Street in the Village. That was Marion. She was much more sophisticated than I was. After all, Marion had been to Europe. Not just Europe, but Vienna! Freud, my God! Here she was rushing about all the time snapping all these pictures of Group people, so independent, so serious about it, so—what is the word—*engaged* with life. When we first met her, she may still have been teaching at that school up on the Hudson. She'd come in on weekends with these great big boots and men's overstuffed gloves—I guess it must have been wintertime—and look just awful. But of course underneath was all this sensuality. She'd start to take off the outer layers and there it was in front of you. I wanted to be an actress, but found myself with a young child and worried about the financial responsibility. But Marion was always so full of life. I envied her, I loved her. We just became very close. I never felt that way particularly about her sister, Helen. There was always something more pinched about Helen, if you ask me. There were periods in the years afterward, when Marion and Lee were abroad and so forth, when we'd be out of touch, but then we'd always refind each other. When she first went with Farm Security, she used to come to our place with her fresh prints. She would be writing captions for them. She'd come into the city for a day and stay with us and show us these pictures. It was so damn exciting and of course she was so stimulated by what she was doing. I wouldn't say she was bursting with confidence when I first knew her. But she had something that could make men nearly swoon."

SO THIS BRINGS A LIFE, at least in cameo, up to the summer of 1935. Call it the camera curve of the story. There's a terrible depression in America. Twenty-five-year-old Sis Post—who doesn't really like the name "Sis" anymore—has resigned her teaching job at Hessian Hills to try and storm the barricades of big-time New York photography. The newly declared free-lance has about thirty cents to her name, but the first thing she does, after moving in with her sister, is to get some fancy stationery printed up: MARION POST, PHOTOGRAPHER. ME-DALLION 3–1233. Almost no one in the photography world, Manhattan or otherwise, has ever heard of her. And yet you might say she has been unwittingly provided—from the pain of Bloomfield to the sensibilities of the Group—with just what she needs.

She borrows money, wangles an assignment at *Fortune* (gets paid but the pictures don't get published), talks story ideas to *Parents, Vogue, Woman Today, Stage, Building America*. Her enthusiasm for free meals knows no bounds. She has a friend who is a wirephoto chief at the Associated Press—Ed Stanley, smitten, soon sends some work her way.

She attends meetings of the Photo League on East 21st Street, a split-off from the Workers' Film and Photo League, whose sensibilities are evident in the name. She studies the photographs of Jacob Riis, who documented New York slums in the 1890s; of Lew Hine, who took a camera to Ellis Island in the years before World War I to get portraits of immigrants stepping from steerage. At the League she pays ten cents for chemicals, supplies her own paper, gets darkroom time free. One night—the exact date is lost, but it seems to be late thirty-five or early thirty-six—she hears a lecture by the noted photographer and filmmaker Ralph Steiner. Steiner has brought along slides of the work of his friend, the great Paul Strand. Steiner, a craftsman as well as a respected teacher, says something that night that Sis will quote often in the years to come: "Keep in mind that behind every sincere photographer is a person with a head and a heart." Strand, of course, is one of the most famous photographers alive. He has helped reorient photographic aesthetics from the pretty and stylized to the almost brutally pure and direct. Strand has said that if a person is going to use the medium honestly and intensely, he must first exhibit "a real respect for the thing in front of him, expressed . . . through a range of almost infinite tonal values which lie beyond the skill of human hand." He is credited with fusing the formal concerns of abstract art with the factual accuracy of the camera.

Steiner, then in his midthirties, lithe and curly-headed and with much
sexual energy in him, poses some questions to the audience that evening
at the Photo League during his slide-talk on Strand. The cheeky twenty-
five-year-old at the back of the room keeps raising her hand to try to
answer. Afterward Steiner comes up to her. Is she a photographer? Well,
she's trying to be one. Would she be interested in meeting at his loft on an
informal basis with other students to discuss their work? Yes, she would
be very interested in that. In fact, how about tonight?

It doesn't happen quite that fast. But some days later when Steiner does
get a chance to view her photos, he sees the promise. But he tells her, "It's
a little too arty, I think, Marion." The student makes experiments, reads
chapters in books on photography, meets Strand himself. Both Steiner and
Strand have connections with the Group Theatre (the Group's earliest
members used to meet in Steiner's studio), so many of these lines of learning, friendship, and influence are now crisscrossing. Strand and Steiner
seem to be taking special pains with their newest student. Is there some
ardor here? The simplest answer is that there's romance and physical love
almost everywhere with Marion Post. This isn't to suggest she's hopping
adventuresomely in and out of bed; actually, she's pickier than most in this
libertine thirties time.

*"Well, I don't think I ever slept with someone just because I felt it would
further my career."*

Time passes. The apprentice is invited to make the stills on a Strand-
Steiner documentary film to be shot on location in Tennessee. It's an activist piece about labor organizing. Gadge Kazan will be going along.
Marion not only gets to see the Cumberland Mountains for the first time,
she gets to learn from three pros close up. She's taking things in now
almost faster than she can inhale.

And where is Helen? The shift between sisters seems to be occurring
in overt ways. The two are still close, so neither talks about the shift very
much. But it's almost as if Helen has slowed up in the art race because she
senses she cannot win. In another year Helen will marry a charismatic
Jewish Austrian émigré, and this will alter much about her life, although
it is also true that some of Helen's most lasting photographic work will
come after she has married Rudi Modley and begun traveling with him
through Indian country in the late thirties and into the early forties. Mod-

ley is an economist and management consultant who does government stints at the Soil Conservation Service. (Later he'll work for the OSS.) On and off for five years Helen Post will crisscross the American West and Southwest, recording intimate scenes among Sioux, Navajo, Apache, Hopi, and Pueblo. With *her* eye and *her* charm and *her* ability to get in, the older sister will find medicine men putting buffalo blood into Coca-Cola bottles, will snap the Slim Battle Cattle Association in stony-faced session. In 1940 Helen will publish a government-sponsored book with the noted Southwestern writer Oliver La Farge. *As Long as the Grass Shall Grow* will get a generally admiring notice by Margaret Bourke-White in *The Saturday Review.* And then Helen Post will stop—almost like that. Years later, one of her two adopted children will ascribe the stopping to the war, to parenting, to family illness, to Jewish refugee work, to the need to be a fully supportive wife to a powerful husband. The supercharged husband, according to the adopted son, was never threatened by his spouse's camera work, indeed would have enjoyed seeing it go on.

But Sis: Well, all this experience and connection and influence and intellectual/artistic/leftist New York talk to the middle of the night is bracing stuff, but on the other hand twenty-six-year-old Marion Post is now close to broke. In late 1936, Ed Stanley, the Associated Press wirephoto chief (he is deeply in love with Sis by this time, and they're about to find their way to bed, or maybe already have), says he knows of a newspaper job in Philadelphia. It's at the *Evening Bulletin,* a good sheet. She charms them in the interview, where she's informed she'll be the only female shooter on staff; in fact, she may be the only female photographer on a major daily in America. That's okay by her, she replies.

She finds an apartment at 2310 Spruce near Rittenhouse Square. It's in an old brownstone walk-up and she fills it with Salvation Army furniture. The paper, at Filbert and Juniper, is twelve minutes away on foot. There are nine other photographers on the *Bulletin* staff, and they're going to give this dame the treatment. They pee in her photographic chemicals when she leaves the room, they throw spitballs at her back when she bends over the water cooler, they squash cigarette butts in her developing trays. "Look, you bastards, I'm staying, so get used to me," she yells at them on about the fourth day. This brings a truce. Each of the nine comes up surreptitiously to tell the new hire, "Now, I'm going to be your big brother, don't you worry. These other guys are wolves. They're out to make you."

She learns how to slap out prints on deadline from wet negatives. She covers fires, she does fashion and society out on the Main Line. It isn't great work, it's a paycheck. But she's learning about speed and economy and discipline and productivity. In terms of what is just down the road it's more valuable experience than she could possibly know. Ink-stained Philly photogs of the midthirties don't get credits on their pictures, and so a viewer through the time portal many years later has to try and imagine which ones are hers—that crisp shot of forty-five debs impersonating movie stars at the Bellevue-Stratford Hotel? It's under Evening Chat on the woman's page.

The painter. Even more than her late passion for Eugen of Vienna is her new passion for a bespectacled, balding, leftist Philadelphia artist named Joe Hirsch. The two are almost exactly the same age. Hirsch, son of a urologist who ministers to the working class, is one of the leading WPA artists in Pennsylvania. He paints proletarian themes and says his determination is to make contemporary art meaningful by endowing it with a social conscience. He has just finished a canvas entitled *Two Men,* in which a pair of workingmen, one white, the other black, sit on the same side of an elongated table, smoking and listening intently to each other. (In 1941, *Two Men* will hang in Hirsch's first one-man show in New York, at the union headquarters of the Amalgamated Meat Cutters of America. Marion Post, in from the FSA road, will attend the show.) Hirsch, a gentle person as artists go, though burdened with a deep possessive streak, is from a cultured Philadelphia family. He is modest and scholarly. He plays tennis, he practices the piano for many hours a day. As a child he had been taken to the symphony, where he sat three rows in from the orchestra pit, drawing with his crayons, not knowing he was absorbing—almost by osmosis, or even something more mystical—complex musical pieces. By the time he meets Marion, Hirsch can sit down at a piano and let Beethoven pour out of him from unconscious memory. His painting studio is on the top floor of his father's house at 900 Pine Street, which is convenient to the Salvation Army apartment at 2310 Spruce. Within several months Hirsch finds himself wildly in love with the photographer at the *Bulletin.*

But once again the relationship proves too intense and cannot sustain itself. Marion is the one who breaks it off. She is afraid marriage will result, an almost terrifying idea, at least at this time.

Hirsch marries on the requited rebound, has a child, tries to come back. Briefly, he and Marion rejoin, but it is too complicated. They break off, come together again. Even after Marion is on the road for the government, the two will still find ways of getting together. It will not be finished between them—at least in their minds—for many years, even though eventually they will lose contact with each other. When he is an old man, happily married to a second wife, Joe Hirsch will talk now and again of his early passion for Marion. "I don't know," he'll say. "I think she married a farmer or something like that." By then his own works will be represented in the Metropolitan Museum of Art, the Museum of Modern Art, the Whitney, the National Gallery. In addition, he will have achieved a measure of curious renown as the artist who rendered the symbolic drawing for Arthur Miller's play *Death of a Salesman*. His sketch of Willy Loman, stooped and faceless, lugging his salesman's suitcase, becomes a poster recognized around the world.

One day—it's the late spring of 1938 and she's about to turn twenty-eight—the photojournalist takes the train up to Manhattan and has lunch with Ralph Steiner. "I'm sick of this job," she says. "I don't want to stay in photography if this is all I can do." Timing and luck: Steiner just happens to be on his way down to Washington to visit Roy Stryker, head of the FSA photo project. Does she know about the FSA? Not really, she answers. Well, they're documenting America on the New Deal payroll. Walker Evans and Dorothea Lange and Ben Shahn have worked for the agency. Steiner says he will hand-carry her work to Stryker; he will help her get her best things together.

A letter of recommendation is prepared. Actually two letters are prepared, one for the photographic section of a government housing bureau, the other for Roy Stryker's unit. Paul Strand also drafts a letter in her behalf. Strand can be standoffish when it comes to helping other people, but not in his letter to Stryker of June 20, 1938, which seems to inflate the truth a tad:

> Dear Roy:
> It gives me pleasure to give this note of introduction to Marion Post because I know her work well. She is a young photographer of considerable experience who has made a number of very good photographs on social themes in the South and elsewhere. Incidentally, the stills for our recently released film, 'People of the Cumberland,' were made by her. I feel that if you have any place for a conscientious and talented photographer, you will do well to give her an opportunity.

She writes to Stryker herself on *Bulletin* letterhead on June 26, 1938:

Dear Mr. Stryker,

At Ralph Steiner's suggestion I am writing you concerning a job. He showed you some of my photographs last weekend, and I am very anxious to discuss the possibilities with you. Could I make an appointment to come to Washington to see you and Mr. Gutheim this coming Saturday, July 2nd? However, if either of you are going away over the holiday weekend, perhaps it would be more convenient the following Saturday, the 9th. I might be able to arrange it some other day during the week, but only with difficulty, as Saturday is my regular day off. Thank you for your interest. I would appreciate hearing from you, or Mr. Gutheim, soon, so that I can make plans. I can be reached either here, c/o the Bulletin—or at my home address, 2310 Spruce Street.

The letter is almost forward. An interview is arranged for Saturday the ninth.

R O Y

HE WAS A MORALIST and a tyrant—a kind of friendly and efferves-
cent tyrant, as one of his shooters said of him in a loving portrait in *Har-
per's* magazine shortly before he died. He couldn't take a picture of his
own for beans; didn't need to, either. He could be garrulous and capricious
and generous and cryptic and kind—sometimes in the same letter. He was
an old-style Democrat whose father had fought in the Civil War and
stumped for populism. He was an antibureaucrat's bureaucrat. He was the
grand compositor. He was the mind linking the far-flung minds. He was
the spymaster at his desk keeping his temperamental artists just enough
off balance to do their finest work. His name was Roy Emerson Stryker
and he didn't love anything but America, as someone once rightly put it.

In the summer of 1935, a forty-two-year-old irascible man with spindly
lensed glasses and white hair that stood up in girlish curls on his pale
forehead came to work in a grubby government office on Farragut Square
in downtown Washington, D.C. Ten million people in the country were
jobless that summer, and you could get a fountain breakfast at Schrafft's
for twenty-five cents. In the Deep South the annual income of the "aver-
age" American sharecropper, whoever he was, was $312.

For the next seven-and-a-half New Deal years this unlikely federal bureaucrat presided almost single-handedly and often autocratically over a
small, quirky, and soon-to-be-mythic army of photographers who fanned
out across America taking pictures of radiator caps and cracked spittoons
and rag dolls and corn testers and blue-tinted Mason jars, though mostly

of people. "I had no idea what was going to happen," he said many years later when he was an old frail man back in his native West. "I expected competence. I did not expect to be shocked at what began to come across my desk."

Photography wasn't a new American language in the middle of the Depression; it only felt like it. Indeed photography, or at least photojournalism, must have felt something like the gale force of television when it stormed in a decade or so later. In his planning memos for *LIFE*, Henry Luce had spoken of the "mind-guided camera." He also said with the air of a prophet: "Thus to see, and to be shown, is now the will and new expectancy of half mankind." That inaugural issue of *LIFE*, dated November 23, 1936, had the gigantic Fort Peck Dam in Montana on its cover—Margaret Bourke-White, the celebrated American photojournalist, shot it—and Winston Churchill on the inside fingering a sore tooth. The presses could not keep up with the demand—the phenomenon: photographs presented not as muddy rotogravure items or adjuncts to the news columns but as the center of gravity of a new kind of journalism. The American picture essay had been born, the *photostory*.

Right behind *LIFE*, in January 1937, came the Cowles brothers with *LOOK*. There followed some Lucian and Cowlesian imitations whose successes weren't so signal: *CLICK, PEEK, PIC, FOCUS, SEE*. They tended to perish about as quickly as they spawned.

Camera clubs were everywhere in America in the mid-1930s, in spite of ruinous times, maybe because of them: In a world of impermanence and loss, the glossy reality of a handsomely photographed object—say, Yankee Stadium or a Christmas window at Marshall Field's or just your cousin's Timex—might provide the illusion of something rich, something to last.

There were an estimated 100,000 "little cameras" in the country by the middle of the Depression—Leicas and Contax, mainly. The 35mm Leica had come over from Europe the decade before (which is where large-format slick photo magazines had gotten their start). The Leica recorded thirty-six pictures the size of special-delivery stamps on what looked like a roll of movie film. Paul Whiteman was a "minicam" bug, and so, too, were Eddie Cantor and Charles Lindbergh—all in thrall to what an explosion of light could do to a piece of sensitized emulsion.

In his landmark thirties fiction trilogy, *U.S.A.,* John Dos Passos named sections "The Camera Eye" and "Newsreel." It must have been more than just technique.

Vicki Goldberg, Margaret Bourke-White's biographer, relates a funny
story about a photojournalist of the thirties who was sent to photograph
Man O'War. No matter how he tried, the shooter couldn't get candid pictures: The racehorse was so photo-literate he kept looking straight into
the lens.

In the prose-and-picture documentary masterwork of the decade, *Let
Us Now Praise Famous Men* (not actually published until 1941, and then
just barely), James Agee wrote of the "keen historic spasm of the shutter,"
of a street in sunlight that "can roar in the heart of itself as a symphony,
perhaps as no symphony can. . . . That is why the camera seems to me,
next to unassisted and weaponless consciousness, the central instrument of
our time."

And straight into this photographic Zeitgeist, in the exact middle of the
decade, rode the ex-Colorado cowboy and former low-level teacher of economics at Columbia, Roy Stryker. "I'm the guy who sat in the middle," he
once said. "I kept the store. . . . My goal was to write the history of the
Farm Security Administration. We didn't collect many documents. We
collected pictures. Many think I went down to Washington with a big
plan. I didn't. There was no such plan. . . . I was one-half editor, one-half
papa, one-half hell-raiser, one-half purchasing agent, and occasionally
psychoanalyst without portfolio."

Walker Evans thought him a philistine. In a way, he was. He had few
aesthetic principles and no artistic pretensions—and was apparently happier for it. "Perhaps my greatest asset was my lack of photographic knowledge," he said in the introduction to a wonderful 1973 book of FSA
photographs called *In This Proud Land*. (He compiled it with a photographer and writer named Nancy Wood; twenty of Marion's pictures are in
it.) What he seemed to have had instead were just the right hazy three or
four inarticulated things in his brain, plus a powerful belief in his own
intuitions, and, not least, a genius for spotting talent and making it go to
work for him. All of it came together in the grubby confines of that first
office on Farragut Square.

Which was forever spilling over with curling celluloid rectangles. At
night he'd take them home on a streetcar to his apartment in Glover Park
in big manila envelopes and pore over them again by lamplight. "I didn't
need a drink, I didn't need a highball," he once recalled. "I looked over
those pictures; I could hardly wait until I got my hands on them. . . . But
no matter how much came in we still saw the gaps in the file. We wanted
more things. I think that many a day and many a night we dreamed of

being able to reach out further. We dreamed of an enormous file. We had our dreams."

He liked Stetsons and rumpled suits. He was a triphammer talker afflicted with perpetual writer's block—he never could get onto paper all he felt about his dream. "You must learn to look at the world through tiny little rectangles," he used to say with that great big Western laugh of his. He loved picking up the phone and barking "Stryker speaking!," hoping there'd be a fight on the other end of the line.

There is a story about how a man once insulted some of his office girls. (He'd left government service by this time and was running another documentary photography project in private industry.) Stryker heard about the incident and called the guy up. Look, knock it off, he said. It happened again. Stryker called the man up. "God damn your dirty soul," he said. "You ever come in this place again ... if I'm not big enough—I don't know how big you are—if I'm not big enough I've got two photographers that will just kick the shit out of you." The guy tried to say something. "Aw, go to hell," Stryker said and hung up the phone.

He once wrote to Marion (she'd been on the road six months and was still feeling a large need to prove herself): "Where in the hell is that summary regarding the remainder of the work you have yet to do for Schmuck? He is practically driving me into the insane asylum about the whole business. . . . God help you if you don't get it done." A paragraph earlier he had been telling her to take a little time off in New Orleans when she got down there, eat some good food, see the sights.

In a more widely quoted letter, in the fall of 1940 to Jack Delano, he said: "Please watch for autumn pictures, as calls are beginning to come in for them and we are short. These should be rather the symbol of Autumn ... cornfields, pumpkins. . . . Emphasize the idea of abundance—the 'horn of plenty'—and pour maple syrup over it—you know, mix well with white clouds and put on a sky-blue platter. I know your damned photographer's soul writhes, but to hell with it. Do you think I give a damn about a photographer's soul with Hitler at our doorstep? You are nothing but camera fodder to me." It was the first assignment for Delano, who was even more of a latecomer to the agency than Marion was.

Stryker once asked for a picture from Kansas with this instruction: "There is nothing in the world that matters very much but wheat." When the picture came in, it was pretty good.

He hectored and he hailed, he leaked with his biases. Leaked, hell. "You seem to be a little ahead of the crops," he once wrote to Marion. "I am sure you can find plenty of other things to work on while you are waiting for actual harvest to start. A little of some of the tourist towns, which will show us how the 'lazy rich' waste their time; keep your camera on the middle class, also."

On the October day that one of his more fetching itinerants found a silhouetted moviegoer on a segregated Mississippi stairstep, the chief posted the following via air mail:

> Dear Marion:
>   Roy Dixon says to tell you that you are finger marking your negatives while loading the magazine. The marks are up by the notches in the film. Exposures are all o.k.
>   Sincerely yours,
>   Roy E. Stryker, Chief, Historical Section, Division of Information,
>   Farm Security Administration

He was morale-keeper, he was time-keeper, he was whereabouts-keeper. "Arthur is due back the first of next week," he once closed to Marion. "Russell is down near Brownsville now. Dorothea is heading out shortly." He must have been using pushpins on a color-coded wall map of the continental United States.

I WAS ONCE AT MARION'S HOUSE when she got up without warning, went to her bedroom, rustled through drawers and papers, emerged with a curling snapshot. "Here he is," she said, "the son of a bitch," flicking her finger at the margins. Then she laughed. She turned it over and on the back was written in her hand, "Very typical of Roy S. in his fun genial mood our friend & godfather."

Nothing about his history, never mind his project, seems chained to logic. He once worked in a settlement house on East 105th Street in Manhattan. This is after he had attended the Colorado School of Mines and punched cows and served nine months in the infantry in France. One way or another the cowboy who'd been born in Great Bend, Kansas, in 1893, found the bright lights of the big city. "No greener kid ever hit Manhattan," he once said. There is another story, perhaps apocryphal, about Stryker and his wife checking into the posh Murray Hill Hotel: The poke from the plains caught a smart aleck in a funny suit trying to cart off his suitcase in broad daylight. It was the bellboy.

Roy Stryker, third from left,
early 1940s, Washington, D.C.
(photographer unknown)

Columbia University in the twenties was where Stryker first began experimenting with photographs as a way of putting flesh on abstract ideas. The grad assistant in the economics department threw away textbooks—said he didn't understand them—and decided to show his students real American economics. He was making $1,000 a year then. He took his charges on subways to slaughterhouses and slums and union halls and printing plants and produce markets. "And that's where the use of pictures really began," he once said. "I got impatient because the bright boys at Columbia had never seen a rag doll, a corn tester, or an old dasher churn. I dug up pictures to show city boys things that every farm boy knows about."

He did the photographic research for a book called *American Economic*

Life, published in 1925. It was coauthored by the chairman of the economics department at Columbia, Rexford Guy Tugwell, who eventually went to Washington to help get the New Deal off the runway. Rex Tugwell was one of FDR's original brain-trusters, and Stryker was Tugwell's unlikely protégé. While still at Columbia, Stryker went to his mentor with an idea for another book: "a pictorial history of American agriculture." The book was never realized, but in a way it was the germ of what followed.

The prairie populist spent more than a decade in the Ivy League and then he, too, moved to the capital. Tugwell had sent for him. It was July 1935. He rode down with his wife on one of the new streamlined trains. He had just been made chief of something called the Historical Section in the Division of Information of the Resettlement Administration. They were going to pay him $5,600 per year, and the job description was about as murky as his title: "direct the activities of investigators, photographers, economists, sociologists, and statisticians engaged in the accumulation and compilations of reports." Tugwell had in mind a visual record of the ravages of the Depression in rural America, and Stryker was his man.

One of the first photographers Stryker intersected with in Washington was Walker Evans, who was already working in the picture section of another government bureau. Evans had been a photographer for about seven years—a specialist, you might say, in elegantly composed portraits of castoff items. Stryker looked at Evans's cool and frontal and almost "surgically precise" pictures, as photography critics have written. Roy walked with Walker at night, took things in. One night close to Christmas in 1935, Roy met Ben Shahn, an artist-lithographer who was painting murals on government buildings. (Shahn and Evans had once been roommates in Greenwich Village.) The cowboy and the artist stayed up all night talking. "Look, Roy," Shahn told him, if not that night, then on another soon afterward, "you're not going to move anybody with this eroded soil—but the effect this eroded soil has on a kid who looks starved, this is going to move people."

Carl Mydans was one of the first to be hired for the project—and worked only briefly but brilliantly. Sometime in that first year Dorothea Lange sent in her early migrant work from California. One way or another the shooters located Stryker, and vice versa. "I really can't say just how we got the photographers," he once said. "I was taken. I didn't know, but I wasn't being fooled. Nobody told me that she was good. I just sensed.

I was getting wiser and more sophisticated and more sensitive to pictures all the time. I said, 'I want her,' and I had room for her and I got her. I got Dorothea—I got Walker."

And eventually he would fire them both. Evans wasn't a team player, he said. Thought himself too much the artist. Dorothea? She took too many exceptions, was always making demands on him for her negatives.

In October 1935, his project less than three months old, Stryker wrote to a professor in the history department at Columbia. He said the time seemed right to "start making an historical picture of America in photographs." In December of that same year, the Washington *Daily News* wrote: "A 'picture book of American economics'—supposed to be the first such thing in history—is being compiled today as part of the widespread activities of the Resettlement Administration. It really would not be a book: it will be folder after folder of photographs. The photographs will attempt to show, in the most artistic and graphic manner, the conditions of life in the hinterlands of this country. Sharecroppers, stricken farmers, slumdwellers, beachcombers—all will be recorded by the government's cameras." Well, that was sort of it.

Years later Arthur Rothstein—he had the distinction of being the very first person Stryker hired—looked back and said: "It was our job to document the problems of the Depression so that we could justify the New Deal legislation that was designed to alleviate them." And out of that prosaic mission fell the encyclopedic portrait of a people.

The Resettlement Administration, and its successor agency, the Farm Security Administration, were set up by the government to help bring relief to the poorest one-third of the country. (In his second inaugural, in 1937, FDR would intone the famous line, "I see one-third of a nation ill-housed, ill-clad, ill-nourished.") The RA and then the FSA ran migrant camps and resettlement communities, made emergency loans and rehabilitation grants, constructed flood control plains, built model "greenbelt" towns on the edge of cities. Because many of these Rooseveltian emergency relief programs and communal rehabilitation projects had socialistic undertones (the idea of collective farming, for instance, is said to have come directly from Soviet models), the idea was quickly hit on to establish an information bureau that would help win over both Congress and the American people. In other words: PR. Or, if you prefer, propaganda.

But something funny was happening. In addition to publicity shots of the agency's works and progress, Stryker's shooters were sending in other kinds of images. Walker Evans made a picture of a cemetery and a stone cross and some steel mills in Bethlehem, Pennsylvania. This was very early. The photograph was released to newspapers. A little later a woman came into Stryker's office and asked for a print. He inquired what she wanted with it. "I want to give it to my brother who's a steel executive," the woman said. "I want to write on it, '*Your* cemeteries, *your* streets, *your* buildings, *your* steel mills. But *our* souls, God damn you.'"

John Vachon—who was nearly as good a writer as he was a squinter through a box, and who started out for Stryker as a messenger boy, no, *assistant* messenger boy—once put it this way: "Through some sublime extension of logic which has never been satisfactorily explained to anyone, Stryker believed that while documenting these mundane activities [housing loans and farm co-ops], his photographers should, along the way, photograph whatever they saw, really saw: people, towns, road signs, railroad stations, barbershops, the weather, or the objects on top of a chest of drawers in Grundy County, Iowa."

It's a vault that seems hard to explain now, but if you look up the *First Annual Report of the U.S. Resettlement Administration* you'll find tucked away on page ninety-seven, across from a picture of a lonesome cowboy looking down on a valley of cattle, this thirty-word justification: ". . . not only in keeping a record of the administration's projects, but also in perpetuating photographically certain aspects of the American scene which may prove incalculably valuable in time to come."

It's almost as if they slipped it in, which I think they did. It permitted, or at least rationalized, the wider reach. And the wider reach must have had something to do with Roy Stryker's personal dream of recording an America he sensed was vanishing. FSA historians have since remarked on this. The small-town agrarian past of Stryker's own childhood explains much about FSA photography, I think. The technicians of reform in their New Deal corridors might have had one agenda; the shooters out on the road and the hard-to-figure man who kept after them always had another. Artists always have their own agendas, often enough subversive ones. You can sense the two-tiered tension by browsing in almost any drawer of the file.

There seems a perverse and wonderful illogic about what we know today as FSA photography: That is, the most burning of these images, which were commissioned by the U.S. government, could be expected to make a person despise his country and its greed-centered capitalist system.

From that revulsion, so far as the Washington healers were concerned, would have to follow a crucial mental step: Here's how bad it is out there. But it's not going to be this way long. We're fixing it right up. As the critic and novelist Glenway Wescott wrote in a 1938 piece about some FSA pictures appearing in *U.S. Camera* magazine, "For me this is better propaganda than it would be if it were not aesthetically enjoyable. It is because I enjoy looking that I go on looking until the pity and the shame are impressed upon me unforgettably." In essence, the documentary technique had been hit on to embarrass a morally bankrupt status quo.

The chief sent his people down the road with maps, USDA pamphlets, his own years-past experiences of the land. He insisted they look up experts in the regions where they were working. He made them carry Professor J. Russell Smith's socio-economic tome, *North America,* a 1,016-page guide to the continent filled with lore and esoterica. He assigned them "shooting scripts." Actually these were closer to free-association word prods, concepts, ideas, feelings. They went like this: "Bill posters; sign painters—crowd watching a window sign being painted; sky writing; paper in park after concert; parade watching, ticker tape, sitting on curb; roller skating; spooners-neckers; mowing the front lawn."

Stryker didn't have time for sentence structure.

In the early days, some of the shooters were permitted to develop and print their own work. But this got stopped—there just was no time. So they Railway Expressed their film back to Washington, where the chief quickly got contact sheets printed up. He'd send back prints and contact sheets for his people to proof and write captions for, and sometimes he'd tear off a corner of ones he wanted killed. Sometimes he'd even punch holes in the negatives of the pictures he thought not up to his standards. Dorothea Lange, for one, regarded that as an act of vandalism by a know-nothing. It didn't stop the chief.

In its ever-threatened existence, the project gypsied itself from the RA to the FSA to the OWI (Office of War Information). But whatever the alphabet-soup name or administrative jurisdiction, the basic reason for being—at least insofar as a fragile, underwriting, coalition government was concerned—was this: to compile accurate, sympathetic images of America that could be channeled into news releases, exhibits, magazines, newspapers, even movies, to show that New Deal programs were desperately needed, to show that hope out there was alive.

The shooters came and went, some staying for no more than a few months, others for nearly the life of the project. Always things were underfunded and understaffed, though never underimagined. Sometimes Stryker loaned out his people to other government agencies (U.S. Public Health borrowed them the most)—and then quickly billed those agencies for services. Red-baiting editors and FDR bashers in the Congress said the rectangles were just another aspect of the well-known Communist-inspired welfare dole. (Three weeks before Marion was hired, a Washington newspaper denounced the "livid pink" photographs.) There were investigations aplenty. At one point the shooting staff got down to two. Yet even in flusher budget periods there were hardly ever more than half a dozen photographers out combing the country for images. That is one of the misconceptions about the FSA's "Historical Section," its legend being so large now: Organizationally you could have fit almost the entire unit into one large room. It was a film lab, some secretaries and clerks and exhibit people, Stryker and several other administrators, the file cabinets, and the takers themselves, who seldom were around. Some never knew each other at the time—it was only later, during reunions, after the acronym FSA had entered American mythology. Marion, for instance, never met Walker Evans, and Dorothea Lange just once, for a few minutes, in an outer office.

In their own day the pictures were published—usually free of charge, often without a credit line—in *Midweek Pictorial* and *LIFE* and *Survey Graphic* and *Fortune* and the *Birth Control Review* and the Lubbock *Morning Avalanche*. They were hung in union halls and at the Museum of Modern Art and in Grand Central Station and also at the Royal Photographic Society in London. They got into a display window on G Street Northwest in downtown Washington. They made the Democratic National Convention of 1936. They were published in at least a dozen books. And they got things *done:* Two pictures by Dorothea Lange in the San Francisco *News* in the cold spring of 1936 resulted in an order that food supplies be quickly trucked to several thousand starving pea pickers in San Luis Obispo County, California.

Another aspect that seems to defy logic: Of the roughly twenty people who shot for the project in one or more of its phases between 1935 and 1943, only two, Lange and Evans, arrived with a real reputation in photography—and then not huge, not at the time anyway. Ben Shahn arrived with a considerable reputation, but not as a photographer; he barely knew one end of a camera from another, which didn't stop him from framing some amazing pictures once he got on the road. He used a 35mm fitted with a right-angle viewfinder so that he could work unobtrusively. Sometimes his images weren't even in focus—it was just their power.

Stryker used to say he preferred hiring photographers who were either amateurs or novices.

And yet every one of these twenty or so people emerged as skilled documentarians—almost overnight, or so it seems now. Not that their photographs are of equal quality by any means. But the influence of their collaborative effort on the documentary genre in particular and on photography in general has been profound. You could say with only a little exaggeration that the motley crew of the Farm Security Administration invented the word "documentary," but what they really did was more sharply define it. Besides Lange and Evans, four or five other FSAers— Vachon, Russell Lee, Mydans, Gordon Parks, and, right near the top, Marion Post Wolcott—can justifiably be called twentieth-century masters, or at least masters of documentary.

What were the odds of this happening? It could not have happened by accident, although much serendipity, even a kind of perfect dumb luck, seems to have prevailed. It was the alchemy of art, the mystery of a moment. It was Stryker, and all that was in him. It was the glimpsed potential, not to say the immediate availability, of those he hired. (Like nearly everyone else in the thirties, they needed jobs.) It was where photography, and America, and social-conscienced liberal-leaning art all happened to be at that moment. Someone once explained it to me as a chain reaction of fortuitous events.

Before the project was over, 270,000 images had been produced. Not every rectangle survives. And yet the ones we have! If we think now, and rightly, of the Works Progress Administration (WPA) as achieving some lasting Depression art—all those post office murals, federal theater projects, and writers' guides to the states—it is nonetheless the photographs of the FSA that provide us with the enduring image of what this country looked, felt, and tasted like during the bitter years. You can say "FSA" today and people will nod. What they are assenting to is our collective memory of the Depression. They may have long forgotten, or never known, what the letters stand for. But they can still see the bleached wood on the false front of the U.S. Post Office at Sprott, Alabama. They can see the bony farmer with the bib apron getting his ears lowered on Saturday

morning at W. M. Scott's General Store and Feed Emporium in Farring-
ton, North Carolina. That's one of Marion's.

The thirties were a time when a lot needed to be said. "We introduced
Americans to America," Stryker said not long before he died in 1975. And
Marion herself once said in a talk about the FSA, "Individually, I think
we all believed that we were in some small way contributing to alleviating
suffering, and possibly, hopefully, influencing government policy and programs for change."

I remember asking her once about her old boss, who was seventeen
years her senior. "What I remember most is the volatility," she answered.
"That roaring with agitation. Yet seconds later there would be only the
patience and sometimes even his tenderness. I think he felt possessive of
all of us. He could be so supportive, and he also could be so damn tyran-
nical. I'll tell you what I remember about him. Rail fences. He always
wanted me to photograph some damn rail fence or other—any kind of
fence."

The Barr Building on Farragut Square is where Stryker, the well-
known fence-lover, sat and waited for his first rectangles. Its neo-Gothic
façade is still there, and so too are these words cut in gold on the lobby
directory: NO CANVASSERS. NO BEGGARS OR PEDDLERS ALLOWED. But the tenants now are a big Washington law firm and the Adams Denture Service,
and blue streetcars don't run by the door.

ONE WONDERS WHAT SHE WORE to that first meeting with the
chief—a Schiaparelli suit in nubbly brown tweed fastened modestly up to
its Chinese collar? Did she doll herself up with layers of eyeshadow and
lipstick? I can almost picture that.

Years later Marion remembered for an oral historian that one of the
first things Stryker did was sit her down in the middle of his rows of
beloved file cabinets and tell her he'd be back later. Later was about three
hours. Afterward he gave her some sociology books to look through. Then
he gave her the third degree, in a fatherly way.

Timing and luck: The next day one of Marion's photographs was published on the cover of *The New York Times Magazine*. It was a shot dating
from her work a year earlier on the activist film *People of the Cumberland*.
She had sold it to the *Times* through a photo agency and had no idea it
had been picked by the editors to accompany a lead story on the Tennessee
Valley Authority. The photograph showed five haunted Tennessee Valley

The New York Times Magazine

JULY 10
1 9 3 8

eople of the Tennessee Valley—"They are proud and determined in their independence; they would rather remain masters of their own destiny than submit to decrees."

TVA'S DOMAIN: A LAND OF INDIVIDUALISTS

By RUSSELL B. PORTER
Knoxville, Tenn

The Congressional Inquiry Touches a People Who Are Slow to Accept a New Way of Life

People of the Tennessee Valley, The New York Times Magazine, *July 10, 1938*

(rephotographed 1991, courtesy Molly Roberts)

faces—a father and four children—staring out of a log cabin window. It was FSA material, all right. Stryker was impressed, and said so in a subsequent letter.

Apparently the job was won in that first meeting and yet wasn't confirmed in writing within the next day or so as Marion had been led to think. So the cheeky, semineurotic, yearning girl photographer from the *Bulletin* fired off a cable: "HAVE EXPECTED LETTER FROM YOU. GIVEN NOTICE HERE. IS ANYTHING WRONG?"

No, nothing was wrong. Four days later, on July 14, 1938, the job offer was formally extended. There would be a three-month trial period. The chief went on: "You will start at $2300 a year, with $5.00 a day expenses for the time you are in the field, away from Washington. You will receive four-and-a-half cents a mile when you travel in your own car. This is to pay gasoline, oil, and a certain amount of depreciation. We supply you with film, flashbulbs, and some equipment. If you desire a special camera, or cameras, I am afraid you will have to supply it at the present time. We are able to add new equipment from time to time, and perhaps later on we can arrange to get some things that you particularly want for yourself. However, it is our desire to standardize as far as possible on the Leica, Contax, and the three-and-a-quarter by four-and-a-quarter Speed Graphic."

Then he turned paternal. "There is still another thing I raised with you the other day, that is the idea of your traveling in certain areas alone. I know that you have had a great deal of experience in the field, and that you are quite competent to take care of yourself, but I do have grave doubts of the advisability of sending you, for instance, into certain sections of the South. It would not involve you personally in the least, but, for example, negro people are put in a very difficult spot when white women attempt to interview or photograph them."

Finally Stryker asked that she send her correspondence from the road directly to his home at 3000 39th Street Northwest in the District. The mail to government offices always seemed to be delayed; this would speed up his replies to her.

Several days later Marion answered:

Dear Mr. Stryker:
    This will confirm my acceptance of the conditions of employment as you stated them in your letter of July 14th. Is that formal enough

to bind us, temporarily, at least? I'm sorry not to have written sooner.
There have been so many things to arrange. It doesn't look as if I will
be able to begin before the 9th [of August]. This week I expect to get
everything finished up in Philadelphia, including my apartment,
lease, furniture, etc., difficulties. . . . This coming week I would like
to get my own camera equipment in shape, my car serviced & gone
over, let the dentist get in a little of his dirty work—and spend a
couple of days with my mother. She has been quite ill recently & I
am able to see her only about once a year. She works very hard, must
travel most of the time, & is seldom near enough for me to visit her
for a weekend. I haven't had any vacation for a long time so that I
would like very much to spend this short time with her.

She didn't start until the twenty-second. It turned out that in addition
to the dental work, there had been a sudden tonsillectomy. Finally,
though, she was aboard. The rummage sale of her Philly furniture went
quite well, she reported to friends.

LOOKING BACK, it almost seems like a gift and a work fallen into—as
if the magic now about to reveal itself had gathered inside her with only a
minimum of preparation. Probably this is the point about genius. The
bend of any life toward its moment of true giftedness must be a confluence
of uncounted forces and fates, all of it ambiguous finally, never quite de-
cipherable, at least in any slide rule sort of way. Apparently it was like this
with Eugène Atget, a photographer whose early years are mainly a mystery to the world. Then at about age forty Atget became a portraitist of
Paris streets and worked at it masterfully for the next thirty years. Marion
Post Wolcott's light was to prove far more evanescent, and then afterward
came her long-hidden other decades, not without their own beauty, not
without their own grace, although it would take me awhile to understand
them that way.
    One other point. For many years Marion tended to be remembered in
photography books—when she was remembered at all—as the great FSA
lyricist, the maker of "positive" images of the Depression: America the
bountiful. There's no doubt she could take such pictures—and liked it
fine. In an interview several years ago with a West Coast critic, Marion
said: "The fact that I did take pretty pictures, landscapes, etc., was a result
of my own feeling about the country. I would do them as I drove along

*Daughter of mulatto family returning home after fishing
in Cane River, near Melrose, Louisiana, 1940*

because I felt good, I thought it was beautiful and I thought we needed that kind of thing in the files, particularly to use as contrast material and in exhibits."

But for too long there was a false impression among the FSA chroniclers that all Marion ever shot, or wanted to shoot, for Stryker at the agency were the fertile farm and sleepy New England town, not to say the shiny new hydroelectric dam project: "FSA cheesecake," as it's been dismissed. There isn't any doubt Stryker was interested in pictures demonstrating beauty and success, nor any doubt he was always trying to read the political waters of the moment, nor any doubt the New Deal had begun to stall badly about the time Marion joined up. (The stall had really begun the previous year, 1937, and then worsened in '38. Unemployment rose; stock market prices fell sharply; the gross national product dropped.) The truth is that Marion has somewhat confused the issue herself through the years—telling some oral historians that, yes, she was primarily hired to document the positive side of things, while insisting in other places that the nature of what she was to shoot never came up per se as a topic of conversation between herself and Stryker.

Probably the chief *did* convey to her in some way in that initial meeting that there was a general feeling around Washington that the American people needed to see what they'd already invested in Mr. Roosevelt's recovery programs before they'd be willing to invest more. Hence, the need for positive material. Marion needed a job. She knew she was going to have to get along with a difficult man. She recognized the need to be a team player. So she certainly would have understood any messages tucked between the lines. But all that notwithstanding, it is ludicrous to suggest— as some have—that because the project had begun to change its emphasis in these prewar years Stryker extracted a commitment from Marion that day to document only the successful side of things. Stryker certainly didn't want that himself, no matter how much he wanted his project to survive in the bureaucratic shark waters of Washington. And of course the record of what Marion shot is unarguable. She shot what she saw. It's all there in the files, perhaps as many as 15,000 photographs. Some of the best pictures were buried. It took years for them to come to light.

*Coal miner's child taking home kerosene for lamps, used
in company houses—coal tipple in the background.
Pursglove, on Scotts Run, West Virginia, 1938*

FIRST CLICK

Before going out on my first trip there were many discussions in the office—about the necessary equipment, what I might need for the car on bad roads and in the mountains, what clothes, and finally whether or not I should carry a *gun!* This caused much controversy, much teasing, and some serious arguments. A girl not much over twenty-five had different problems. One of the veteran photographers, Arthur Rothstein, decided to settle this foolishness and said he was taking me on an official shopping tour to Sears, Roebuck. We would return with all necessary implements. We had a hilarious time and came back with only two pairs of boots, one leather and one rubber, some socks, insect lotion and bug powder, tow rope and cable, chains, tire repair kit, first aid kit, can and bottle openers, sheepskin jacket, car blanket, small portable radio for lonely evenings (at Arthur's insistence), a good jackknife and a small axe, to take the place of the pistol and/or gun. So far the axe has been used for almost everything but I still have to commit my first hatchet murder.

—from a fragment of Marion's unpublished writing

S H E   H I T   P U R S G L O V E and Cassville and Jere and Chaplin and Maids-
ville and Caples and Bertha Hill and Scotts Run and Tygart and Osage
and Laurel Point and Bluefield and Davy and Mohegan and Maitland and
Westover and Granville and Elkins, too—the names alone must have
seemed like a kind of poetry. All of them were, and still are, in the almost-
heaven of West Virginia. To cover so much ground in so short a time—
about two-and-a-half weeks in September 1938, as I calculate it—she
must have slept very little and pumped her own gas on the run. One
woman, flying solo, first time out, trying to refract an entire mountain
state through a Kalart Synchronized Range Finder.

The exact itinerary of Marion's maiden field trip for the Farm Security
Administration is lost now. But from what can be gleaned and recon-
structed from three telegrams and one letter and certainly the images
themselves, it appears she started shooting about September 14 in the
Morgantown area, up near the Pennsylvania border, five hours from
Washington, then sliced southward, cutting west to Charleston, moving
on to Welch at the bottom of the state, and finally heading back up toward
Washington via Beckley. She would have been traveling—they all did—
with a government I.D. and a continental "letter of authorization" and an
expense advance known to the accountants on the Potomac as the "encum-
brance." Only two of the places she stayed at are known. The first was the
Hotel Morgan in Morgantown, which was fireproof and even had phones
and from which she filched a wad of stationery she employed down the
road—a trick to be repeated over and over for the next three years. And
the second was the Hotel Carter in Welch, no dump apparently, but nothing to plan a vacation around.

What is astonishing is not only the quality, variety, and sheer bulk of
what the novice brought back, but that she managed to get it all in little
more than a fortnight. Walker Evans and Ben Shahn had photographed
more leisurely in some of these same West Virginia valleys and hollows
and switchbacks three years before, and I think a case can be made that
Marion's first field work for Stryker and the agency came right up to
theirs.

"RAIN AND MORE RAIN. DENSE FOG WORST HANDICAP. NOT VERY HOPEFUL
FORECAST. REPORTED SAME ENTIRE WEST VIRGINIA," she reported in her first
wire. That was from Morgantown, on the Monongahela, home of West
Virginia University, center of one of the world's greatest bituminous coal
fields. Her hotel had a dark-paneled lobby and a marble front desk with

rounded cut-glass bank-teller windows. The elevator boys, in their wire cages, had blue suits with "Hotel Morgan" stitched in gold script on their sleeves. But the poverty and hard times of the leaden thirties were right outside her door.

The president's wife, Eleanor Roosevelt, had been to Morgantown four months before, dedicating a school for black students. A month following the shooter's visit, three Morgantown miners were to die in a cave-in of a roof section of the Number 5 at Scotts Run.

Fifteen days after the first wire, on September 29, a Thursday, Marion cabled Stryker from the bottom of the state: "ARRIVED WELCH YESTERDAY AFTERNOON. FOGGY RAINY ALL DAY TODAY. REMAINING THIS TERRITORY FRIDAY SATURDAY IN HOPES OF BETTER WEATHER. WONDERFUL MATERIAL HERE. NEED AT LEAST ONE GOOD DAY. ADDRESS HOTEL CARTER. RETURN SUNDAY. IN OFFICE MONDAY. MARION."

She didn't make it into the office on Monday. She stayed through that weekend, waiting for the sky to clear, closing her one surviving letter of the trip with this: "If it hadn't stopped raining, I'm afraid I'd have been driven to the Christian Science Reading Room or Myra Deane's Elimination Baths (both right next to the hotel), just for a change or purge, you know." It was a harbinger of jokes to come.

The week before, when she was still in the northern sections of the state, Roy had mailed her a two-page letter. "I know full well no photographer ever really gets through in any region, but at least he wants to have a satisfied feeling of putting together at least a few of the rough edges. . . . I suggest that you go ahead and do the thing you are finding interesting and do not worry about getting back here in a hurry. . . . Then come on in and we will get your stuff printed up and go over your pictures and make plans for your next month's work." The infamous Stryker bark was being held in check—for now.

What one essentially has from this trip are the images themselves. Maybe that's exactly as it should be—nothing else to distract, just the work itself: that little girl bent to her can of kerosene in the darkening Pursglove afternoon. She is framed between a row of blackened clapboard houses and some New York Central freight cars loaded with mounds of precious black gold. The caption on FSA Print 30180-M2 reads: "Coal miner's child taking home kerosene for lamps, used in company houses—coal tipple in the background." The road bends to the right, the blonde-haired child bends to the left, the day seems streaked with something

deeper than sadness. Because of her load, the child isn't able to raise her
eyes off the stony road and thus can't make out the outline of hills and
trees up above the coal cars. They look like blighted trees and hills anyway.

That erotic-looking miner's wife propped on the porch of her falling-
down company shack in a place called Marine. (It's near Welch but not
listed on maps.) Has she got syphilis and Jesus both? Leaving town, the
photographer made a note that four or five families were living in the
same space and that the place was just about a ghost town: The company
had moved to other mines.

That lit-up Rexall Drugs window in downtown Osage crammed with

Unemployed miner's wife on porch of company-owned

house, Marine, West Virginia, 1938

Children on bed (cornflakes boxes and dolls), coal miner's
children, Charleston, West Virginia, 1938

its potions and lotions and sundries and signage, not least the cardboard
stand-up display for Mi-31 Antiseptic Mouth Wash: WILL KISSING BE OUT-
LAWED? SOCIAL CUSTOM VOTES "NO!" GARGLE TO HELP PREVENT INFECTION.

That pair of children sitting on that filthy bed in Charleston, the state
capital. The wall behind them is papered with the wrappers from Post
Toasties corn flakes boxes. At the top of the photograph, two dolls seem to
be hanging by their *necks*. (You can't quite tell, because of the way Marion
has composed it.) The feet of these two suspended dolls—which are
cleaner than the two children—are tied with thin white cord. There is no
explanation, just this caption: "Coal miners' children in their shack; no

water, sanitary facilities or electricity, Charleston, West Virginia." Maybe the caption does explain.

That come-on carnival lady opening her silky front to some gawking Mountaineer boys out in front of a nudie sideshow in Granville, just across the river from Morgantown. On the back of a proof sheet a couple of weeks later, the shooter will pen: "'That's what you wanna see and that's what you will see and don't bring bashful with you 'cause he can't take it.'" Stryker probably didn't like that.

That child with a cap shooter coming through the "cathole" in a bedroom in Bertha Hill. You can make out Mussolini's name in a headline from the Morgantown *Post*—which is wallpaper, of a sort.

Coal miner's child coming through the "cathole." Bertha Hill, Scotts Run, West Virginia, 1938

Coal miner who is known as a "lady's man" and "smart
guy," Bertha Hill, West Virginia, 1938

That man taking a shower in a homemade bath in his cellar in the town
of Westover. All you see is his naked backside. How did she get in? It's not
a great shot at all. Did she take it in the first place to show the boss she
wasn't afraid of nuttin' out here?

That supine lecherous miner, in his jumpsuit and lantern helmet, biting
off a cigarette as he waits for his shift to start outside the Bertha Hill
mines. He is lying on the ground, and his body seems to be describing not
a human form but the letter S. The picture is captioned: "Coal miner who
is known as a 'lady's man' and 'smart guy.'"

And on and on. Nothing in her past could have predicted this output.
To me it only says how stimulated she was by what was on the other side
of her lens and how badly she wished to succeed. She'd succeeded all
right, with her clunky black photographic box. A three-year highway had
begun to unreel like a national documentary.

FRAME TWO

ALTERNATING DOTS
OF LIGHT AND DARK

It seems likely that the change that occurred in photography around 1930 was fundamentally a matter of formal evolution. . . . It was at this moment that sophisticated photographers discovered the poetic uses of bare facts, facts presented with such fastidious reserve that the quality of the picture seemed identical to that of the subject. The new style came to be called documentary.

—JOHN SZARKOWSKI
Looking at Photographs

ODE TO AN INSTRUMENT

IT HAS A LEATHER-COVERED BODY made of high-grade Honduras mahogany. It has a leather bellows on a sliding silver track, known as the bed scale, which essentially turns it into an 8 × 10 view camera, although without all that weight and bulk. It has three separate focusing systems, with Houdini-sounding control functions: the *knurled focusing pinion;* the *spring tension escape lever;* the *parallax-corrected viewfinder.* Fully rigged, including the monstrous flash, it weighs nine-and-a-quarter pounds, which must feel like 109 pounds when you've been holding it up to your eye all day. Folded shut, the thing resembles a woman's pillbox purse—or maybe a carton of TNT. It swings open like a Murphy bed. The way you get it to open is by depressing the hidden bump on its top side. Suddenly you're not gazing at a black box with a leather side belt for your left hand, but at an accordionlike instrument tricked out in handsome Art Deco designs and featuring a state-of-the-art movable lens. It has all kinds of little nifty gizmos—a folding magnifying peepsight, for instance. It looks a little like what D. W. Griffith might have used to make *The Birth of a Nation.* It first hit the market in 1912, manufactured by Folmer and Schwing, a division of Eastman Kodak. And by now, late thirties, with the quarter-century anniversary model about to appear, this ingenious box is so universally revered and employed by members of the fourth estate that it's nearly of icon status. It's a little like the card that barks PRESS in the hatband of the crumpled fedora: It gets you the nod right past the police barricades.

This is the one that clicked the Hindenburg in flames in Lakehurst, New Jersey. This is the one (in the next war) that'll get the marines planting the Stars and Stripes on Iwo Jima. This is the one you can stand out in the rain with all day and know the rubber is going to meet the road. Such is its fame that the New York *Daily News* carried a picture of it for years on its masthead—with wings.

The flash attachment is a long, shiny tube with a saucer-sized reflector bowl. The flash bulbs themselves are as big as light bulbs; you cart them around in heavy cases. The flash gun can just as easily be removed and held by hand, over the top of the box. This is known as the "off-camera" technique and is especially good for getting rid of indoor shadows. Working with a G. E. Mazda photo lamp, the photog is not only freed from the tripod and slow film speed, he can work virtually anywhere at any time of day. With this camera, *you* control the light.

The instrument takes sheet film in four-by-five-inch holders, two exposures per holder. On deadline editors can go with the contact prints, the hell with waiting for negatives. The holder—no one who uses the camera professionally would bother to say "film holder"—snaps into place at the back. The sound of a holder snapping into place is the good, clean air-compressed THUNK of a Mercedes door slamming.

Now, to make a picture you withdraw the first slide card in the holder (silver side is out), cock the shutter, frame the shot, hit the release, reinsert the card you took out (dark side must be facing out this time, very important), turn the holder around and withdraw the second slide card, cock the shutter again, frame the shot, hit the release, put the slide card back in. Then you remove *that* holder and slap another holder in.

All these steps—for just two shots.

It's a rhythm, it's unconscious liquid motion, and the great ones can do it in their sleep: card out, the cock, the click, card back in, the cock, the click, the next holder: THUNK. And of course during much of this you're supporting the camera out in front of you, squinting through its various finders, your back bent, your legs flexed: the classic, ready, romantic, press-photog slouch: *Please, please, Miss Dietrich, just one more for tomorrow's paper!*

If you're working from a tripod, you open up the back of the camera and focus through ground glass under black cloth—just like Mathew Brady in the Civil War. From the rear, the image before you appears upside-down. Really, the image is upside-down on the back of your eyeball, but that's either physics or semantics. Even if you were carrying a dozen holders in the cargo pocket of your khaki camera vest—and that would be a lot of holders—you'd still only have an absolute maximum of twenty-four shots to make. With this camera you're not firing off rolls of film. You're not building up to something. It's the discipline of waiting. It's the terrible tension of getting it right the first time. It's the difference between taking and making. There is truth to the saying that these new sleek 35mm jobs have turned bums into shooters and shooters into bums. Although Marion Post is skilled with her Leica and Rolleiflex and Contax, employs them, admires them, it is *this* camera, this bulky, funny, oblong, antediluvian American-made box, with which she is now performing some of her most amazing sleights of hand, time after time, frame after frame, town after town.

Its name? It has a wonderful name. The Speed Graphic.

On the nicked shiny sticky table, next to the ashtray and the half-empty Coke, is a spent bottle of dreams. It's Old Grand Dad. (I used a magnifying glass.) You can almost feel the texture of the plywood wall on the flat photographic page. Is there a fingernail of moon out? Is Ethel Waters throating through *Stormy Weather* on the lime-green juke? If you look closely at the tootsie on the right, you can make out not only the fume on her smartly held smoke, but the wrinkle in her off-white nylons. I love the cookie-cutter cuffs and the locked collar on the chaste thirties dress. You wouldn't call her anorexic. I think she's just gotten back from the ladies' room where she leaned three inches from the mirror and sticked on another coat of ruby-red and then hitched quickly at her girdle. But she missed a little.

This is Moore Haven, Florida, on the southern sandy rim of Lake Okeechobee: cane country. All these picker towns hereabout—Clewiston, Lake Harbor, South Bay—are cabbage and rock-tomato but most of all sugar towns. Route 27, the Sugarland Highway, leaves the flat fields and cuts right through their grimy hearts. Over in Clewiston, eighteen miles east, there's a sign at one end of the main drag that reads WELCOME TO CLEWISTON, AMERICA'S SWEETEST TOWN. Moore Haven doesn't have a sugar sign, just these two sweeties caught in the prewar amber of a Saturday night gin joint in the winter of 1939.

Marion's been on the road a couple of months now. She's sending her dispatches to Stryker on the letterhead of the Clewiston Inn. In a recent one she breezily reports: "More wildlife trouble. Other day in the middle of a field where I was photographing the pickers, there was a terrific commotion & sudden screaming & yelling & before I knew what was happening, one of them pushed me in one direction knocking my camera out of my hands, & literally dragged me with them to the road. Two of the foremen fired some shots with a rifle, & the biggest rattlesnake you've ever seen—about 10 ft. long & as big around as a small stovepipe, went tearing along."

*Two couples in a booth in a juke joint, near Moore
Haven, Florida, 1939*

Another gin joint, another town, another state. She has stopped them right at hip-swivel, right at shoe-scrape. She's been working all week at a plantation near Clarksdale in the Mississippi Delta and on Friday afternoon says on impulse to the straw boss (like all the rest, he's taken with her), "Say, what do these folks do on Saturday night when they're not working for you?" "Well, they go to the dance place, for one thing." "Could I go there?" "No way." "Well, if your son takes me on a sort of date, could I go there?" "Well, maybe." The son is pestering her, too. He's a lousy dancer and uglier by half but he gets her in.

The room—paper streamers looped from the ceiling, body-to-body perspiration—stops dead. *A white woman come in here, with the boss's son? Shooee.* There's an old cruel saying among whites in Mississippi: "Nothing like being a nigger on Saturday night." And the shooter is going to experience the truth of the remark from the inside.

The plantation owner's son says, "Go ahead, have a good time, she's just going to snap a few pictures. We won't be long." She doesn't say she's working for the government—that would have made everybody even more uncomfortable. The dancing starts again. She eases around, smiles, keeps the box down at her belt. After about twenty minutes she starts to shoot. She uses lots of flash and frames it tight, probably at a speed of about 1/500th of a second. At first she can barely keep her fingers from trembling. By the end they like her fine. They even invite her back. Fifty years later, remembering all this as an old woman, she shakes her head and says, "I wish that guy's son could've danced better, though."

Negroes jitterbugging in Juke Joint, Clarksdale, Mississippi, 1939

Ostensibly the lenswoman is documenting a fifteen-foot-high ad painted on top of brick at the corner of Third and Main in Wendell, North Carolina. But other things seem to be going on here. That man in the cardigan in the foreground—you wouldn't call him menacing, not exactly. And that woman hurrying in the long coat: Is that a baby or a sack of flour she's cradling? And those two boys, are they getting out of her way because they know their manners—or has the woman with the baby just spoken sharply to them? Off to the left, beneath the scalloped canvas awning, this sign: WATCH THE CHANGE TO CHESTERFIELD.

The caption she later puts on the picture says only: "An advertisement on the side of a drugstore."

It can't be known from the photograph whether Paul Brantley, the town chemist—he has red hair and a temper—is inside the drugstore at this moment, although probably he is, standing in his copper-colored cage down from the soda fountain and doing what he always does: spreading the gray Livor-Kap paste onto the white marble rectangular slab before him and then working it back and forth with a pearl-handled putty knife and then using a tiny rubber spatula to wedge it bit by bit into the dozens of celluloid capsules around the slab and then taking those stuffed capsules and counting them out like raisins into the flat white boxes with the handwritten directions glued on the top.

Brantley has the patent on Livor-Kaps. Thought up the name himself. Never gets rich. Is the local agent for Philco Radio. Dies in Wendell.

As it turns out, I once stood around with my hands in my pockets at Third and Main in Wendell, North Carolina. (It's named after Justice Oliver Wendell Holmes, but they still say Wen-DELL.) I was hoping in my foolish way for lightning to strike. It didn't. No one I showed the picture to could remember the man in the cardigan sweater. The best guess was that he wasn't even from those parts. The trip wasn't a complete wash, though. I learned that Jakie May, southpaw submarine pitcher for the Chicago Cubs who once struck out Babe Ruth, used to send his paychecks back to the Bank of Wendell. I also found out about Mr. Brantley and his Livor-Kaps. "Whole town used to take them," the lady at the chamber of commerce told me, deep regret in her voice. "Even the beagles. Purge you in the spring. Wish I had one right now."

An advertisement on the side of a drugstore, Wendell,
North Carolina, 1939

Same town, same day, same street, just down a few doors. It's the swirl of that old cane chair, and those lard buckets with their metal bands, and the Compeer Snuff cartons behind him, and the way he's got that five-cent cigar cocked, and the popped buttons on his vest, and the silver dollar watch fob, and the flecks of ash on his shiny gaberdine, and the ribbon tie, and the bashed rolled hat—why, all of it says instantly that this is Mr. R. B. Whitley, Mr. Rayford Bryant Whitley, Pioneer Citizen, Builder, Man of God, Friend to Man. Actually, that's what they put on his tombstone after he died, five years after this picture was snapped.

There almost wouldn't have been a Wake County, North Carolina, if it hadn't been for Uncle R.B., which is what everybody in these parts calls him. He's the president of the bank. He'll tell you he cut down the trees and pulled up the stumps out of Main Street. Maybe it's true. He controls the general store and the drugstore both, the drugstore being the one with LIVOR-KAPS painted on its side. Uncle R.B. only finished fourth grade. When he talks, his tongue likes to come out and lick his lip like a lizard. Every morning Uncle R.B. takes his constitutional down Main to buy himself a cigar and a fountain Coca-Cola. Then he settles in his cane chair next to the blackened potbellied stove. All day supplicants come in and ask for extensions on their loans. Uncle R.B.'s general store (there's a milliner on the second floor, and you access her by a catwalk) carries everything from lye soap to bamboo rakes to Green Spot Orange-Ade to Bloodhound Chew to Finck's Detroit Special Overalls. ("Wear Like a Pig's Nose. The Man Who Thinks Invests in Finck's.")

Uncle R.B. and his wife, Marietta, live in the big brick twelve-room house on Selma Road that got turned into a hospital during the influenza epidemic of '18. Uncle R.B. is seventy-six when the photog from Yankee-land comes in and takes his pic. Five years from now, after his passing, a Wake Countian will tell the local paper: "If we were down and out, we could go to Mr. Whitley and he would see us through. He was a friend to the farmer." That's when the tombstone inscription just comes to Uncle R.B.'s son, Philip. He has the letters cut carefully in: *Pioneer Citizen, Builder, Man of God, Friend to Man.*

*R. B. Whitley, who was one of the first citizens of the
town and is one of its leading citizens, owner of the
general store, president of the bank, and owns a cotton
mill nearby and a farm, Wendell, North Carolina, 1939*

Who are these fully clad believers getting cleansed in the middle of this Ganges-looking stream? On the bank, the faithful of Primitive Baptist Church in Morehead, Kentucky, are witnessing the event. Actually, several of the faithful seem to be witnessing the picture-taker and her rude uninvited box, who may be standing on a railroad bridge or hanging from a tree. Marion manages to get into the shot that child haunched down on the extreme left—it's as if he can't wait for this holiness to be over, while yet another child on up the line, closer to the baptisms, has his hands on his hips, as if he will have to be convinced. Out in the saving waters, the man second from the right seems like he'll be next to go. Perhaps the penitent to his immediate left has just finished going, because concentric rings are spreading to the shore. In the foreground is an ugly old board, barely afloat: the despoiling mote in God's eye.

The precise date of the picture is unknown, although a fair guess would be August 17, 1940. On August 16 from Morehead—which is in Rowan County in eastern Kentucky on the edge of the Daniel Boone National Forest—the infiltrator pens a letter to the folks in the home office. She sounds almost intoxicated: "You will have to make allowances for me—there's a full moon, a clear, cool, beautiful nite in the mountains.... I'd at least like to be able to go for a little ride in the country with the top down on the car, but no—good girls in the mountains in this country don't ever ride around alone after dark! And since I'm trying to make a 'good' first impression, I must do as the natives do. Ain't it awful."

Two pages down she says, "I'm going to get a creek baptizing here tomorrow—I hope there will be no objections. Tried to get permission to take pix inside the church (Baptist) of the annual 'feet washing' service, but was unsuccessful." Had they seen this, the congregation at Primitive Baptist probably would have immersed *her* the next day, keeping her head under until she gasped "Savior."

Baptism in Triplett Creek, Primitive Baptist Church,
Rowan County, Morehead, Kentucky, 1940

Yes, but it's the food itself. Of course the country faces and the Melmac dishes and the squirmy kids and the wooden-handled paring knives and the go-to-meeting dresses and the stapled-down paper tablecloths and the feed-store baseball caps and the funeral-parlor folding chairs and the dented aluminum serving pitchers beaded with condensation—all of that. Absolutely. Got to have it, every time, that sort of texture, at least some version of it, otherwise you might not really believe you're sitting down to a genuine church supper.

But the food, the simple, awesome, uncompromised, gorging pleasures of the vittles themselves: That, I think, is what this photograph is about.

Which once again she found in Kentucky: at St. Thomas's church hall, in Bardstown, on August 7, 1940. It's a Wednesday, and they're serving from 5 to 8 p.m. It costs fifty cents to get in. It's an all-you-can-eat affair, as they always are.

Nine days later, still in the Bluegrass State, she writes to Washington: "Post has been drinking only orange juice, milk & beer, & not been sick again. However, the chiggers nearly ate out her bellybutton, among other delicate spots in her anatomy, after sitting on old wooden benches & climbing around in dry grass & weeds at the church picnic supper. It's the church that will do you dirt every time!"

I've wondered about the way these good church ladies, especially the one on the far left and the one on the right, are wielding their knives. The knives are too much out in front of them. It doesn't seem natural. I think they're afraid some of the juices from those delicious late-summer Big Boys and Beefsteaks are going to splash down their fronts and soak through to their Sunday dresses. I have a feeling that the dour-looking parishioner on the left removed her apron the instant the federal photographer said she was going to take a snap.

Parishioners peeling tomatoes for benefit picnic supper at
St. Thomas church hall, Bardstown, Kentucky, 1940

But is it a male or a female hand reaching through this tight and humiliating little wire-meshed opening at the Marcella Cotton Plantation? I don't think it's possible to know, no matter how much you look, and this is part of the picture's brilliance: It has in it all the strangeness and gauziness of the half-remembered dream. About all you can really make out of the payee from this side is the coarse garment on the seemingly disembodied wrist, that and the two-toned in-reaching hand, with its thumb and forefinger spread just far enough apart to lift the little envelope, *snatch* it.

She even gets the dust on the top of the inkwell.

I'd been looking at this photograph for many months before it occurred to me that there is nearly the same angle of bend to the two hands—the white one about to retrieve its cig, the brown one about to lift its pay. I think the hands are mirror images in more senses than one.

The envelope with the measly money inside it seems to have just been put down on the counter and slid forward past the check-off tablet of names. Maybe it has been slid contemptuously, maybe not, but I think the point recorded here in a fiftieth of a second is that no white skin on this Delta payday need come in contact with any dark skin. And yet, partially because of such subtleties as the structural bend of two wrists, what you end up feeling, if only viscerally, or at least I do, is that, yes, the lives here are and were inextricably bound.

On this same tack: If you drew a downward line from the crook formed by the picker's thumb and forefinger, it would lead you straight into the elbow crook of the slicked-back cashier with his wonderfully spindled glasses. But that's geometry.

Old shooter, recalling, fifty years later: "*Well, I think I took it deliberately. I think I knew what I was taking. Originally, I was working from the other side. I could see what was happening, yet I couldn't photograph it. I said to myself, 'How in the hell can I get this across?' Then it hit me: 'Ask them if you can come inside.' They were very nice, I was very sweet. What they didn't think about was how my presence might be to their disadvantage. Maybe they didn't care. As I say, they were very nice to me, but they were also part of a degrading system.*"

Cashiers paying off cotton pickers in plantation store,
Marcella Plantation, Mileston, Mississippi, 1939

The parching ground, the almost 3-D effect of vines climbing legs. Two straw hats shading half-hidden faces. A woman peering over her knuckle at the eye of the instrument. Is it her bashfulness or hostility? Beside her, an Ichabodian figure in a low fedora (canvas or felt?), patched blousey pants stuffed in his rubber boots, belt notched at what is probably the last hole. Why is he staring off the edge of the photo? Because the foreman is coming? Or is this, too, a way of protesting a moment?

She took it in a Louisiana sweet potato patch—I think after a rain—at Bayou Bourbeau Plantation near Natchitoches. It was just before or just after July 4. She didn't think she was getting much. In a letter with a salutation of "Dear Brother Stryker" (she puts it on copped paper from the Hotel Monteleone in New Orleans, where there are 600 rooms, free radios, a garage in connection), the shooter writes: "There has been so much rain, dark heavy clouds, damaging & delaying crops everywhere (in addition to the very late cold spring), that I have not gotten as good or as many pictures as I might otherwise. Many roads, on projects too, cannot be traveled after these heavy downpours, & weeks of rain, until after a dry spell. They haven't been able to cultivate & get the grass out of many of the crops. Ain't it awful!'"

Nope. Something clicked. Consider the formal balance Marion managed to get into this photograph. The three hoes, lightly caked with mud, form an almost perfect fan effect. Each cultivator holds his hoe in a slightly different way, and yet naturally. Perhaps because of the way they're being held and leaned on, these tools seem almost bodily extensions of the tillers themselves. Marion has captured the way a worker in a field places his feet, cocks his hips, holds his head, his hoe.

What time of day? High noon, perhaps. The light isn't beautiful, but there's a range of tones, thanks in part to film loaded with lots of silver.

This picture, which I had a print of a long time before appreciating some of its intricacies, makes me think about the heat and humidity that must have been in that field, though mostly it makes me wonder about the lives in that field: Did anybody find his way out of there and into modern times? Eventually, machinery came in and co-opted this kind of bare livelihood.

Negro men and women working in a field, Bayou Bour-
beaux Plantation, Natchitoches, Louisiana, 1940

FRAME THREE

PARABLES OF IMPROVEMENT

Those few photographers who understand this correspondence between outer and inner state read the world as if it were an allegory and pass through it as if they were pilgrims on a journey, looking for signs. . . . Such photographers also share an understanding of the kind of luck known to gamblers and hunters. It is luck, based on desire, that takes the form of being in the right place at the right time. Carl Jung observed such coincidences in his practice for thirty years.

—MICHAEL LESY
Bearing Witness

*"Rickets." Tenant farmer's children, younger one with
rickets from malnutrition, tobacco-cotton culture. Poor,
eroded land, Wadesboro, North Carolina, 1938*

RICKETS THEN

A CHILD IS COMING DOWN a scabbed hill in North Carolina. He looks bald. His legs are bowed outward like barrel slats. He has on a one-piece dresslike garment that may be homemade. There is wariness in his face, as if something he hasn't seen before is just in front of him. He is being led by an older child, who may be his big sister and who is about a half-step ahead. Her face doesn't have the instinctual caution of the younger child's, more a curiosity perhaps.

About what? A black box on a tripod? A white woman stopped by the side of Route 109 in Anson County to take a picture?

It's about a week before Christmas. A documentarian is enroute by macadamized rural roads to the sunny migrant climes of central Florida. But what she sees, she shoots; what she feels, she frames.

Up above these two Carolina Negro children is an unpainted pine house with a high-peaked twin-gabled roof. It looks solid, looks tuck-pointed and tight. It isn't some tarpaper shack stuck up on cinder blocks—she's shot some of those already. Perhaps this visceral pleasing sense of a thing well made, sitting on a washed-out hill, is what has pulled her over. But that doesn't matter anymore. Because two children, one with bowed legs, one in a stocking cap and a too-short-at-the-sleeves coat, are now coming down, straight into her lens.

Next to the house are some light-colored clothes flapping on a line. Beside them are several small dirt mounds, and sitting on top of these mounds are what look like wash tubs. Actually the mounds are sweet

97

potato hills, and the warm womblike space inside them—which the photographer cannot see or even know about from down here—is bedded with pine straw and cornstalk. The galvanized wash tubs serve to keep the winter weather off and also to provide ventilation: There's a hole in the bottom of each tub, and a stake through it, and the stake runs down into the sweet potato cavern.

When the caption comes into headquarters some weeks later, it's nineteen words, straight factuality, which is just what the chief wants.

And Marion Post never sees those kids again. . . .

"I WAS THE EARLY BIRD KIND," he is saying. "Daybreak came, I'd milk the cow, feed the mules, stoke that fire before Mama got up."

"Tell him about the calf you put the coat over, so's she wouldn't freeze," his wife calls in from the other room.

He smokes Newports, though not in chains anymore. In his driveway is an eight-passenger Dodge Ram with cranberry seats and a seven-inch TV and a CB radio in it. (Had the toggle switches for the CB installed over the driver's seat, so he can flick them on and off as he cruises.) He wears small gold glasses, rectangular in shape; they almost look like hippie glasses. He lives behind the high school, just out of town, right where the blacktop begins to curve—these were the directions he gave me when I called last night from Charlotte. They worked, too. To reach him I had called his neighbor and she ran under the hedge and got him. Jerry came over puffing. His phone's been out. I kept wondering how his legs were.

"There was a well right over here," he says, his thumb at the outer edge of the picture, past the sweet potato caverns. "And there's a spring down here. That water was so good. Like I was telling you a minute ago, we were rich, really. We never did suffer from anything. Back then you didn't have a light bill to pay. See where I'm coming from?"

His blood pressure is high and he's had a bad back since he was twenty-two. But his legs aren't bowed outward like barrel slats anymore. "Would you look at those legs," he says, grinning at the self he once was. "Mama and Daddy took me to a clinic over at Gastonia. The doctors wanted to break both my legs with mallets and reset them. Not enough calcium in my bones. Vitamin D deficiency. Mama and Daddy told the doctors they figured I'd outgrow it. They said they'd pray on it. I think they brought me home and wrapped me, gave me some special exercising. What I'm saying is my folks were right and all those doctors at the clinic wrong."

Once he lived somewhere up in New Jersey, but that was too cold. Besides, it wasn't North Carolina. He's lived in Charlotte, he's lived in Greensboro, he's lived in Ohio (where he first carried hod), he's lived in Washington, D.C. (where he made good dough at union carpentry). But none of them was Wadesboro, none of them was home. So Jerry Little came on home to this poor town and this scrub county near the South Carolina border, where the land doesn't charm the eye, where the moon can go blood red at harvest, where the economy—what there is of it—is built on textiles and lumber products, and where the old Seaboard Air Line Railway tracks lash along U.S. 74 like a Carolina blacksnake.

The roots of Anson County go back to 1754. Once this county stretched all the way to the Mississippi River. The name Little goes back a long and prominent way here, too—but those are the white Littles, not the black ones. Their name is on the hardware store. Also the park.

A couple of years ago Hollywood drove in some big trucks and shot *The Color Purple* in this county, a story about racism and violence and usurpation and accommodation in the 1930s Deep South. It's a story about a black child writing letters to God. Its message is that meanness kills, love redeems. Jerry Little could have had a job as an extra in that movie, but the more he thought about it he didn't feel like standing around in the Wadesboro sun all day for minimum wage. He said he figured there was more gold in Beverly Hills banks than that. He sort of liked the picture when it came out, though, has seen it a few times on the cable.

"See this window glass?" he says, pointing to the front window on the first floor of the house where he was born. "That was the room where my mama and daddy slept. I remember a twister coming through and the window glass fell out and my baby sister, Edna, sleeping right through it in her crib. She wasn't hurt at all."

He is a bulky and muscular man, over 200 pounds, with a gold chain around his neck and a black mesh golf hat sitting on the back of his head—which isn't bald. The hat has a kangaroo emblem on it. I just noticed this. He has six fingers on each hand. I just noticed this, too, when he was pointing out the room where his parents slept and where baby Edna dreamed through the twister. The extra finger looks like a little toe and also feels something like that. It's about an inch and a quarter long and just sprouts outward from the ridge of each palm. All his brothers and several of his sisters were born with a sixth finger tucked behind their little finger. So was Jerry's daddy. So was his mama, although she had the sixth on only one of her hands.

He must have seen me eyeing his toelike addition, even though I was trying not to show my surprise. "Go ahead, squeeze it," he says, extending his left hand across the sofa. He rests it nearly in my lap. His voice is kindly, beckoning. He isn't afraid; I am. "Naw, go ahead. It's all gristle, it won't hurt you, try it."

I do try it. It feels oddly pleasant, as if I've just been inducted into family mysteries. The nail on the finger is perfect, with a half moon of cuticle. "Here, I can hide it," he says, folding it under with his other hand, as you might bend a piece of putty. He presses his left hand flat against his knee and, sure enough, the finger is gone.

On the sink in the bathroom is a small leather volume of proverbs from the New Testament.

On a freezer top in the dining room are a pair of white Reeboks.

On a hook in the kitchen is a curing ham.

The chairs in here are covered with cellophane.

And the former bald child with rickets coming down a rutted hill, straight into a hunter's lens, is in his fifties now: a builder, an odd-jobber, a talker. Far from just surviving, Jerry Little has prevailed.

"I knew I was going to have to be the one," he says. "You know, take care of my family when they needed it. My daddy took me out into the field just before he died and taught me how to make terrace rows. He said, 'Son, I ain't going to be with you very long. I want you to take over, I want you to take care of Mama.' There were all kinds of strange signs those last days. One night he said, 'See that big moon, Jerry? That means something.' Then he died."

We've been talking all morning. It's a Sunday morning, hot as blazes. Jerry's wife, Vera, has just fixed up a plate of scrambled eggs cooked in fry grease, giant links of hot pork sausage, slabs of toast that got burnt a little in the oven. "You always burn it, Vera," says Jerry, leading the way to the table, not sounding upset.

His name is really Edward Little, but for some reason everyone calls him Jerry. I keep looking at the burly man and seeing the wary child with the crooked legs. He isn't wary at all. He is only eight years older than I, but somehow he seems old enough to be my uncle. He has seven children and nine grandchildren, and one of these grandkids, Corey Teal, who lives in Atlanta, just scored 602 on an aptitude test—which put him in the 99th percentile. The grandfather is powerful proud of these numbers, has them committed to memory, can glide on "percentile" like a high school principal.

"Look at those shoes," he says. "Floppy. And I think that's a flour sack dress I'm wearing. I remember how Mama would boil and bleach the lettering out. They could turn about anything into something else, they set their minds to it."

He is the fourth of twelve children. Ten are living. One is a cabbie in New York City. One got shot outside a Wadesboro grocery. One died in infancy. One is in a state institution for the retarded. One went to cosmetology school in Charlotte and then got a practical nurse's license up north. Her name is Anne, and she is the other child in Marion's photograph, coming down in her too-short coat and unafraid gaze. Anne Little was almost seven the day the picture got taken, Jerry shortly to turn two. Anne is in her late fifties now and her last name is Grady. She is the first-born in this family, although she wasn't the first child to get off the land. All the children of James Franklin Little and Willie Mae Little got off the land, eventually. The land was too hard. And yet they miss it now—well, sometimes.

"I never miss being out there in that field," Jerry says. "I remember our rent to Mr. Brower was three bales of cotton a year. Had to work to get it, too."

"I wish we would've had those kids of ours on a farm when they were growing up," says Vera. "Then they'd know something about work."

"I wonder what were the names of those mules," her husband says, studying the picture again. "I think one was Bill. And Mary. Tom? Was Tom the name of that third mule? Anyway, we used to race 'em to town, make it in fifteen minutes, leastways when Daddy wasn't around. You know how that is."

"Jerry won't be doing anything, he has to rush himself," says Vera. "Just like the addition he built on this house, had to get it done before he even started."

"I think it was because I couldn't walk good till I was almost five," says Jerry. "Been trying to catch up ever since."

Grover comes in. Grover is Jerry's brother, right below him on the ladder of kids. Once Grover Little was an MP at Fort Bliss, Texas, with shiny shoes and a snap latch on his holster. But that was a long time ago. Grover lives with Jerry and Vera. He walks slope-shouldered and has a spray of chin beard. Jerry buys him his beer, tries to keep him off the street on

Saturday night. Grover is good people, to use an idiom, but he's been unlucky at life, which isn't an idiom as much as raw common black Southern fact, what James Agee (and Marion, too) might have called "the cruel radiance of what is."

"Look at the old home place, Grover," Jerry says, handing the picture to his brother: found treasure. "Remember how we used to work to stop the boll weevil? Used to mix molasses and arsenic and go right down the rows, mopping."

"Raised oats for the mules, had two milk cows and lots of chickens," says Grover, nodding.

"Didn't Daddy love to see things coming out of that ground?" says Jerry. "He'd be out working in the fields on Saturday night."

"He'd be out in the field and just sit down in the rows, his asthma got so bad," says Grover. "He'd go to town and get a shot."

"Said he got it from working on peach farms as a kid," says Jerry. "All that fur and dust give him the asthma."

"Doctor gave him an atomizer," says Grover. "He'd be sitting up nights with that atomizer, scuffing for his breath."

"Work all day, sit up all night," says Jerry.

"I remember the boll weevil came bad the year he died," says Grover.

"Died at forty-two," says Jerry, shaking his head. "Twelve children and gone by forty-two. Nineteen hundred and fifty. Christian man. You should have heard him sing in church. I would have been fourteen that December."

"Seems to me we made six bale the year he died, if I got it right," says Grover.

"After everything was paid, I think we had about two or three hundred dollars left over," says Jerry.

"Do you know Daddy would give food to people he knew didn't have as much as we did?" says Grover. "He said the Lord blessed him with enough so that he could give some away."

"He bought a brand-new forty-nine Chevy, tan, year before he died," says Jerry. "He was so proud of that car."

"After he passed, we moved down to Uncle Silas's place," says Grover.

"I kept wondering if we were going to make it," says Jerry. "Did, though."

"Mama lived to seventy," says Grover.

"Hemorrhage in her brain," says Jerry.

"Never married after Daddy," says Grover.

"Said she didn't want a strange father rearing her little ones," says Jerry.

"Remember how we used to dream about finding money inside those old walls?" says Grover, laughing, handing the picture back to his older brother.

"Yeah, we thought there was some kind of mystery about those walls," says Jerry, also laughing.

A STORY, HIDDEN inside a mystery: Just at the point I wanted to find *them*, they found me. Luck based on a kind of Jungian desire? Who knows. Never mind. What I do know is I had written an article about Marion in the Washington *Post*, and the Wadesboro "rickets" photograph had appeared with it. I hadn't written anything about the picture because I didn't really know anything about it—other, that is, than Marion's two-line caption—and hadn't had time to try and find out. But anyway there it was in the paper one Sunday, those two tenant farmer's children, that raw-board house under that ether of Carolina sky. The picture moved me, and I was very happy it had been used to help illustrate the piece. I think it was the particular scabbed ugliness of the rutted hillside that moved me most.

And the bent legs of the bald-looking child.

The picture had the authority of a document, and its meanings were clear.

Then one day several months later, just when I was struggling anew to understand the puzzles in an artist's life; just when I had begun thinking in more direct ways about this particular photograph; just when I was wondering which response to my several emotions about it might be the "correct" one; just when I had begun forcing myself to try and think about "correspondencies" and "interrelationships" and "synchronisms" and other abstract, theorizing, Jungian-like words; just when I had begun feeling less and less sure about any of the things I thought I knew; just when I was wondering how in hell I might find someone to lead me to those two children on that ugly piece of Carolina real estate—assuming, as I did, that there was a fifty-fifty chance that one of them was still alive, somewhere, in this wide, startling country—the phone rang.

And a voice said: "You know that picture you ran in the paper with your newspaper article? Well, that's my brother Jerry and that's my big sister Anne and that's our old house on top of that hill. They'd like to talk to you."

Almost unable to comprehend, I said, "But are you sure it's them?" To which Effie Simpson, who is the seventh-born in this family, about hooted back: "You think I don't know my own sister and my own brother? Annie lives right here in D.C. So do I. So do three more of us from the family. I'll tell you what else. That house is still standing. I don't think anybody's been in it for years. It's just sitting out there in the weeds on 109. You could go see it. You could probably climb around in it. Jerry lives down in Wadesboro. Shoot, we were all just down home this summer for a family reunion."

That seemed almost spooky to me. And even more did this: Effie Simpson, my open sesame, lived a five-minute car ride across the Anacostia River from where I lived. Which, from another point of view, meant she lived in another country, for any realistic chance I ever had of meeting her. At the point Effie called me up, I had been a journalist in Washington for nearly a decade and a half. But during the whole of that time I had never once—well, almost never—ventured southeast from my own reasonably secure and racially mixed neighborhood on Capitol Hill into the historic, and predominantly black, and supposedly far less secure quarter where Effie Simpson lives, a quarter that everyone in Washington, black or white, knows by the encoded name "Anacostia." It is a name something like Harlem: What it means depends a little on who is using the word. Like Harlem, it is a place of landmarks. (The great early-twentieth-century black educator and writer W. E. B. Du Bois, for one, lived in Anacostia.) But I had almost never been there, except on quick drive-throughs with the locks down. I was afraid of Anacostia. It glittered in my mind, but like broken glass.

A few evenings after Effie called, I went over to meet her. Nothing to it, just got on South Capitol Street and drove across the bridge. Effie was waiting for me on the steps of her apartment building. It wasn't in the least a beat-up building. She was wearing slacks and a pretty blouse and had an umbrella under her arm. I think her red-tinted hair was newly permed. In her left ear was a flesh-colored knob shaped like a small oyster: She suffered, she told me, from partial deafness due to an accident several years before at a telephone switchboard. She got into the car and smiled and put her seat belt on and the two of us then rode out to Oxen Hill, in the near-Maryland suburbs, to the well-kept ranch-style house in the integrated neighborhood where her big sister Anne lives, a sister who once got her picture snapped coming down an eroded hillside in Anson

County, North Carolina. On the way out, we fell into talk, a little awkwardly. Effie took out the ear knob and rubbed it in her fingers. She told me that her daughter had been set upon the night before by some thugs, but that they weren't neighborhood thugs. Some of them may have been from across the river, in fact. Over my way.

The two sisters, high school graduates, both grandmothers, both supporting themselves, embraced at the door. The three of us sat around a kitchen table that evening, talking and looking at a photographer's magic. It was soft and rainy. The table was lit by a pale yellow lamp. Under the lamp was a straw basket with some artificial flowers and Roy Rogers coupons in it. In another room a television set was on. Jesse Jackson, candidate for president, was orating about Rosa Parks and the bus boycotts of Montgomery in 1955, about how he, Jesse, Jesse of South Carolina, Jesse of the long struggle, had known the slop jar by the side of the bed, had known all kinds of hard and depriving things in his life. And I kept saying to myself that night, a pilgrim trying to shake water from his ears: *So what were you expecting exactly? And you mean all you had to do was come across a bridge? But it's so damn normal here.*

"I'm not expecting to make a bucketful of money out of this old life, that's okay," Anne Grady said that night. She is a powerfully built woman with a rich rural accent that a lot of years in the urbanized North haven't been able to change. Lately she had been laid up from a hip operation and was getting around with the help of an aluminum walker. She told me she had worked as a nurse in Washington for twenty-eight years and would like to work as one for twenty-eight more—except that she'd like to go for her R.N., because a practical nurse's license just wasn't enough. She said she didn't mean only the money.

"My father only got to third, couldn't really read," she said. "Mama went to seventh, though. I used to do all Daddy's bookkeeping." She said she was the one who raised up her siblings, while her parents were in the fields behind the mules.

She told me how her father eventually moved his family out of the house on the top of the hill and into another one down closer to the blacktop, out of sight of Marion's picture: James Franklin was determined to be a tenant farmer before he died, not just a sharecropper. And he made it, too. (In Marion's caption, Jerry and Anne are identified as the children of a Carolina tenant farmer, which means James Franklin would have been paying his rent in cash, not with three bales. But James Franklin was still sharecropping in 1938. Also, the date of the picture has been misidentified in subsequent years—but this isn't Marion's error.) She told me about her mother, Willie Mae, who was broad in the shoulders and big in the heart and who could work all day in the cotton rows and who was the kind of parent who would have been inclined to tell her fidgety, extroverted, and unafraid first-born, "Okay, go on now, if you have to, child, take your little brother and go down there to see what that white lady's doing with that big box. But you mind your manners to her, Annie, you hear?"

The grown Annie—who still bears a strong resemblance to the six-year-old one—said she had no memory of the day Marion stopped. I said I had been able to locate several other pictures of the Little family in the FSA files and that Marion apparently came up to the house that day, or at least onto the porch.

"Well, if she came up, Mama invited her in, that's sure," Annie said.

A week or so after we first met, Effie and Anne went to a faith healing service in downtown Washington. I asked if I could meet them at the church and sit in the back. They said sure. The service was held in a building I had walked past many times but had never entered. The two sisters wore starched pink summer dresses that night and stood in the pews with their hands over their heads, their bodies swaying, their voices raised, as the Reverend Frank Garris of Montclair, New Jersey—Marion's birthplace—whooped and prayed and healed all about them with a cordless microphone. I felt like a man on a strange journey, trying to interpret signs—if only I could believe in them, if only I could know them. "Do you believe?" the healer screamed, his face awful in its holiness. People with cancers and goiters and other ills came forward. The Reverend Frank Garris of Montclair has given Effie Simpson the gift of her hearing back, or so she now believes with every bolt of faith in her. Not that the healer performed the miracle by himself. He was just the instrument Jesus was working through.

THE FORMER BALD CHILD with rickets is piloting his eight-passenger Dodge Ram with the CB and the seven-inch color TV and the plush cranberry seats through Wadesboro. It is middle afternoon, still broiling, and we are on our way out to the house on 109. But first Jerry Little wants to show me his town. It's the county seat. Grover and Vera are along for the ride, too. We've just passed a billboard with an advertisement for a bank: WE CAN OPEN DOORS FOR YOU. We've rolled past Hardee's and a Bojangles

The Allen Plantation, an FSA cooperative. A Negro woman and her children taking a rest from hoeing in the field, Natchitoches, Louisiana, 1940

fried chicken out on the strip. Now we're touring in the core of the old town, where Beck's Lunch (billiards) is out of business but Little's Hardware (cast iron sinks) isn't. There's a sign on a drugstore Marion wouldn't have missed: WE SELL SNAKE SULPHUR. You park some vintage cars against these high concrete curbs and you'd have a ready-made set for a Depression-era movie.

"Those are the other Littles," says Jerry, nodding toward the hardware store, leaning on his steering wheel. "The rich ones. We don't mix with them."

Down Rutherford, past the big houses on Camden Street with their canvas awnings and wide porches. Out to the Y at the edge of town, where Little Cotton Manufacturing is. There are about a dozen and a half textile mills and knitting plants in the Anson County of modern times. Its people are patch tobacco growers and poultry farmers and public assistance recipients, but mainly they are mill hands. Little Cotton's superintendent used to be, a man named Mr. Charlie Brower, who is the same Mr. Charlie Brower to whom James Franklin Little always owed his three bales at the end of growing season. Mr. Charlie, like James Franklin and Willie Mae, has passed on.

"You know how some white folks always have a picture of the black man as lazy and no good?" Jerry says. "And how some black folks think the white man is reaching at us with his whip? Well, the truth is Mr. Brower was awfully kind to my parents. I think he was happy to have us living out there on his land. He didn't have a whip. He didn't stand over us for those three bales. I used to come in town and mow his lawn. For good money, too."

These days the cotton that gets spun into quality yarns at Little Cotton Manufacturing isn't grown by Anson County black men cropping on the share. The mill's cotton comes in by rail from Alabama and Mississippi, mostly. A lot of the mills aren't even locally owned anymore—they're held by conglomerates in other parts of the state, other parts of the country.

Anson County's population is barely holding at 26,000 and its per capita income is a little under $7,000. This classifies the county as "very poor and very rural," although not *the* poorest or *the* most rural in the South or even in the Carolinas. But poor enough and rural enough by any yardstick, given the half century that has fallen away since James Franklin Little and his cache of kids were breaking the land. The federal government sponsors something for current Anson County farmers called the CRP—the

Conservation Recovery Program. It sounded to me like an FDR New Deal James Franklin would have signed right up for.

The home place is about two and a half miles out of town; in ten more minutes we are there. I remember reading how John Vachon of the FSA photography team once found himself in Atlanta with a three-hour lay-over between trains. Vachon spent the time trying to find two identical unpainted frame houses that Walker Evens had photographed several years before. The old houses with their curlicue woodwork were sitting behind a pair of movie billboards, on one of which was Carole Lombard's face with a sultry black eye: caught tension between Georgia reality and Hollywood illusion. Vachon hunted up the address, saw that the old houses still stood, positioned himself, clicked his own photo. The only thing different was that Carole Lombard's face was gone. Both pictures are now in the FSA file. Vachon later wrote that he felt a little like a man finding a First Folio Shakespeare.

The house where Jerry Little was born is about three hundred yards up from the road. It's Marion's photograph, all right: same hill, same erosions, same etherized sky. I am ready to jump out the van window and start running, lest this vision vanish on me. Jerry pulls off onto a side road. He leaves his engine running, with the air on, so that Vera, who says she'll wait, who says she doesn't need to go rummaging around inside some old abandoned house in this kind of heat, can stay cool. Grover leads the way, taking us in from the side, through some barbed wire, past a pond, under some tall pines whose browned-out needles would do just fine for a sweet potato cavern.

There are clumps of wild rose bushes in what was once the front yard. I see cow pies, an old bald whitewall, some rusted machinery parts. The front porch is buckled nearly in two. The ground around the foundation is split with green weeds. Stalky plants are sticking up through the rear, where the kitchen used to be. The clay earth down the rutted hillside where the children came that day is now like red pulverized moon dust. One of the two windows on the second floor, on the front side, below the sharp V of the roof, is nailed over with a sheet of corrugated tin. Grover slept in that room; Jerry, too. The tin sheet covering the broken window is full of .22-caliber bullet holes.

"Target practice," says Grover, disgustedly.

"Cotton here," says Jerry. He is back about twenty yards, where the sweet potato caverns were, surveying. He is pumping a little for his breath, a 200-pound black man with six fingers on his hand, wearing a mesh Kangol hat and standing in a weedy North Carolina field you wouldn't call purple. The field feels on fire, almost.

"We about had it all in crops, didn't we?" calls Grover from around the side.

"Snug up around the house," says Jerry. "Any place we could find a space. What'd we have, Gro, thirty-six acres?"

"Right over yonder under that tree's a cemetery," says Grover.

"I remember I'd be planting and the school bus would come by and I'd just jump down and lay flat," says Jerry. "Didn't want the kids who lived in town making fun of me 'cause I had to stay out of school that day."

"I used to climb up in a tree and the driver would get out and come looking for me," says Grover, coming over with a rusted doorknob and a couple of chipped Nehi orange soda bottles.

"See, a clay soil will hold a hard rain for a couple weeks," says Jerry. "It's not like a sand soil where you can get in there and plow it the next day. Sometimes we'd have to wait two weeks to get in there with the mules."

Three rooms up, three rooms down, a hearth in every room. All the fireplaces are intact, including the carved mantles, which are smooth and bone-dry to my touch. The window weights, made of rope and iron cables, are still sitting in the window wells, as if ready for a rehabber. The banister on the staircase looks in mint condition—I could probably lug it up north and get a thousand dollars for it in a Georgetown antique store. Some of the walls in here still have wainscoting on them. White bird poop spackles the stairs. Wasp nests adorn corners. Jerry Little, father of seven, grandfather of nine, born into a half-cropper's brood of twelve, kicks at an old malt liquor can. He is standing in a window without any glass, staring at the highway glistening down below him like just-laid tar. He hasn't been inside this house in at least twenty years. He seems contented and very weary. Sweat is rolling off his nose, steaming the small gold rectangular glasses. His legs are giving out.

"I think it must have been our parents," he says softly. "You know, that gave us something rich, something to make us lift ourselves."

THAT EVENING, when it was several degrees cooler, after I had bought Grover two six-packs of Bud (I felt funny handing them over, but he high-fived me), after promising Jerry and Vera that I would try to keep in touch, I drove back out 109 and climbed through the barbed wire and walked up the scabbed hill and onto the buckled porch and into the eight-by-twelve front room where James Franklin and Willie Mae used to sleep and where earlier in the day I had spied an old rotting piece of burlap sack with some printing on it. What did I think, it was a First Folio Shake-speare? That night, in another part of North Carolina, I excitedly spread the burlap out on the bed in my room at a Days Inn and tried to read it. But time and the sun had all but boiled and bleached the lettering out. I decided to bring it on home, though, and I have this piece of rotting and mite-infested old burlap with me now, just several feet from where I'm writing this down. Maybe I'll pitch it out, and then again maybe I'll hold onto it a little longer.

"*Biscuit Lady.*" *Member of the Wilkins family making biscuits for dinner on Corn Shucking Day. At the home of Mr. and Mrs. Fred Wilkins, near Stem and Tallyho, North Carolina, 1939*

AUNT MARY

CONTENTS OF A KITCHEN in Stem, North Carolina, going clockwise, left to right. The walls in here are tongue-and-groove eight-inch pine, painted white, with layers of gleam on them:

- a towel on a hook
- a measuring scale with a spring-needle indicator
- a two-tone stone crock with a speckled porcelain pan sitting in it (there's probably lard in the crock, though possibly cucumbers in brine)
- a bucket of Swift's Jewel shortening (the small print on the label says: "A shortening made from vegetable and animal fats. Swift and Company. General Offices Chicago. U.S. inspected and passed by Dept. of Agriculture. Net weight 8 lbs")
- a half-empty jar of preserves, though it could be molasses (the inside of the jar is mottled, indicating something sugary and sticky)
- a white oval pan, with a quarter-sized black spot on the lower left, where the enamel has chipped off
- a spray of cut flowers (they look like marigolds)
- a canning jar of something dark, with a metal screw-on cap
- a box of Premium Crackers, salted
- a narrow-necked bottle of vanilla (possibly vinegar, though vinegar isn't generally so dark; the bottle has a glass-hook handle probably just big enough to get your second finger through)

- rubber sealers used for canning (they're hanging on the nail in the window frame)
- a large aluminum pot, with a black-handled lid, sitting on a side table covered with an oilcloth
- a few towels
- two more aluminum pots, the larger one with a pressure valve on its lid, for steaming purposes
- a stone butter churn, with a cloth draped over it, and on top of the cloth an oblong white porcelain pan with black trim, and, sitting inside this pan, another black-knobbed lid (which suggests how tight they were for space this particular day)
- thirteen biscuits in a black baking pan
- the biscuit dough itself, in a concave wooden container
- a water bucket and a wash-up bowl (The rim of the wash-up bowl is just visible at the lower left corner of the frame. The water bucket next to it has the requisite ugly chip in its porcelain. You can't see the bucket's dipper, but it must have been there, and if it wasn't made of tin and bought in town at Coley's General Store—"Credit Makes Enemies, Let's Be Friends"—then it probably came from the backyard garden: a long-stemmed summer gourd, with its fat end hollowed out into a bowl. That's still a common practice in this part of Carolina and probably elsewhere too. Country folks know to grow their gourds from the top of fences, to take full advantage of gravity and thereby get the best home-grown dipper handle possible.)

But these are things, items, ways, lore. Who is this broad-beamed old girl in the white apron and size sixteen print dress and the ribbed hat jammed so comically low? Well, her name is Aunt Mary Wilkins, and she is the wife of Uncle Thad Wilkins, who is one of the eight Wilkins brothers—a whole civilization of Wilkinses—who cultivate tobacco and grow corn for their mules and live fence row to fence row, flue barn to flue barn, along this unpaved and sweet-scented stretch of Granville County road about half an hour north of Durham. The eight Wilkins brothers are the sons of Tump Wilkins, and the road here is named after him, or will be one day. The reason Aunt Mary has a hat on is because her hair is fine, almost exquisitely fine, and she doesn't want any of it coming out and getting into her biscuit dough, certainly not today. Today is Corn Shucking Day, one of the benchmarks in a seasonal year. Carolina tobacco farmers like to say they work the leaf thirteen months a year, and if it isn't the damn drought, it's the hail, and if it isn't the hail, it's the blue mold sure enough. Today, a celebratory and clan-gathering day, Aunt Mary's biscuits will be piled five high on wide plates of blue crockery. Wilkins men eat biscuits at every meal and give the leftovers to their dogs. The dogs love them, too.

The entire Wilkins family, plus hired hands and neighbors, are coming to dinner today, dinner being what folks in the country always mean when they're speaking of the noon meal. There will be sweetened tea and fried chicken and green beans and sliced tomatoes and apple sauce and heaps of steamed corn, plus a huge stack cake for dessert. The eight tobacco-growing brothers—John, Cale, Hellon, Roosevelt, Lee, Fred, Elvin, and Thad—will come into the house after their morning of husking and joke-telling and politics-talking. They will take their places at the table in the dining room while their wives line up behind them, holding several of the little ones. The necks of the men will be scrubbed, their hair licked back, several of their collars locked at the throat. Aunt Mary will come in from the kitchen and stand to the right (her right) of the Armours Big Crop Fertilizer calendar while the photographer from the Farm Security Administration works to get a group picture. Aunt Mary wears glasses, thin little spectacles, and her face has a kind of soft pensive look, but of course you could never know this from the backside biscuit-making shot. By the time Aunt Mary gets into the dining room to pose with several of her sisters-in-law, the ribbed hat is sitting on the back of her head. From the front, she doesn't look like a crusher at all. She looks gentle, she looks shy, she seems reflective. Two of the little ones in the family are leaning up against her.

So let fifty years swim away. Yes, the name Wilkins is still stenciled on RFD mailboxes up and down the still-unpaved and sweet-scented Tump Wilkins Road in Stem, North Carolina. But this is deceptive because the land here is increasingly in lease now to part-time farmers-turned-security guards at the Research Triangle, to people who clock time over at the No-Nonsense pantyhose plant in Creedmoor for their six-something an hour. And none of their names happens to be Wilkins. And some of these part-time grangers live in mobile homes, which are eyesore beyond eyesore, abortion beyond abortion, although no Wilkins, not even a fifth-generation Wilkins, which is how far it comes down—this family, this road, this way of life—would ever really use such a word to vent his or her anger, his or her fear at what is going on.

When Marion came to Stem, there was another place, called Shoofly, just down the road.

Nearly all of those eight scrubbed brothers, Tump's sons, who sat down to dinner and Marion's camera in their buckled overalls on Corn Shucking Day, 1939, are gone by the time I find my way into Granville County. Aunt Mary, Uncle Thad's wife, is alive, but she seems both present and not present: a tiny fine-haired form sitting in a rocker in her daughter-in-law Myrt's stifling front room. I think I had first looked at Marion's rear-view photograph and thought—not so generously, not so intelligently—of someone stolid and stuck. "There's big ol' Ma Wilkins in her kitchen," I probably said, or something like it. That ribbed hat was so comic, those shoulders so mannish. Perhaps I was also thinking in semiconscious ways of my own long-dead Kentucky grandmother, a lifelong country woman named Martina who was broad in the beam and stumpy in the legs and who was known, certainly to grandkids, as something of a crusher, whether from front or rear. I can recall the loud-talking and stockings-rolled Martina Hendrickson standing at wooden counters in her sweet-scented Union County kitchen, in one corner of which was a chipped porcelain water bucket on a green wicker stand. She always seemed to be busy getting dinner for my Uncle Lonnie and Uncle Jimmy and Uncle H. C., all of whom had been on tractors since nearly dawn and wouldn't be in again until half-past noon—that's how they said it. "Go on now and get out in the yard before Grandma has to get after your rags," Martina would say midmorning to the lingering Illinois city child standing at eye level with the water bucket. That child would git.

Perhaps a small forgiving part of me had first looked at the backside photograph of Aunt Mary and thought not so much of someone's bigness or loudness as of someone's damn hard life. But in truth I think I was also fascinated by a kitchen barren of anything resembling a modern appliance. (The pot with the steaming valve on its lid seemed about the only candidate.) How did these folks get by? It was the wonder of all those old ordinary things. And then, too, I suppose I was just letting myself be pulled toward a face I couldn't see, the hiddenness of it feeding my hunger once again to find out something, anything. In a way it was like the hiddenness of an artist's life.

And not least what was drawing me to the photograph was its beauty. I have since discovered literate pieces of writing in photography columns that speak of the "horizontals and verticals" of this image and how they are "as well placed as in any photograph by Walker Evans." I once saw another interpretation of the photograph that spoke of "images of archetypal order and industry, showing matriarchs among their canned goods, making biscuits among their gleaming pots, like peasant heroines by the 17th century painter Zurbarán."

I wasn't relating like that at all.

"DO YOU REMEMBER ANYTHING?" I am shouting one midday to a half-deaf woman in North Carolina, waving a picture in front of her she cannot see. Aunt Mary Wilkins is as old as the century.

"Well, I made the biscuits that day," a voice says. It seems thin as sparrow egg. It seems back from beyond. She is looking past me, not at me. "Took several pans to satisfy them, I suspect. We had colored folks helping and white ones, too."

That's all she says. She sits and rocks.

Later that afternoon, down the road, the backside biscuit-making shot and several others that were taken that 1939 day (there are about eighty altogether in the files) are being pored over by myself and a new generation of Wilkins wives. They are trying to help me identify some of those things around Aunt Mary.

"Now, that oilcloth," says one of these latter-day wives. "You bought that stuff by the yard. If you needed fifty-four inches, they just rolled it off."

"Yes, and I think that's a meal chest she's working at," says her cousin by marriage. "It looks like a counter top, but it's a meal chest, I'm pretty sure. It opened on hinges and had three big bins for your flour, sugar, and corn meal. Back then you bought your provisions in one-hundred-pound bags."

"See how she's rolling and cutting her dough?" answers the first. "Now, my own mama never cut a biscuit that way. She just pinched off a bit and worked it with her hands. Don't you figure Aunt Mary had been standing there for hours that day? That's some devotion."

"Yes, and that butter churn has a dasher in it," comes back the second. "You'd pour in your sour milk and work it till it clabbered. I don't know why a towel laid over the churn seemed to keep the butter so much cooler. But it did."

The phone rings. It's the married daughter of one of these Wilkins women. The daughter lives just across the road. Once you could call your mother or your neighbor or your first cousin across Tump Wilkins Road in Stem, North Carolina, without bothering to dial all seven digits. "No, Daddy's not here," her mother tells her. "He's in the field laying irrigation pipe. Should I run and get him?"

I am trying to record the fleshy faith of all this, but after a while I put away my pencil and just join in the talk. One of the wives brings in tomato sandwiches, along with a pitcher of sweetened tea and a plate of cold muskmelon cut up into bite-sized cubes. Who would have thought that a home-grown tomato, picked a few hours ago, sprinkled with pepper and served between slices of white bread that have been coated lightly with mayonnaise, could taste so wonderful, let alone seem so elegant an idea.

Wilkins clan assembled in the dining room, Aunt Mary standing, third from left. Stem, North Carolina, 1939

The tomato sandwiches, cut in halves, are sitting five high on a piece of blue crockery.

"That way of life is about extinct now," says the Wilkins wife who told her married daughter across the road that her daddy was out back laying irrigation pipe.

"And it'll never return," says her cousin by marriage. "I don't know, everything just got so changed around. But, say, you did get to meet Aunt Mary today."

Just in time, too. Because late one night several months later, when I was plagued by other thoughts, when I was adrift in other voices, floating in other Wolcott images, E. B. Wilkins of Stem—who is the son of Elvin Wilkins, who is the grandson of Tump Wilkins, who is the nephew of Aunt Mary Wilkins—called and informed me that Aunt Mary had breathed peacefully and moved her head down toward her breast and died that very morning.

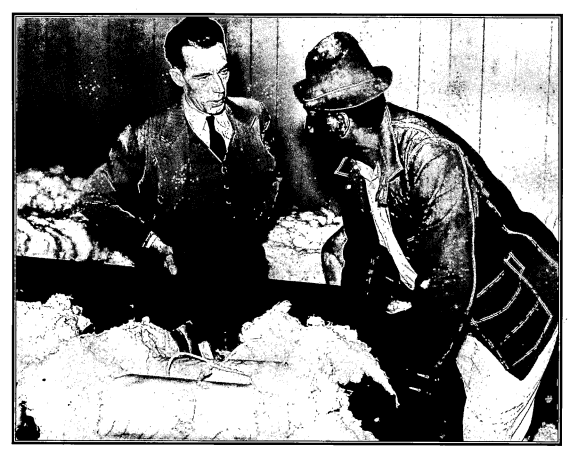

Tenant farmer brings cotton samples to buyer and discusses price, Clarksdale, Mississippi, 1939

·E R W I N C . M O O N E Y

I WOULD HAVE LIKED traveling back with her to one of the places where she shot. Clarksdale, seventy-seven miles south of the Tennessee border, would have done fine. The town used to bill itself as "The Golden Buckle on the Mississippi Cotton Belt," and I have been there when the light looked clear as gin. They don't put on the Delta Staple Cotton Festival anymore, but you can still connect with history at Friar's Point or out at Yazoo Pass, where U. S. Grant and the Yankees cut the levee and watched the Mississippi pour out like Niagara Falls.

Marion and her husband and I might have taken adjoining suites in the Alcazar—if the Alcazar still existed. The Cotton Boll Tourist Court, where I think she also put in a time or two, is now the Howard Village low-income housing units. The brick, overhanging carports have been cut into extra bedrooms.

I have come across dozens of Clarksdale photographs in the Library of Congress archives with a Marion Post Wolcott credit line, in addition to the one I've already described: that uplifted, jitterbugging black couple in their bare-board and ribbon-draped Saturday-night juke joint. I never found that place, although it's true I didn't look very hard. I'm not as nervy as Marion was.

On the other hand I did locate the razor-nosed Clarksdalian you see on the page across from this one. Or at least I found his bones, and that was enough to convince me of a late truth I've come to prize. It's a statement by a photographer/critic named Allan Sekula: "The photograph, as it stands alone, presents merely the *possibility* of meaning." Lance Morrow, essayist at *Time* magazine, once wrote: "All great photographs have lives of their own, but they can be as false as dreams."

His name was Erwin C. Mooney and he brokered cotton. Almost all of the old cotton men of that time and place are gone now—Albert Metts and H. J. Murff and L. L. Ledbetter and Ira Lane and Jack B. Cunningham, who was E. C. Mooney's partner at 284 Sunflower Avenue down on Cotton Row. The Clarksdale firm of Cunningham & Mooney had its name beautifully scrolled on its storefront window. Back then Cotton Row was a horseshoe of streets hard by the dribbling Sunflower River. The cotton men, which is what everybody in town called them, used to meet for poker and gin rummy in the torpid Delta afternoons, used to go for ham sandwiches and navy bean soup at the It, used to stand at long low wooden tables and make quick judgments on wads of fluff tied up in brown butcher paper. It was the "grade and staple" these important men were after, and they made their decisions by pulling apart the samples in their fingers. They were examining color and fiber length, mainly. Maybe the offered price was twenty cents. Cotton at twenty cents a pound means $100 a bale. Maybe the man who had brought the sample in, who had spent three quarters of a year growing and picking and ginning his crop and was now getting this crappy twenty-cent news, only had three bales to offer. Of course, he was perfectly free to go on down the street to the next storefront buyer if he thought he might be able to get a half cent or even a full cent more down there.

All sorts of hazy criteria seemed to come into play atop the sample table—soil conditions, the amount of rainfall that year, what the Memphis market was paying this particular week. Maybe the man who had brought in his butcher-wrapped wads had been "furnished" by his broker, in which case he wouldn't even think of going down the street. A furnished farmer is one who has accepted a cash advance—at interest, of course—for that year's seed, tools, and family necessities. The black cotton grower in Mississippi in the thirties had an expression: "From can to can't." He also had a rhyme: "A naught's a naught/ Five's a figger/ All for the white man/ None for the nigger." Which is just another way of saying you could never get ahead of last year's furnish.

I once saw that rhyme above Erwin C. Mooney's photograph in *12 Million Black Voices,* a book written by the great midcentury black novelist and essayist Richard Wright. The book was published in 1941, just as

Marion was getting off the road, never to take another professional photograph, though no one really knew that then. *The New Yorker* described Wright's book as "a burning commentary on three centuries of slavery, persecution, and want"—which might tend to influence a person's thinking about some of the real-life people whose pictures were and are in it.

Ever since I had first gazed at Marion's photograph in the FSA files, I had felt fascination for Mr. E. C. Mooney. I can think of one hundred other Wolcott pictures I like better—easily. It's probably not a "great" photograph by anyone's critical yardstick. But Mr. Erwin Mooney of Clarksdale, Mississippi, held me fast from the start. He looked almost like a character out of Dickens with that hatchet nose and swept hair and pointy face. I loved the way the bottom of his pinstriped vest slitted to an inverted V.

I didn't have so much as his name in the beginning. All I had was Marion's caption: "Tenant farmer brings cotton samples to buyer and discusses price, Clarksdale, Mississippi, 1939." I felt some not-so-sly irony in her use of the word "discusses." The picture was telling me the old Delta story: Here's whitey beating up once more on his poor black brother. The brother in the bashed felt hat and the denim jacket with the stitched piping is leaning in with what seems to me like plaintive though not prostrating body language.

Erwin C. Mooney, Clarksdale burgher, has his thumbs smartly hooked in the hind pockets of his Humphrey Bogart trousers.

But who really was this man?

I was once on an airplane, sitting next to a woman who told me she taught art photography at a museum on the West Coast. I pulled out E. C.'s picture, told her about the book I was trying to write. "He's sleazy, he's oily," the female professor said. "It's all surface. Whatever authority he has is stolen. The black man in his beat-up clothes looks far more dignified. I think if you're tracking this one down, you won't be very surprised."

The professor was wrong. What Mr. Mooney's life, as opposed to Mr. Mooney's picture, revealed to me was the brittleness of certainty. Because I found in Clarksdale some additional truths, some extra facts, connected with, if not necessarily contradictory to, the alluring pattern of alternating dots of light and dark that made up a Marion Post Wolcott image in the Library of Congress archives. In a sense what I found out about Mooney was little more than what a nickel fortune on a scale under a drugstore awning had once warned me: Watch your step. Consider every side.

Things will be more slippery here than you originally thought. I got that fortune at Turner's Drug in Belzoni, which is only down the road a piece from Clarksdale.

Erwin C. Mooney, who died in 1972 at the age of seventy-seven, was an alcoholic. You wouldn't get that from the picture. Nor that he died of a ravaging cancer—got it in January, was gone by early summer. Nor that he had a reputation for being far more decent to Clarksdale blacks than some of his fellow brokers on Cotton Row. Everyone I talked to, and that included several black men who don't chop cotton any longer, had positive things to say about him. Not that they were ready to press his case in Rome for canonization. But what each was telling me, I think, was that a photograph, like a statistic, doesn't lie, and yet like a statistic, the realities and "truths" it imparts can be elusive and warping in the light.

Mr. Mooney wasn't Bill Sykes with a Delta accent—which isn't to say he didn't press the hardest judgments he could at the sample table. But he never had this life knocked. He may not even have had that *day* knocked.

"E. C.? Hell, yeah, good fella," said Bernie Smith, who had a tennis match going on the tube when I knocked. Smith used to broker for Anderson & Joiner, which was at 311 Yazoo. On the day I knocked, the front door of his house had iron bars on it: Crime had grown bad in Clarksdale. "Course, Erwin's idea of a workout would be a match you had to scratch twice," said the retired cotton man, breaking up. Then Bernie Smith said, "Hey, you should've seen that life. The idea was we wanted to get it picked, ginned, but especially *sold* by duck hunting season. Then you had the rest of the year off."

I asked about Mooney's three-piece suit—did everybody go to work that way? "Now that's an interesting point," he said. "Those damn little flecks of cotton would get all over your clothes—you had to brush 'em off all day long. That's why some guys changed into jackets or windbreakers when they got down to work. But this is exactly how I remember Erwin dressing. He was willing to do the brushing."

Then Bernie Smith added, a little slyly, "I suppose he wanted to show that other guy in your picture something from the get-go."

My first Clarksdale hint that things may be more complicated than what they first seem in a photograph—no less, possibly, than in a photographer's life—came when I spoke on the telephone to Nancy Easley, Mooney's daughter. She is upper-aged herself now and has the same lean body and prominent nose her father had. She has lived in Clarksdale all her life; lives, in fact, in her daddy's house at 1406 Cheyenne Street, which is still in one of the best neighborhoods in town. On the phone from Washington, trying awkwardly to describe what I was doing, I had said something to the effect of, "Well, you must have been awfully proud of your father in his lifetime."

"Well, yes, sometimes," she had said.

And on that Sunday morning a few weeks later, when I took out Marion's photograph of Nancy Easley's father, Nancy took one look at it, almost a sniff, and said, "Well, that is old Daddy, sure enough. I wonder if he was sober that day." The sentence stunned me.

She told me many other things, how alcoholism seems to have a way of running down through families, and how she has come to view the world, and her father, a little more complexly now. She said her father, who'd been born into a family of nine children in 1895 in Pine Bluff, Arkansas (he would have been either forty-three or forty-four when Marion photographed him), was a fervent Catholic. That in itself was an anomaly for any Deep South white man of the thirties. "Even when he was loaded, he could get up and go to mass," Nancy said. "I think we about prayed him into it. His sobriety." Then she said, "You know, I never understood how he could eat like a horse and still be thin as a rail. And as far as the blacks went, I know he was fair. Oh, heck, he used to carry on and get mad at them, as all of them do, and you know, call them 'nigger' and whatnot, but the fact is, I think *they* took advantage of *him*."

She said she could see Erwin falling in a Mississippi minute for the photographic wiles of a young Yankee woman who'd just stepped in off the sidewalk. "He was naive that way, even if he was a salesman himself," she said. I was thinking suddenly of some of my own journalistic wiles and how I have managed one way or another to get people to say things they might not have any idea they're saying. She told me how her father had pretty much quit drinking when she was in high school, then sort of came back on, then stopped again, and then licked it almost completely before he died. "I can picture him pulling that cotton apart between his fingers," she said, some sadness getting into her voice. The two of us sat around awhile longer that day in her pleasant living room at 1406 Cheyenne, where there are fine old wooden ceiling beams and curved hallways and big trees out in the yard to keep the heat down. I told her I wasn't really sure what I had come for, but in a way I might already have found it.

FRAME FOUR

GOVERNMENT LADY PHOTOG

The scientist tries to examine the 'real' nature of the photograph; he tries to get away from the psychological configuration, the meaning of the image, to move down to some other, more basic level of patterns of alternating dots of light and dark, a world of elementary particles. . . . We rummage about in our minds in search of a feeling that was there before the first fact was deposited. But searching for facts won't help, for it is not so much a matter of what we think, but what thinks us. In the interval between each thought, in the interval between each heartbeat, in the place where there is no breath, we recall what we always knew.

—WILLIAM IRWIN THOMPSON
The Time Falling Bodies Take to Light

FIRST PHASE

FROM THE END OF 1938 to midsummer of the following year, Marion Post Wolcott traveled and photographed almost nonstop in the Deep South. Not all of the roads were bad and not every night was the blue-plate special in a fly-specked diner and then back to the funnel of frowsy room light—though enough of it seems to have been that. Primarily, she documented in the Carolinas, Georgia, Florida, Alabama, and parts of Louisiana. She spent Christmas Eve driving in the rain between Columbia and Charleston, South Carolina. She spent Easter week laid up with a head cold and fever in the Henry Grady Hotel in Atlanta ("550 Rooms, 550 Baths," it said on the stationery). And she spent the 4th of July heading back north, having just cleaned up some U.S. Public Health contract work in Savannah—which she found a mindless kind of shooting, even though she knew it helped pay Stryker's bills and keep the FSA photo unit afloat.

Of all the photographers who ever shot for Stryker at the FSA or the RA or the OWI, only one, Russell Lee, stayed out longer at the beginning of his or her tenure. This wasn't Marion's absolute start, of course—that brilliant fortnight in the coal fields of West Virginia was. But still it was awfully close to her very first work for the agency, and the toll must have been terrific. They had stuck her right into the deep end. If the twenty-eight-year-old who left town in late November of thirty-eight was eager and rested for the road, the twenty-nine-year-old who came back almost eight months later was experienced and spent. But she still greatly cared for the life and wanted more of it, at least then. To dip now into the prolific, raw correspondence that dates from those thirty-odd straight weeks of asphalt and starchy food and amazing camera angles is to feel up close a shooter's exhilarations and exasperations, her loneliness and her guts. And, not least, her chronic sense of never having enough time. Because no matter what mood or state Marion is riding in, that is the cry: "*If I just had a little more time, Roy.*"

The humor of these letters often seems a mask for what's just below their surface.

So here's an uncelebrated American artist, two days before Christmas 1938 (I figure she's left the rickets child and his sister on their Wadesboro hillside about three days earlier), venting spleen to Toots Wakeham, Stryker's girl Friday, with whom she has struck up a fast friendship:

> Toots dear: You were sweet to send me a Xmas card, & I *do* appreciate it—plus all the mail forwarding you've been doing. You should see all these southern towns, decked out fit to kill, with more lights & decorations & junk than you could find in the 5th ave. big 5 & 10 cent store. The houses too. But damn all the firecrackers, everywhere, all the time, day & nite. Especially every time I'm ready to click the camera. I jump like I'd been shot, time after time. Can't get used to it, especially if I'm concentrating on something. I wish that they'd celebrate & serve a *decent* meal in one of the restaurants, just for a change for the holidays! Vegetables for one meal are usually fried potatoes, mashed potatoes, sweet potatoes, rice, grits, or turnips!

She goes right on:

> So far I've been mostly dashing around from one tenant purchase farm to another, with one idiot or another (each in their own way, of course), & from cancer to syphilis—my malaria jobs haven't come through yet.

Her compass is aimed at Florida, but at the moment Marion is still in the Carolinas. About two weeks later, having made it deep inside the Sunshine State, the thought of those rockheads back in Columbia and Charleston with their little wads of holiday dynamite is still getting her goat. "I'm sure even friend Jesus might be slightly surprised or scared if

Mosquito Crossing, near Greensboro, Georgia, 1939

Bennie's grocery store, Sylvania, Georgia, 1939

Signs in Bible Belt, Greene County, Georgia, 1939

Torso of old Negro man, ex-slave, seated (lost fingers on
hand, ragged patched clothing), Camden, Alabama, 1939

he happened along," she writes to Stryker from Homestead early in the New Year, adding, "They use cannon crackers." Perhaps crackers has a double meaning.

This first long report from Florida goes fourteen pages, and in it she unwittingly pries open a can of Stryker worms:

> Some said they didn't understand why I was riding around in that kind of country & roads all alone. [She is referring to the Carolina low country.] A couple thought I was a gypsy—(maybe others did too) because my hair was so "long & heavy" & I had a bandanna scarf on my head & bright colored dress & coat. All of which I remedied immediately, but it didn't seem to help. All the things in the car seemed to awe them too.

A few pages later, describing an animal she'd run over on the way down:

> I ought to be getting sort of toughened to such things—the roads are so full of squashed rabbits & dead dogs being eaten by a lot of those big black vultures. Pretty, yes? I hope you've had lunch. Or maybe you're not such a sissy.

And then toward the close:

> I hope you'll send me *all* first prints on this first batch of stuff so I'll know what turned out & what didn't—also the bad negatives so that I can get some things on my return that were worth it. The locating of the places & people really takes just as much, sometimes more time, in the beginning.

The reply is immediate. Maybe that "sissy" line has gotten somebody's goat up north. Stryker's letter is dated January 13, 1939.

> I am glad that you have now learned that you can't depend on the wiles of femininity when you are in the wilds of the South. Colorful bandannas and brightly colored dresses, etc., aren't part of our photographers' equipment. The closer you keep to what the great backcountry recognizes as the normal dress for women, the better you are

going to succeed as a photographer. Russell and Arthur learned this
too: When Russell bloomed forth with his sky-blue jacket covered
with all manner of pockets, I raised my eyes unto heaven, but said
little. The back-country people solved the problem. Russell doesn't
wear it any more. I know this will probably make you mad, but I can
tell you another thing—that slacks aren't part of your attire when
you are in that back-country. You are a woman, and "a woman can't
never be a man"! If you could just see me stroking my gray whiskers
while I am giving all that fatherly advice, you would take it in much
better form.

Stryker is right about one thing—his letter raises her temperature. The
answer to *his* answer starts right in, no real salutation. Nor is there a date
at the top, something that drives the chief to distraction in these first
weeks of their correspondence. Marion puts in the top right-hand corner:
"c/o General Delivery, Belle Glade. Wednesday." It's probably the following Wednesday, January 18.

Now grandfather—you listen to me for a minute too—all you say is
perfectly true, *but* I just wish you had been along with me for just
part of a day looking for something, particularly with POCKETS. Let
us assume that we agree on the premise that all photographers need
pockets—badly—& that female photographers look slightly con-
spicuous & strange with too many film pack magazines & rolls &
synchronizers stuffed in their shirt fronts, & that too many filters &
whatnots held between the teeth prevent one from asking many necessary questions. Now—this article of clothing with large pockets
must also be cool, washable if possible, not too light or bright a color.
Try & find it! Even a simple overall "jumper" or jacket! ... Where
did I finally find one? In a *drug*store! After scouring several towns &
a city or two. You can see you touched on a sore subject.

Is she finished? Hell, no, she's not finished.

About slacks—you can't make me mad. I learned you can't wear
them in the stix when I was in Tennessee, etc., a couple of years
ago—But—Florida, in *most* sections—is an exception. Everyone
wears them—idle rich, winter & year round residents, migrants &

negroes. Especially picking, & if you'd seen the results of the pleasant
feast the insects & briars & sticker grasses had on my legs the first day
I took photographs of tomato & bean pickers you'd know why. I
wore a skirt & heavy stockings & socks, & was still a mess. But not
again. And I DIDN'T use feminine wiles, & I usually wore an old
jacket & sweater, but it was too cold that day. But I'll be a good girl &
buy an old brown swagger coat next winter. My slacks are dark blue,
old, dirty, & not too tight—O.K.? To be worn with great discrimi-
nation, sir.

But then, very next paragraph, down to the work, as if she's filing intelligence cables to agronomy spies:

Child in doorway of shack of migrant pickers and packing
house workers, near Belle Glade, Florida, 1939

The situation in Homestead was thus. Fewer transients than they've ever had before—about half the number, & most of them working in packing houses. Most of the pickers this year are being brought in from Key West, Miami, & nearby towns. I stuck my nose in every back yard looking for people living in chicken coops & found practically none. Scoured the glades & canals & ditches. . . . This year, the season is a little late. The very early "rock" tomato crop, planted in small sections of higher, rocky land, came in late Nov. & Dec. was not so good, & they have to wait, to plant the next crop, until the lower glades are no longer flooded.

Toward the close, she reports:

Today in Belle Glade—Okeechobee area, find things still very slow, but much more to photograph. There'll be plenty to do here, & more transients should be coming in soon, & I'll prob'ly find more too as I get around. . . . One has to hunt for these things, & they're not always so close together, & sometimes one must go back again. Many people are so superstitious—or suspicious—others require or demand explanations, etc.

She does find more, no matter an artist's standard neurotic worry that she won't. Apparently not too long afterward (the dates assigned to the negative are confusing and indeterminate), she encounters a ten-year-old migrant child holding up his little brother. She has come on the pair far back in the Belle Glade cane clearings. The older child has the younger one balanced on one arm and is showing him in the way you might exhibit a carnival doll. The doll-like face of the held-aloft one is clotted with something black. It's the muck rash, around his eyes, his lips. The ten-year-old tells her: "This little un's fell off so since we come here. Hit was so fat before. Hit's had colitis and muck rash so bad. Now I don't like it here so well. But I reckon we'll have to stay a smart while. My daddy had to turn back the car. He'd paid a lots off on it. But he didn't get enough work here. Now we can't go nowheres else."

Those words turn up in pen and ink on the back of a mounted image in an FSA file. The number assigned to the print is LC-USF 34-51187-E, a government clerk transcribing it word for word as she sends it in. Such emotion doesn't often make it onto the back of Roy Stryker's factual photographs.

*Baby's Sore Eyes. The children of a migrant laborer, Belle
Glade, Florida, 1939*

   After she gets the picture, the photographer speaks with the mother
of the children. She tells Marion she's thirty-two and has given
birth to eleven kids but six are dead. She tells Marion the bosses sent
her home because they think she's pregnant again, even though she swore
to them she wasn't. She says she has a pet name for her ten-year-old:
"Grandpa."
   It isn't known where Marion goes from here, but it is known that in
this same general period she has been slipping down into Miami whenever
she has the time, taking amazing pictures with such wan captions as
"Brunch being served to member of private club." She goes to the races at
Hialeah and catches its straw-hatted splendors. She gets into basement
bars in the homes of Gold Coasters, where the Depression must seem like
merely an inconvenience. (In one of these private tippling preserves, she

finds the brother of Mrs. Ira Gershwin.) At the Jockey Club, she gets the crispness of the tablecloths and salad leaves, she gets the general squalor of an upper-class affluence sitting less than seventy miles from her clotted-faced child. About six dozen permanent prints will result from these off-hours infiltrations into the south Florida wintering zones, and years hence photo esthetes will regard them as some of her most original and enter-prising work.

But her primary material is documenting the dispossessed. About January 28, 1939, she writes to the chief:

> A woman the other day told how she'd been waiting around the packing house all day long. They were told there'd be *some* work, finally something came in & she got 9 *minutes* work. They never know, so they not only don't get paid, but they can't stay home to take care of the "house" & kids either. Then at the peak of the season they have to work 12, 16, 18 hrs. straight with 15 minutes rest every 3 hrs.... There's good material for me here, conditions are awful at all times, just more of it & easier to find at the busy seasons. It takes time, Roy, but you'll see that it's worth it. Talking, & listening to people, going back again to persuade them, or returning when the one (sometimes either the mother or father, *not* both) who objects to pictures will surely not be at home, or returning when the light is right. When you are shown around by other people, almost always a good deal of time is lost as well as gained too.... You have to see so many other things that you don't want to photograph & explain why not, & then return another time to try to get the people to be less self-conscious with you, alone.... The roads are awful & often one must go back & try another way, or walk across the field & muck because the car is too low.... Be sure to let me know if there's any dust, etc., in the negatives. It's an awful struggle to keep this black muck out of the cameras & film. It's as fine as powder or flour & blows so. I keep everything covered & wrapped up, & brush & clean everything several times a day & every nite. By the time I get that done, my film loaded, the car brushed out, my clothes shaken out, my underwear scrubbed, the muck out of my hair & ears & nose & neck & arms & feet—it itches so!—there's not much time left for reading.

She isn't referring in this last sentence to books of poetry or the thought of plumping herself up in bed with a box of chocolates and some movie

Entrance to Roney Plaza Hotel, Miami, Florida, 1939

Spectators at horse races, Hialeah Park, Florida, 1939

Brunch being served to member of private club, Miami,
Florida, 1939

A typical scene on a private beach club boardwalk,
Miami, Florida, 1939

magazines. She means finding the time to get through Professor Arthur Raper's *Preface to Peasantry*. Stryker feels it's a must-read.

Incidentally, here is his answer to that business about the muck:

We really don't care what the black dust does to you as long as you can work, but I hate like the devil to see it get into your camera, because it hurts your negatives—the good employer!

On February 3, she writes:

I want to get the people, mostly women, working in the packing houses until 2 & 3 a.m. . . . I mean the life of the packing houses— the hanging around, the "messing around," the gambling, the fighting, the "sanitary" conditions, the effects of the *very* long work stretch, the rest periods, their "lunch"—etc.

Same letter, dander suddenly up, regarding the plague of Bible-toting social workers she's encountered:

Maybe I'm intolerant in my own way, & I suppose these women are at least aware of a few more things & interested & active, but goddamn it I can't stand their approach to problems or their unrealistic & sentimental way of handling it. After a whole day of that crap & listening to them playing Jesus I could just plain puke! Just a little daily Bible reading for the kiddies & a service on Sunday for all the folks.

This tickles Stryker no end: "It just goes to prove my theory," he writes, "that once you get in the services of God, you [are] seldom ever able to free yourself of those damnable traits."

Marion now learns her mother has been fired from the Sanger organization. So many things have seemed to go wrong in Nan Post's life since the divorce from Walter back in Bloomfield. She has been canned for trying to stir up union activity at the Planned Parenthood Foundation, although the stated reason for the dismissal is consolidation of the staff and amalgamation of the several birth control organizations in the country. "Dear Mrs. Post," the oily termination letter begins. "It is my very unhappy task, as the new Acting Managing Director of the Federation, to tell you that these changes in the field program affect you. It would be impossible for me to put into words how deeply distressed one and all are. . . . This letter is official 'notification' and is to tell you that the Executive Committee voted a full month's pay as an expression of its debt of gratitude to you." Nan is traveling for the federation in Oklahoma when the news comes. Marion receives a copy of the letter in the mail from her mother, swears at it beautifully, throws it down, stamps on it, picks it up, smooths it out. One way or another, it will find its way into FSA archives.

Sometimes as much as ten days or more can go by before the shooter and the chief find each other. On February 24, following a flurry of back-and-forth communication by both cable and letter, she reports:

> Received another package of prints & also one more box of negatives. Am setting out today for some quiet spot where I will be a completely unknown quantity & not be disturbed. I'm going to put on *very* dark glasses & hang a typhoid fever sign on my front & back & *dare* anyone to come near me. Whether or not it's very obvious that one is working, there are always a million blokes who want you to either teach them photography, explain the mechanics of your & their cameras, or else they're sure they have some valuable information concerning the country. If you have any prints around, god help you! I tried working in my room, but it was so damn cold & damp that I eventually decided to brave the chiggers on the grass outdoors. There's been another cold spell here—freezing, & frosts, but because there was such a high wind too, there wasn't as much damage to crops as before. . . . There's no heat in these homes or hotels down here so when it does get cold it seems much worse. The changes are so sudden and extreme. Everyone now has a cold or grippe—so far I haven't succumbed seriously.

Next page:

> The two main reasons for my taking extra exposures with the Speed Graphic were because for quite a few days I had no confidence in the lasting effects of the rangefinder repairs & adjustments, & I had a general feeling of insecurity & lack of confidence. It's hard to get over that in the beginning unless you see your negatives or prints immediately. I'm getting used to it now.

March, she's in Alabama. April and May, it's Georgia. Back to Alabama. Back to Georgia. She's in Camden County, Coffee County, Greene County. It's Atlanta, Lincolnton, Irwinville, Orangeton, Birmingham—two days here, one day there. That's not the exact order, this isn't the entire list.

One day in Coffee County (this is lower Alabama, near the Florida panhandle) she shoots the Ellis Adkins clan. Ellis, head of a family of nine, is a rural rehabilitation client. Miss Hesterly and Miss Christian, two FSA home economists, are present. Ellis has holes in his shirt and needs a shave; Miss Hesterly has granny glasses and pinched sleeves. On the dinner table are biscuits, beans, and cake. There's nothing remarkable about this series of photographs. It's Marion's lawn and she's mowing it. Even with this dreary project work, however, her eye manages at least one powerful shot. It's of two of Ellie Adkins's boys. They look about ten and twelve and are wearing railroad-striped overalls. One son has his hand raised to his forehead, the other has a hand stuck deep in his pocket. It's their twin gazes that haunts: faraway, prematurely old.

The chief keeps pushing her for more, including a possible return to

The two sons of Mr. and Mrs. Ellis Adkins, a rural rehabilitation family, Coffee County, Alabama, 1939

the Florida migrant fields. On May 8, 1939, from Montezuma, Georgia, she writes:

> But how can I get all this done, even excluding Florida & migrants, & be back by June 15th, in one month. Only with wonderful luck & no hitches, *if* it's at all possible. Driving at nite is definitely *not* a good idea for a gal alone in the South. And you know I'm no sissy. I've done it some, but no more than absolutely necessary. Everything closes up, including gas stations, & everyone goes to bed, & the only ones who stay out are bums who are pretty drunk or tough or both—negroes & whites. If anything goes wrong you're just out of luck & no one understands it if a girl is out alone after dark—believe it or not!

This letter must bring Stryker awake, for he quickly cancels several jobs. "By no means drive around the South at night," he writes. "I would feel very much upset if anything should happen to you while doing our work. To hell with the work. When night comes find yourself a nice safe place and settle down."

Ten days later, though, the bark is back, this time by night letter via Western Union: "WHY HAVEN'T YOU PICKED UP FLASHBULBS GENERAL DELIVERY ATLANTA? CAPTION AND RETURN IMMEDIATELY PRINTS MAILED GREENSBORO GEORGIA TODAY."

Two days later, the softness again:

> If you happen to be in a small town over Memorial Day, you might watch out for a set of pictures. . . . You haven't done much small town stuff, so if you get a chance, you might add a little to our collection. Watch out for Court Day; hard to find, but you may just stumble on it.

She receives the letter in Greensboro, Georgia, and shortly afterward a great small-town photograph is snapped. She captions it "Playing checkers outside a service station on a Saturday afternoon." Marion not only catches a move just about to be made in this intensely watched game, she subtly catches the social order between two races: The blacks in the picture have a seat on the watching bench all right, but they are down a little from the action and must crane their necks. Of the seven people in the shot, only

Playing checkers outside a service station on a Saturday
afternoon, Greensboro, Georgia, 1939

the child beneath the Goody's Ice Cream sign seems to know of a stranger's presence; everyone else is too buried in the match. You can fairly feel this old stucco filling station hanging in the roadside dust and late afternoon Georgia sun: a pleasurable tangle of hoses and gas cans and deflated inner tubes. One of the combatants is sitting on his cane and chewing on his H. L. Mencken cigar. In the foreground, an overturned ice-cream Dixie Cup.

On May 21, she writes:

In the meantime, I've been struggling with my damn car, & think I've found the answer to all my troubles with it. At first I thought that the banging it took getting across the Gee's Pond Ferry, plus getting stuck bad twice in Flint River (once when the project manager was driving & once when I was) were responsible for it. The rear axle housing line which resulted also in one tire being worn out. When they took the rear end out, they found it had at some previous time been *broken & welded!* In two places! So I evidently didn't get a new car when I bought it. Either it was a demonstrator's, or had been in a wreck & turned back to the agency who fixed it up for new—*or* it might have been badly assembled at the factory, since I bought it right after the strike days when cars were in great demand & very scarce. Anyway, somehow, I got royally gipped, & am going back to the agency with it as soon as I return.

Four days later Stryker writes:

Camera received. You just raise hell with equipment. Reg is on the warpath. He tries to keep each camera unit intact—flash equipment and synchronizer. We will let you off this time, but don't ever do it again. Incidentally, the camera was terribly dusty; looked as if you'd been out in the worst dust storm the Great Plains ever had. What happened? Where is the back? If it is broken or lost, we must get a report out at once. Try to find it if possible. If not, make a memo to account for what happened.

Next paragraph:

I am terribly sorry about your car. Be sure to get a statement from the garage where the repair work was done. This is very important when you get ready to make a row on your return. I will be glad to do anything I can in the way of letters when you go after them, and you can scare hell out of them if we "play like" we can get the Government after them.

In late May she's due in New Orleans for a Public Health project job at a marine hospital on State Street. But on the way down, there's a delay in Atlanta—car troubles. On June 7, her twenty-ninth birthday, she's in Mississippi. She sends a wire from Meridian that she's leaving immediately for New Orleans. It's about a five-hour roll down to the sea, via U.S. 11. Does she go to the French quarter for red beans and rice when she gets in? There's no record of it. Probably she just takes a room, the hell with turning twenty-nine in a romantic and jazzy American city.

A feature clip about her regarding her New Orleans stay. It's from the *Times-Picayune* and among other things notes that she's staying at the Hotel Monteleone on Bourbon Street.

At least the scribe from the paper could have gotten her damn name right:

> Miss Miriam Post, pretty girl photographer whose work has been published in such slicks as Fortune and Vogue, is here taking pictures of the Marine hospital and the Quarantine station.
>
> Miss Post is now employed by the information division of Farm Security Administration in Washington, and has been temporarily loaned to the U.S. Public Health service.
>
> Before this job she was a staff photographer on the Philadelphia Evening Bulletin, but found that a gal has a hard time persuading policemen and firemen—in emergencies—that she is an official photographer. "While the building was burning down or the shooting was going on, I was usually trying to dig up my identification cards to get by the lines," she said.
>
> Miss Post, of course, didn't say so, but her looks are against her. She is too pretty and young looking to be taken seriously as a news photographer. "They were always trying to keep me from getting hurt or pushed around in crowds and saying, 'Stand back, little girl, you'll get wet' or something," she complained.
>
> So she quit the newspaper and went to work for the government—taking pictures of sharecroppers or building projects or health projects or anything they wanted.
>
> On a recent trip through Florida she took pictures of the itinerant workers around Lake Okeechobee who live in the most primitive conditions. Some of them don't even have grass huts to crawl into, but live under burlap bags, or in the marshes and woods. . . .
>
> She took up photography as a hobby while in school in Vienna, and decided later to make it a vocation. She is staying at the Monteleone hotel, and will leave Monday for Washington.

On June 22, a Stryker letter reaches her at the DeSoto Hotel in Savannah. She's finding her way back north; the two have been out of touch for three weeks. ("I haven't heard from you for so long that I have begun to wonder if there is such a person!" grumps the man in Washington.) For seven and a half months she has been crisscrossing a dozen states. Stryker has praised her work here and there but never quite enough:

> Let us know how long you expect to be on the road, and give us the approximate date when you expect to be in Washington. There is no great rush—it will depend a lot upon yourself.

In the final furlong, last communication of the journey, July 5, 1938, ribaldry ever intact, Marion writes:

> Dear Roy—the P.H. [Public Health] jobs are cleaned up as well as possible. They certainly are a pain in the neck, & I don't mean neck either. I still haven't recovered from the mass of Savannah mosquitoes. . . . The damn mosquitoes we were trying to photograph in the insectary wouldn't "feed" off anyone else so I had to pose, & the next morning my arm was so swollen & blue I couldn't use it. I was actually sick from it, among other things, for days. No need to tell you I'll be glad to get back—if only to get rid of my athletes foot—no, it's really not bad. . . . I'll also be glad of a rest from the daily & eternal questions whether I'm Emily Post, or Margaret Bourke-White, followed by disappointed looks—or what that thing around my neck is, & how I ever learned to be a photographer, if I'm all alone, not frightened & if my mother doesn't worry about me, & how I find my way. . . . I'll probably get in Saturday sometime, providing the weather stays reasonably good the next couple of days.

Yes, she has found her way. Three days later she hits town. It's caption time, it's reunion time with old friends and lovers in New York and Philadelphia. She'll get some clothes out of mothballs (they're in the back of a closet at the apartment of Stryker's secretary) and she'll get her car tuned up and she'll take the monthly rate at the Blackstone Hotel and she'll dawdle over late-night dinners in places where they don't serve grits. She'll sleep on Willy and Tony Kraber's couch in the Village and then in two months she'll be back out again for more Stryker camera marathons: Chapel Hill. Memphis and Clarksdale for the cotton harvest. Back to Florida. Into the blizzards of New England. But for now it's sleep and rest and love. Ah.

SECOND PHASE

Chief Stryker! Calling all cars. Caution all photogs! Never take picture of pregnant woman sitting in rocking chair on sloping lawn while visiting family on Sunday afternoon! Consequences are—lady doesn't want photograph taken in present state, starts hurriedly to get up & run in house, but chair tips over backwards dumping (& embarrassing, not seriously damaging) her. Photog is surprised, sorry, tries to apologize, inquire after victim's health, etc., etc., & succeeds only in almost being mobbed & beaten & driven off by irate & resentful & peace loving members of family—DOZENS of them. (P.S.—Camera was saved.)

>   —*From a letter, July 28, 1940, Louisville, Kentucky*

THE JOKES WERE JUST AS RIBALD, in fact, more so. The shots were just as brilliant, in fact, more so. Only now you could plainly hear the other stuff, too: the ache to stop, the longing for permanent connection, the night fears, the war fears, the self-doubt, the nerves that tended to fray like bad rope. Which isn't to say these things couldn't be heard in her earlier letters. I suppose you just had to be willing to listen a little closer for them, read between the lines for them, and I didn't. I was still clinging to my illusions about Marion's romantic photographic life. I was too in love with the piss-and-vinegar aspect, that high-toned American flyer who could sit down at midnight in the Claridge Hotel in Memphis and rip off, "Jesus Christ, these social workers are fierce inhuman stupid prigs. I can't call them enough names!"

Reason can destroy reason, truths can block out other truths.

Because it turns out that the very same hilarious Jesus-Christ-fierce-inhuman-stupid-prig letter, which I've quoted often to my friends since I first found it, is the same one in which a shooter walked downstage and said:

> The drive over here was beautiful. I was sorry I hurried so, after I arrived & found that no arrangements had been made for the pix here. It wouldn't have mattered if I had taken my time & gotten some photographs of the spring & planting, etc., on my way. Perhaps it was better so—the lab might have gotten too many apple blossoms & budding trees & spring clouds to print. More FSA cheesecake. Or if I *had* stopped, I might have begun to dig in the red brown earth in some farmer's garden & just stayed there.

Perhaps to deflect that paragraph came an immediate stab in the next at a pale joke: "I can see so much more with the top down in my new car—it's wonderful. The dogwood trees so white—my nose so red when I got here—a very hot sun."

And yet . . . two paragraphs from the bottom, the fear getting in again: "Parts of the country driving reminded me of France which I drove through one spring. War news, international & national happenings, always seem to be even worse & more terrifying when I'm away and don't have anyone I know to talk to about it."

Stryker's reply? "Dear Marion," he wrote three days afterward. "Your delightful letter arrived. I enjoyed it particularly because I, too, feel as you do about social workers. I just don't let myself turn loose on them in the presence of polite people—they never understand what I'm talking about. Roy E. Stryker."

He was as thick as I am.

She mailed that letter on May 15, 1940. (She had learned to date her correspondence—well, most of the time.) By then she'd been traveling alone for nearly two years, with only brief time-outs in Washington. Most of the other photographers who shot for Stryker managed to travel with someone on their assignments, at least part of the time. Jack Delano's wife, Irene, often went with him, taking notes for captions, keeping a diary. Dorothea Lange, who was halt in one leg, nearly always traveled with her husband, the Berkeley economist Paul S. Taylor. Russell Lee went out alone in the beginning, but then he met the woman who was to become his second wife. In the interim she served as his traveling "secretary." Ben Shahn would sometimes take his wife, Bernarda, on assignments. Even the aloof, fastidious Walker Evans, with his tailor-made clothes and English shoes, had the mournful and poetic James Agee for company when they went to Hale County, Alabama, in the summer of 1936.

Two weeks after a traveler let out her anxieties about global destruction, she let them out again. On May 30, 1940, different state, different stationery, Marion wrote: "If I'd only stop having dreams & nightmares about the war & the 'human' race I'd be a little happier—Sorry I'm somewhat depressed. Maybe it's just the rain—I doubt it—Best regards & love to all—Marion."

By the end of May 1940, the Germans had invaded Luxembourg, the Netherlands, and Belgium. The evacuation of Dunkirk had begun. France was about to fall. And Hitler's U-boats were sinking Allied ships virtually at will. By the end of that year, Christmastime 1940, Britain would be under constant barrage, Japan would have taken over large parts of China, and America's own entry into world war would be considered something inevitable.

Marion once wrote a very moving essay about her experiences as a photographer in the Deep South; I have already quoted from parts of it. The opening pages of the essay are missing, and the date is gone, and Marion can no longer remember why she wrote it in the first place. (She thinks

Colored maids with white child in stroller visiting together on street corner, Port Gibson, Mississippi, 1940

Uncle Joe Rogue, a Cajun, Natchitoches, Louisiana, 1940

she may have composed it for a pay upgrade, which seems pretty ironic, given what she had to say.)

She put much of it in the third person. "One has the feeling of not belonging anywhere, of having no roots or base. It is a kind of numbness. One never really participates in anything. At times nothing seems real, to you, or part of your life. Nothing affects your own life. One has a feeling of being suspended, of never being relaxed, or at home, or accepted for who or what one really is, or has been, and what one believes. One never has the same feeling of belonging as one does when with former acquaintances and friends. It is a need to be with familiar people, to walk known streets, and recognize familiar places. It is not good to feel always that one must go on, leaving everything unfinished and incomplete—both work and human relationships."

She spoke in this fragment of losing "any vital reaction to the material or subject . . . almost empty or dead inside . . . becoming just an observer of life . . . one has forgotten slightly, or the edge has worn off. One does not remember so acutely or distinctly what one felt, or thought about the material at the time, nor what one wanted to project. . . . It is discouraging, disappointing, and aggravating never to be able to return to a place."

That almost sounds like a cry for help. And the first time I read it, I read right over the kind of pain it must have represented. I am not suggesting I missed it entirely—no one could be that blind to plain English. But somehow the truth of her words never sank in. It was as if I had heard and not heard, read and not read. It was as if I had willed myself to be opaque to a truth: that there was always a sense in which Marion couldn't wait until the work was over.

I once looked up the name "Marion Post Wolcott" in the clip files at the Washington *Post,* in the room that used to be known, before computer microdot NEXIS printouts, as the morgue. There was only one clipping on her in the *Post* morgue, quite short, about to disintegrate, folded into fours in its old yellow envelope. The story was published above an ad for Heinz Plum Pudding and alongside this featurette: "How to Exclaim About Centerpieces."

The headline on the article said, "GIRL PHOTOGRAPHER FOR FSA TRAVELS 50,000 MILES IN SEARCH FOR PICTURES." There was a thumb-cut photo of a not-particularly gorgeous woman with thick shoulder-length hair. This was the lead: "It takes considerable courage, not to mention credentials galore, to venture into the hinterlands with a camera these days—particularly when you're a comely young girl. 'People in small towns take one look at me and admit Hitler's getting pretty smart,' says Marion Post, Farm Security photographer."

I laughed the first time I saw that. That's Marion, I said. And the next time I looked at the clip I wondered if the flippancy wasn't just the underside of some thinly concealed anxieties.

At the time the piece was published, February 19, 1940, the shooter was deep in New England. She had come in the previous July from that initial and exhausting seven-month Southern trip, had left again in the fall for Carolina and Mississippi and Tennessee, had returned to home base, had traveled to Florida in January, had come back to Washington, had departed for New England. On the morning the newspaper feature appeared on Washington's doorsteps, the girl photographer for the FSA was in the vicinity of North Adams, Massachusetts, facing down a blizzard. She was trying to make Vermont, where among other things she was going to click the transcendently peaceful "Snowy Night, Woodstock, Vermont." The afternoon of the newspaper story, at 2:45, Marion wired Washington that she hoped to reach Brattleboro by nightfall. The next day, February 20, she wrote to Stryker: "You are a cruel and heartless master. I feel like a Finnish boyscout ... am fingerless, toeless, noseless, earless. Wish you were here with the wind whistling through your britches too." Four days later she was telling the chief, "What really ruins my disposition are the icy cold toilet seats."

But that's New England in her second winter on the job, and one could spend much more time on it than this. But catch up to her at the moment in a different clime. It's two months later, end of May 1940, the South once again, and the land has turned gorgeous. The traveler has documented the experimental food stamp program and the Cotton Carnival in Memphis and right now has dashed to Louisville, where she'll stay only four days before turning around and hauling straight back to the Deep South, to Lake Providence, Louisiana. (At the Hotel Maben in Lake Providence, the chiggers are in convention.) Before she departs Kentucky for Louisiana, she writes to Stryker:

> Mother is still feeling depressed about her new job. Probably insecure too. She undoubtedly finds it difficult to remember her sales talk for her line of the 39 varieties of contraceptives. Imagine it! She's very disturbed because the drugstores & supply houses are interested

Barnyard in snow outside Woodstock, Vermont, 1940

Main Street during blizzard, Brattleboro, Vermont, 1940

Proprietor of pool hall playing cards on pool table, Wood-stock, Vermont, 1940

in selling only the ones which are *not* recommended by the clinics, since they're in greater demand because of wider publicity. Somehow it doesn't seem too serious to me these days.*

She makes it down to Louisiana, does project work, grabs a train to Florida. On June 19, on letterhead from the Surfside Hotel in Palm Beach, she writes, "Not staying here—just using their stationery." Perhaps she doesn't want Stryker thinking she might have treated herself to something cushy for an evening. She proceeds to report on recent experiences in West Carroll Parish, in northern Louisiana.

I did a whole series on a rehab. family who has been on the program 5 yrs. (Poor thing.) And just to really celebrate the anniversary properly, there were FIVE SUPERVISORS along too! . . . They came in two separate cars—behind us, & in all that dust, you'd never know *what* was happening. I almost got into a *serious* row with the home supervisor. She got very red & mad. Nuts! To continue with West Carroll Parish—I got the co-op veterinary going through his little act, sticking capsules in & out of mules, mares & what have you—he was all dressed up looking like he was going to a Sat. nite dance. . . . LIFE had taken his picture once too, by god. Then came the co-op binder harvesting oats, no less. Next a co-op combine—more oats! The final climax was a new co-op thrasher! Still more OATS! And they almost carried Miss Post home on a stretcher. By all that's good & holy I hereby swear I'll never put in another such day as that for nobody.

That's Louisiana as dispatched from Florida. But here's some Louisiana *from* Louisiana; it's even better. She's in Natchitoches, which is down from Shreveport and up from Alexandria, on the Cane River, hard by Black

---

*Nan Post, having been fired from the Sanger organization, and unlucky in love once more, is now a traveling sales rep for a manufacturer of birth control devices. In a subsequent letter, Marion tells Stryker: "Mother is still in Idaho & writes the most excited & glowing accounts of the country out there. She still hates her job, tho—& just had everything, *all* luggage, etc., & sample cases, display materials, etc., stolen out of her car. Bet the thieves were surprised! But she was sort of downcast, as they got all her unworldly possessions too, her trinkets, her pictures, from years back, of & by her darling daughters—the little things she has dragged with her as only comfort & closeness to people she loves & has been separated from so much. . . ."

Lake, where the fish are generally jumping and the living not particularly easy. The time seems to be around the Fourth of July. (No date on the top.) Yes, it's another great letter, unless you start to think about the almost schizoid emotions in it, then "great" seems not quite apt.

> The other day I got caught in such a storm (small hurricane) when the rain & wind blew so hard that the telephone poles along the road went down one after another in a line just like the Roxyettes, only a little too close to my new automobile with its convertible top, for comfort. And now there are rumors of floods—well, I need my feet washed anyway.

Several pages earlier:

> . . . I just got frantic & unreasonable about it. Every so often I get these jitters & am afraid everything will crash down around my ears before I ever do anything, any job the way I want it to be done. There's always something I'm looking forward to doing, or anxious to return to complete, & I become impatient with any new "delay." I'll try not to.

The next page:

> But how it can still be so goddamn hot & sultry & suffocating & humid (even in cloudy weather) I can't understand. I go around most of the time just soaked thru, the sweat literally pouring off me—my clothes plastered to me. One can't get drinking water very often, & the Coca Cola or beer method is very unsatisfactory. Too many Coca Colas make me sick to my stomach, more than one beer during the day & I get too sleepy & groggy. No wonder people around New Orleans & Terrebonne & south La. drink whiskey & black coffee fairly regularly during the day. I have never felt so completely de-energized & tired. Terrebonne is only 6 ft. above sea level, many places very often it's too hot to sleep well at night. Nobody *ever* moves fast or cares too much how little is accomplished.

A photograph comes out of the Natchitoches stay that will haunt her in years to come. It's of a mulatto artisan who works on the nearby John

One of the mulattos who works on the John Henry
Plantation. He is very skilled in woodworking, weaving,
& other crafts. Near Melrose, Louisiana, 1940

Henry Plantation. She doesn't get his name. The man is very skilled in woodwork and weaving. He has a broad flat nose and deep-set eyes and a two-day stubble, but most of all he has an enigmatic expression—not quite a grin, certainly not an apology. What is in this look, she wonders. Self-confidence? Yes. But tenderness. And dignity. And spirituality. And eroticism. The man doesn't seem nearly as repressed or silent as so many Louisiana black people do. There are children around the man, so probably he is a father. She wonders if he has Indian blood in him. He lives in what is referred to by the locals as an *Afrikander* house. These houses have a peculiar shape with large overhanging roofs. Years later, studying over and over her half dozen images of this man, rubbing her fingers at the border of the prints, a photographer will ask herself, "Was he telling you that day, Marion, 'You're stealing a layer of my soul, lady, a filament of my memory, with your infernal magic box. Perhaps I should lie down with you and take something for myself.'"

She meets a white man named Randall Prothro. He is a government agent and shows her around the bayous a bit. It's the only meeting between them. But five decades hence Randall Prothro, happily married, will one day open his newspaper in Columbia, South Carolina, and recognize some photographs from back beyond. The credit line will read, "Marion Post Wolcott, Library of Congress archives." Prothro will call the Library, plead with somebody to tell him where Marion is, cajole a long-distance information operator in California into giving him a street address, and then sit down and write out his stricken heart to "A big city Yankee girl, career type, sophisticated, well-stacked, charming, beautiful personality, proper, fashionably dressed, with a clever and friendly speech and lovely manners." The letter writer will go on and on, trying to summon the overwhelming thing he felt back then in his patch of scrub South: *I can't believe it. What a female!*

SOMETIMES A SHOOTER'S MOVEMENTS can be closely tracked. Consider the following four days at the end of July 1940. On Thursday the twenty-fifth comes a wire to Washington from the Delta: "LEAVING CLARKSDALE. WILL BE COUPLE DAYS ENROUTE LOUISVILLE. SEND PANATOMIC X AND SUPER XX 120 ROLL FILM LOUISVILLE. AM MAILING EXPOSED FILM TODAY." Four days later, Monday, July 29, at 2:20 p.m., another wire: "ARRIVED LOUISVILLE. STAYING KENTUCKY HOTEL. MAILING YOU PERSONNEL SHEET AND LETTER TONIGHT."

Child in doorway of old mountain cabin made of hand-
hewn logs, Jackson, Kentucky, 1940

Marion Post Wolcott helping change tire, with fence post as jack, in borrowed car, up creekbed road, Breathitt County, Kentucky, 1940

*Children at desks, one-room schoolhouse, Breathitt
County, Kentucky, 1940*

It's impossible, obviously, to know of everything photographically that comes up on the other side of her range-finder between the sending of those two wires. And yet, by studying in sequence the hundreds of pictures framed across three states, by looking at the captions and the notes for the captions, by consulting old forties tour books and AAA highway maps, and, not least, by the evidence of one's own drive through that same region many years later, a *kind* of picture emerges, and this is it:

She crosses the Kentucky line at Guthrie (pop. 1,272). Actually you have to get off the main road, U.S. 79, and come south a mile to get to Guthrie, and even this tiny fact suggests someone determined to document it all. Guthrie, Kentucky, is a railroad town. The L&N (Louisville & Nashville) has a tie-treating plant here, although what seems to interest the shooter most is the number of distilleries you see as soon as you cross the border from Tennessee. The poet and novelist Robert Penn Warren was born here, at the corner of Cherry and Third, but he isn't immortal yet, so she doesn't get his house.

Driving toward Bowling Green—this is Saturday afternoon, July 27— she passes many stone walls, most of them built by slaves. Nearly every other farm has its tobacco patch of one to six acres. The leaves make field-sheets of deep summer green across oblong choppy spaces. This is one of the most solidly built roadbeds in the state, ideal for someone who constantly pulls over to frame something with her eye.

She comes to Russellville (pop. 3,297), sitting in a valley among the knobs. Trees bower the fine old houses on Sixth Street, which are surrounded by flower gardens. Jesse James, imitating a cattle buyer, had once come through this town. That was on May 20, 1868. He and fellow bandits robbed the bank of $9,000 and wounded the president and then fled to Tennessee. Marion's arrival is more peaceful. Farmers in galluses stand under a "Cooksey's Drug" sign on the clogged Saturday streets and watch her as she snaps their picture from across the street. She gets the town blacksmith. Positioning herself on the square by the flagpole and the Confederate monument, she takes a row of cars parked diagonal to the curb.

Skirting Bowling Green (no pictures are in the file), she picks up 31-W toward Cave City and Horse Cave. At Dixiana, smack on the border of Warren County (wet) and Edmonson County (dry), she gets a combination beer joint and gas depot and pool room and roadhouse. The words LIQUOR DISPENSARY are painted on white board. Clouds scud overhead. A man in a ladder-back chair, elbows on his knees, sits in the shadows. No

Russell Spears's tobacco barn, near Lexington, Kentucky,
1940

Pie and box supper, Jackson, Kentucky, 1940

Up Squabble Creek, near Buckhorn, Kentucky,
September 1940

bourboned-up farm boys in their daddies' hot-rod Lincolns are in the picture—it must be too early in the day. Instead what she gets into the photograph is the feeling of small-town, sunlit vacantness.

Coming into Horse Cave, she pulls over to snap a Loose Leaf Tobacco Warehouse. She shoots from the right side of the road. There's a skid mark in the foreground. Numerous signs are in the shot: JUST AHEAD OFFICIAL CAVE INFORMATION, GULF TRAILER SPACE, ROYAL CROWN COLA, US 68, STOP LIGHT IOOOO FT, GASOLINE LEADED TAX TOTAL.

Horse Cave is built over the top of Hidden River Cave, with its flowing underground stream and its freaky pearly-white "eyeless" fish. She frames the locals standing out front of the A&P. Inside the store, Sunnyfield Corn Flakes are going three packages for a quarter. A man, leaning against the store's plate-glass front, is fooling with a package of matches (maybe it's a Barlow knife). He looks to be eyeing her lecherously.

On the other side of Horse Cave, heading toward Cave City (not to be confused with the earlier place—which she will confuse when it comes time for captions), she shoots the Wigwam motel. The Wigwam is a clot of concrete teepees painted white and trimmed with Indian hieroglyphics. "EAT AND SLEEP IN A WIGWAM," it says over the top of the three Standard Oil pumps out in front of the head teepee. The resort offers cheesy little rooms with bark-lashed bedposts.

The place names keep blurring by: Bear Wallow, Linwood, Hodgenville, New Haven, Bardstown, Lawrenceburg. This last, Lawrenceburg, is the site of the Great Rocking Chair Incident. It's Sunday now, July 28, sometime in the afternoon, and my God, the only thing she wants is a shot of a family spread out on a sloping lawn. But sometimes when it goes wrong, it all goes wrong. The rocking chair tips backward, putting the big mama of the clan on her francis. These Lawrenceburgians can turn nasty. Shooter hotfoots it to car, family in pursuit. (P.S., Speed Graphic is saved.) Is she embellishing here? Who cares. It's a hilarious story for the folks at their dreary desks in Washington.

She begins the rocking chair story that evening after she hits Louisville. They have real hotels in Louisville, and the one where she puts in is the Kentucky, 5th and Walnut (phones in every room: WA-bash 1181), which has air-conditioned rooms and gigantic steaks in its famous Kentucky Tavern and also these words embossed on the letterhead of its stationery: "Where Kentucky Hospitality Greets You." The Linker Cigar Company runs the newsstand off the lobby.

Tourist cabins imitating Indian teepees, Horse Cave,
Kentucky, 1940

Her letter, on hotel stationery, started that night but finished the next day (this must be the case, because there's a double date on it), goes seven sheets, fourteen sides, all of it in the familiar big looping Postian pencil scrawl, the scrawl getting a little larger and more furious as she goes. She goes a page on the tipped-over rocking chair, proceeds to other burlesques.

> I certainly was sick a couple of days in Mississippi. Ate some rotten meat & turnip greens, which are bad enough going down—but my God coming up! I didn't know one could be so violently & suddenly ill & stay that way so long. Even a fever & chills, & nothing seemed to help much for awhile. Even when I finally got my stomach somewhat settled, I felt sore & bruised & achey all over for several days. Sort of yellow & green & no pep. I guess you get the idea by now.

Two pages later:

> It's hard to get away with just "taking pictures" any more. Everyone is so hysterically war & fifth column minded. You'd be amazed. So suspicious! Even the little "Cajun" children in La. would run home or hide or run to get their father in the field, scared to death & saying I was a German spy with a machine gun. Seriously.

Two pages on:

> I'll send you a pretty picture of me too—in my usual uncombed sweaty state. What clothes of mine haven't been ruined or rotted by sweat have suffered the same fate from mildew.

Next page:

> Received those boxes of prints today. Such a mess of awful pictures I've never seen—not often. Some of the Florida ones aren't bad, but what upsets me most is that there's not one print in that whole bunch that's really sharp. It's so discouraging and disheartening. . . . Roy, I'm not complaining or blaming anyone else, I just feel sick about it, can hardly bear to edit & caption the things, want to tear up the whole mess & go back again.

*Sunday afternoon in the front yard, near Lawrenceburg,
Kentucky, July 28, 1940*

Three pages later:

My airplane trip over the migrant camps in Fla. wasn't all it was
supposed to be. The only time the guy could take me up was at noon,
there was a terrific wind & the bumpiest he'd ever seen it. We could
only stay up a few minutes. The clouds were thick & big & no help.
It was just a small dusting plane & I felt awfully seasick after just
that short time. He said it was too bad to stay up & he didn't want to
risk it. One of the project engineers knew him, asked him to do it &
I gave him a dollar.

The letter is signed, "With love from Sorry Sue." And then there is this
postscript: "I'm dehydrated, & definitely not under the influence of liquor—just recovering from that day in that fantastic deserted town of
Rodney, Miss."

MARION STAYED IN KENTUCKY into that fall. Altogether she produced about 7,000 photographs for the agency in less than two months'
time. It was perhaps her greatest frantic output. Then she left for North
Carolina. Somewhere in Tennessee she wired Washington. She completed
the work in Carolina, came back to headquarters, left again. On October
1, 1940, she was in Yanceyville, North Carolina. The next day, from Dan-
ville, Virginia, she wrote, and here the fatigue seems almost palpable on
the page: "The prospect of a real honest to God vacation seems so sacred
and important to me now that I'm wanting to make it a good one and
take it at the right time. You may not realize it, but I haven't had a vacation
or leave (that wasn't honest sick leave, or 3 or 4 days after a trip or 'long
weekends') for 3 years! I missed my vacation that I was planning to take
on the Philadelphia Bulletin that summer, to take a new job with F.S.A. I
didn't have the guts to take the vacation scheduled & then quit the day
after without giving them notice."
    And then, deflecting:

Now tomorrow I'd like to wake up in the morning and say I can go
where I damn well please. I don't *have* to let F.S.A. and Stryker
know where I am; I don't *have* to go to Western Union or the Post
Office or the railway express, or feel guilty because I haven't done my
travel reports and can't find the notebook that has the mileages of the

Marion Post Wolcott, fording the
Morris Fork of the Kentucky River
in Breathitt County, Kentucky, 1940

first half of the month in it. I can sleep all morning no matter how bright the sun is shining and stay up all night and not give a damn how I feel the next day. So then, after all this, I'd probably jump out of bed, grab my camera and run off and take some more pictures. What a dope.

Seven more months would elapse before Marion met the high-ranking man at Agriculture to whom she gave her heart, and almost a full year was to pass before she got off the road for good. But it seems clear that, by the fall of 1940, no matter her masking comments, a shooter had already vectored herself toward another kind of life.

WIDOWER AT AG

IN THOSE DAYS he favored tight-cut double-breasted suits and a cock-combed upsweep to his thick dark hair. He stood five-foot-nine and looked brawny as a pit bull. Ladies were greatly attracted to him, and he knew it. He was half Jewish but tended to conceal the fact. In a room, his voice had a strange charged quality, not unlike electricity jumping over water. It made you listen whether you wished to or not. And when he moved it was with a certain subtle feinting force. He was just getting over an immense sadness and shock in his life. It was the wet Washington spring of 1941 and the handsome, muscular, high-ranking federal official's name was Leon Oliver Wolcott.

He was a native of Red Bank, New Jersey, an hour south of New York City on the Navesink River. He, too, had come from a broken home, and his mother, like Nan Post for her second daughter, had long been a powerful if not always serene influence. Mother Wolcott, born Edith Golden, was a willful woman, and after the divorce—the final split came as Leon was finishing high school—she'd embarked on a number of selling jobs in and around New Jersey, appliances and so forth. Eventually she established a children's dress shop in Red Bank. In hard financial times, she'd managed by will and scrimping to raise her two boys—the one who achieved, Leon, and the one who did not, Harry. Harry was something like his father, known as Bop, who was gregarious and lacking in ambition and ended up driving a soft-drink truck. Leon, on the other hand, who'd grafted onto himself his mother's drive and will, seemed to succeed at nearly everything he tried. He'd gone to Brown University (it didn't cost so much in the twenties), where he'd taken the classics and English literature. After college—he'd finished in '27—Leon had begun working at a string of advertising sales jobs in Manhattan. He'd stay at one place just long enough to bury everybody around him with his energy and sales performance. He started at twenty-five dollars a week for the Hearst chain, went to radio sales, switched to an ad jobber, went over to the McFadden papers (they were offering sixty dollars a week), enrolled in night law school, came back to print media (the New York *Evening Journal* was offering the practically unheard-of Depression sum of eighty-five dollars a week, plus commissions), finished law school, passed the bar. This was 1933, belly of the Depression, when somewhere from 13 to 16 million people were out of a job: one in every four American workers. Leon had never really gotten a job in law. Legal jobs hadn't dangled from trees then; he was doing fine, at least in terms of dollars, in the media sales business. He was on his accounts the way white is on rice.

One of his old accounts for the *Evening Journal* was B. Altman's, which is where he'd met Margaret McCulloch. She held a desk position in the retailer's in-house advertising department, and the two would talk when he came in. Margaret, who was brunette and fair, quite shy and extremely inexperienced with men, was from Colorado. In no time she'd fallen for the outside ad man. Leon's mother liked Margaret, and this cemented it. (Mother Wolcott would never seem to accept Leon's second wife to the extent she did his first.) In their brief time together, Margaret proved totally devoted to Leon. Her husband made every decision of consequence and found he liked it that way. In later years Leon would look back and feel he'd probably made a cerebral choice in marrying his first wife, a passionate one in marrying his second, although that oversimplifies it.

Leon O. Wolcott had married Margaret McCulloch in 1935. Probably even then some strain of the cancer that would take his wife's life inside of five years had entered her body. Restless, as always, eager to try something new, the ad man came home one day soon after the wedding and told his bride he was sure he wanted to go back to school. He had never really liked the newspaper sales business, just wasn't high-minded enough. So they'd gotten into their car and headed west. They looked at graduate programs in Ann Arbor, moved on to Madison, where Leon decided to enroll in an accelerated Ph.D. political science program. A man named Stryker had recently gone down to Washington. A free-lance named Post was scrounging camera jobs in Manhattan. A North Carolina sharecropper named James Franklin Little had three kids under his roof, nine more to come. The next to come in those hard-farmed Wadesboro fields would be Jerry, the one who got rickets.

Anyway, Leon and Margaret had stayed a year and a half at the University of Wisconsin, with Leon doubling up on his courses and teaching undergraduates for table money. By the second year he'd secured a research fellowship for six hundred, but in spite of this, finances got tight, Leon got restless again. And besides they had just brought into the world their first beautiful child. Bill Robinson at the New York *Herald Tribune* wired an offer. Leon accepted. In the spring of 1937, with maybe half the degree completed, the Wolcotts left Wisconsin for New York·in a Pullman car with little Gail sleeping beside them in a wicker basket.

Back in the city again, Leon, who'd signed a one-year contract with the *Herald Trib,* handled Saks, Macy's, Altman's. In the beginning he commuted from his mother's place in Red Bank. But the old restlessness came back sooner than even he would have guessed. The low-mindedness of advertising sales was eating at him. He'd studied literature at Brown, he'd read Henry Adams, he had a damn law degree.

Within a year Leon had heard of a job in Washington, with an outfit called the Social Science Research Council, working in conjunction with Henry Wallace's Department of Agriculture. It was a kind of capture-and-record operation, revealing the inner workings of a huge federal agency. The position paid three thousand. The hell with making ten thousand in pressured Manhattan, he'd take it, Leon said. Margaret agreed. Another child was on the way now. Surely there were some—Mother Wolcott among them—who must have figured Leon was a little nuts, all this switching around, such crazy relocation. And now, to top it off, he was going to take a seven-thousand-dollar cut in bitter times to go down to some quasi-governmental thing in Roosevelt's New Deal?

They'd arrived in the capital in the late spring of '38, just about the time a fed-up news and fashion photographer for the Philadelphia *Evening Bulletin* was hearing from her mentor Ralph Steiner about a band of idealistic traveling documentarians at the Farm Security Administration. The FSA, no longer an independent federal relief agency, had come to be reorganized under the Department of Agriculture. But these were huge bureaucracies, and so it was entirely possible for two people to be employees of the same government agency for several years and never run

*Planting corn before storm, Shenandoah Valley, near
Luray, Virginia, 1941*

into each other, in fact, never to hear each other's names. Especially when one of the two was seldom in town. The Ag department had something like 62,000 people then.

Well, Leon Wolcott became a father for the second time in December 1938. This one was a son. During her pregnancy, Margaret, never known to complain about anything, complained much about strange pains in her leg.

Leon proved a skillful Washington operative. He seemed to work like a man killing snakes. Early in 1939 he published a well-regarded piece in the *National Municipal Review* entitled "National Land-Use Programs and the Local Governments." The next year Leon and one of his old Wisconsin profs, John Gaus, brought out a 400-page study entitled *Public Administration and the U.S. Department of Agriculture*. Leon's key chapter on the central command of the Ag department drew the attention of Henry Wallace himself. Leon, the Washington newcomer, appeared loaded with self-assurance, and it wasn't long before he found himself hired directly into the office of the secretary, where he began serving as one of Wallace's four principal aides. During the half-hour interview for the job, the talk between Wolcott and Wallace was mostly about world affairs, not much about farming. There was a tremendous need for improved relations with Russia—didn't he think so? Yes, Leon agreed. At the end of the interview, Leon still in the room, Wallace pushed a button and told his chief aide, Paul Appleby, to come in. "This guy's right for our team, Paul," the secretary said. "Why can't he start immediately?" Leon did.

They paid him $5,600, not princely but enough. It's true he knew next to nothing about agriculture, but he knew a good deal about public administration, about how to sell, about how to talk. Henry A. Wallace—developer of corn hybrids from Adair County, Iowa, FDR's Agriculture Secretary since the New Deal's inception, spokesman for the common man, one-time editor of *Wallaces' Farmer*—seemed to take a special liking to his high-energy lawyer-cum-ad-man-turned-bureaucrat. Some people in Washington thought Wallace an incorruptible visionary, while others regarded him as a naïve political dreamer, but whatever he was, he and Leon got along splendidly their whole time together. Wallace liked to take his four aides down to the cavernous basement of Ag promptly at five o'clock for games of Ping-Pong. On balmy days after work, or before the day started, Wallace and his boys would go out onto the polo field on the national mall in their rolled shirtsleeves and loosened vests to toss plastic

Leon O. Wolcott with
Henry A. Wallace, c. 1940
(photographer unknown)

boomerangs. Much interested in boomerangs, Wallace kept a man in the
Bureau of Chemistry and Soil toiling constantly to refine their pitch. The
lab guy, stuck somewhere in the bowels of USDA, would mold and tip a
new boomerang and then bring it up to the secretary himself, who'd give
it an imaginary stroke in his office air, beam, then press the intercom button and say to Leon and the three other aides, "C'mon, men, we're going
to toss." Henry Wallace also loved strange telephones. His hard-driving
aide, Leon Wolcott, had a special White House phone on his desk and was
listening in on the day FDR called and spoke to Henry about whether the
Iowa delegation was going to put up Wallace's name for the presidency.
As things turned out, Wallace became FDR's vice president for the third
term. By then Leon had risen another notch—to deputy director of the
Office of Agricultural War Relations. The country wasn't into war yet, but
there wasn't anybody who doubted it was coming, and so this was a key
responsibility.

Leon had thoroughly enjoyed his work with Secretary Wallace. And then the cloud, small as a hand at first, had floated into his life. His wife, Margaret, was diagnosed with cancer. It was in her leg and initially they thought it could be controlled. Soon the doctors told Leon there was no hope, although Margaret herself didn't know until the end. Leon was shattered. How could he hope to raise these two beautiful young children by himself? The situation seemed to go downhill so fast. Margaret lay in bed with her suspended limbs wrapped in gauze while her baby daughter ran in and out asking the nurses what was wrong. When Margaret Wolcott died, in early 1940, little Gail Wolcott was three, baby John Wolcott not quite one and a half.

After the funeral, Secretary Wallace, as an expression of how much he thought of Leon, had sent him on a made-up trip out west. In time the old energies began to flood back. Wallace went to the White House early in 1941 and Leon moved over to become the department's Deputy Director of War Relations. The widower, then in his mid-thirties, lived on a small rural holding—a cow and ten acres—in the exurbs of Virginia, a town named Oakton, about forty minutes from his office. He had a housekeeper for his two children, and he was trying to be a mother and a father as best he could, and his own sexual needs were being met from time to time by a willing neighbor. But it was clear to anyone who knew him that Leon's chief goal by the spring of forty-one, roughly a year after he'd buried Margaret, was to discover a new mate with whom he could begin rebuilding his broken family dreams.

Post office in blizzard, Aspen, Colorado, 1941

EROS AND THE LAST CLICK

A MAN AND A WOMAN, the woman pushing eighty, the man well into his eighties, are talking in their California home about the fur of sexual passion that flew between them in six weeks of 1941. One measure of how blinding their passion for each other must have been is that neither seems able to summon very many sequential details of that long-ago courtship and marriage. It's a blur. At the end of their blur of eros, the two aged people sitting here now holding hands got hitched. For life, it turned out.

Marion: "Well, I remember he had this seven-foot-long goosedown couch on the night I first saw his living room. And a five-foot-long fireplace. It was very comfortable. I suppose the lights went out rather fast. I'm not sure I made it back home that night."

Lee: "I also had two white pines in my front yard that caught her fancy."

Marion: "Roy Kimmel was the one who introduced us."

Lee: "He was my neighbor in Oakton. I commuted with him to town. This was before Marion and I got our real farm in Lovettsville. Anyway, Roy had known Marion from prior years up in New England—Connecticut, I think. When he heard she was working at the FSA, he invited her out to Oakton for the weekend. I'm not sure what he had in mind. I think he'd called up FSA a few times that spring and said, 'Listen, is there a Marion Post who works for you folks?' By the way, the Kimmels' goat later ate the top of our convertible."

Marion: "Yeah, we had to prove it to them, didn't we? They were our good friends and we were married then, but we still made them put that damn goat on a leash and bring him over to the scene of the crime."

Lee: "Anyway, on this business of how we met: Kim left his number and the next time Marion came in, she called him. He said, 'Why don't you come out for the weekend?' He invited me over. I didn't really want to go that night. And then I saw the woman."

Marion: "He was so damn confident and smooth. Or that's how he struck me. Handsome as all get out. But I must have found out pretty soon about Margaret. I think he was hiding it in the beginning, or at least the shock of it. He took me to lunch every day for three weeks. I was just trying to do my captions. He wouldn't leave me alone. He over-powered me."

Lee: "I probably had marriage in my mind almost immediately. I re-member we got down to talking about values pretty quickly. Having chil-dren of our own was certainly part of that."

Marion: "I must have told him pretty soon about my leftist friends and some of the meetings I'd attended abroad and other places. I didn't want it to become an issue between us. And then, too, there was his job with the government. He had to be careful. He had to have his eyes open if he was going to marry me. Well, I guess I told him most of it."

Lee: "I remember at one point in that six weeks, Rex Tugwell, FDR's old brain truster, whom I knew from government, came out to Oakton for dinner. Next day in town he said to me, 'Don't pass it up. Grab her if you can.'"

Marion: "He didn't propose on his knees, you know."

Lee: "I proposed in bed. Maybe a week, maybe two weeks, before we actually got married. We were talking about the kids and family, and I was appreciating her interest in my children. I said, 'You know, we seem to have this good relationship, why can't it continue?' Oh, I don't know the exact words. We had certainly talked around it almost from the begin-ning. But that night in bed, I asked. She expressed her fears about mar-riage in general—what she came from and all that."

Marion: "I suppose we discussed it over the course of the next several nights, how we were going to do it, the procedure and so forth. But it was kind of implicit it was going to happen."

Lee: "The reason we were anxious to have the marriage in the Mary-land suburbs was so that it would stay out of the D.C. papers. I was afraid my housekeeper would leave if she found out there was a new lady of the house."

Marion: "You have no idea how hard it was to get and keep help then. All this war preparation was going on. We did end up losing her, too, which only made the pressures that much greater on me to quit."

Lee: "So I got out the yellow pages. We needed a parson."

Marion: "No, no. First, you called up an Episcopal priest you had once dug out of the snow with tire chains and a shovel."

Lee: "Oh, that's right, babe. But he turned out to be almost reactionary, didn't he?"

Marion: "Yeah, he wanted us to come in for this prenuptial examination or something. Organized religion didn't mean a damn thing to us. He started asking us all sorts of things. It was none of his goddamn business."

Lee: "So then I went to the yellow pages and began shopping."

Marion: "You'll have to excuse our language."

Lee: "Actually, we married ourselves with our own ceremony out in the country. We married ourselves on the second of June. That's the wedding we remember. Then four days later, we had the parson's ceremony in Bethesda—in the parson's parlor."

Marion: "Yeah, his wife was one of our two witnesses. She was just fascinated as hell by this whole thing. I remember a yappy little dog somewhere in the background."

Lee: "We made the decision to get hitched in one night. In bed. And know what? I can feel her beside me in that bed right now."

IT WAS A WEEKEND at either the end of April or the beginning of May. The shooter, whose life hadn't slowed down very much, had most recently been documenting Virginia's upper-class horse country. Like her earlier reconnaissance behind the lines of the Miami Beach rich, Marion Post had been able to get striking images among the landed gentry of Warrenton taking its booted ease.

Since the first of that year, 1941, she'd traveled back to New Orleans, back to Florida, back to New England. In late January, the Washington *Star* had done a brief feature on her. The piece appeared on January 21, written by a male staffer who couldn't help himself:

A tall wispy young woman, with blue [*sic*] eyes and a cascade of curly dark-brown hair which she usually binds in a red bandanna, she has been mistaken for a gypsy, arrested for a spy, ordered off farms where the tenants thought she was an itinerant peddler, played the role of mother confessor to scores of farm folk in the isolation belt and numerous times been called a brazen young hussy for traveling about the countryside without a chaperone. . . . For weeks on end she has lived out of her convertible coupe, which not only contains her three cameras and all the paraphernalia that goes with modern photography, but enough of a wardrobe to make her presentable and comfortable from the sands of Florida to the ski runs of Lake Placid.

It isn't known if Henry Wallace's man at Ag saw that piece; one wonders in any case if the offices of the Washington *Star* were a little besieged by horny suitors as to the exact whereabouts of the tall, wispy young woman.

In the spring of that year, Marion had taken a northeastern trip that she managed to make part vacation, part work. Again, you can track some of it by her correspondence. On March 14 (that is to say, about six or seven weeks before she met Lee), she sent a cable from Manchester, Vermont, basically advising the folks in the home office they could stick it. She was on a skiing holiday, her first real time off in three years, and "not even thinking of you people"—except she then relayed how they could get in touch with her.

On April 8 she wired from Stowe, Vermont: A bad head cold had delayed her return. One hopes there was at least a small lie in this and that she had her skis on her back that day instead of her camera.

By mid- or at least late April she had returned to Washington, was doing her captions, filling out her reports, making day runs down into Virginia hunt country. And that's when the introduction to Lee occurred.

On the first night, they snuggled. On the second night, they slept together but didn't make love. On the third night, they made much love. On the fourth night, Marion moved in. That wasn't hard. Most of her belongings were in her car.

Over the next six weeks two people listened to Brahms, Beethoven, Schubert, Mozart. They took many walks. A few evenings they stayed in town after their separate workdays and had supper at the Occidental, where there were dim lights and linen and dark wood. "Do you think this could work?" seemed the implicit subject of all their talk.

Once Lee went on a day trip with her and tried his hand at shooting. Didn't do too bad, he felt.

Marion took one out-of-town trip that lasted about a week. After she came back, she seemed more certain about the possibility of something permanent. She photographed Lee's two children. One of Lee's good friends from the department came out to meet the woman he was so stuck on. Phil Glick was a land-use guy. He pulled Lee aside: "You've got to get her, old boy," he said.

Late May, the in-bed question was popped. Early in June, two blissful, nervous people drove to the Montgomery County courthouse in Rockville, Maryland, and applied for a marriage license. They had to wait forty-eight hours before they could pick it up. They got the license on Friday, were married on Saturday. The Reverend James S. Albertson pronounced the appropriate words over the couple in his parlor at Bethesda Presbyterian. Roy Stryker stood up for them. From the time of her parents' divorce in the midtwenties until now, June 6, 1941, Marion Post, whose name had become Wolcott, had never really known a permanent home.

The day following the wedding, the bride turned thirty-one.

There was no honeymoon to speak of—both parties had commitments. In fact, Marion had to leave almost immediately for a previously scheduled shooting assignment in New England—potato fields and bomber factories. In one of those two, her cameras got pinched. She replaced them several weeks later in Manhattan with a new Ikoflex and a Heiland Sol flash gun. It isn't clear whether Stryker issued her another Speed Graphic. In any case, she wasn't going to do much more shooting in her life, not professional shooting.

The archived Wolcott correspondence turns spotty at this point. There's a wire on June 19, 1941, from West Hartford, Connecticut (she's been hitched two weeks), that suggests a person of upbeat mood who is not traveling alone: "JULIA'S SISTER IN FARMINGTON SAVED US FROM THE PARK BENCH LAST NIGHT. DON'T KNOW WHERE WE WILL LAY OUR PRETTY HEADS TONIGHT. . . . "

She appears to have gotten back to Washington in mid-July. (There was a stopover in New York City to see her sister, Helen, and Helen's husband and also to get the new equipment.) And then at the end of that month came a sixty-day trip out west.

Almost from the start of her time at the FSA, Marion and Stryker had talked of such a trip. (You can find mention of it, in fact, in that first correspondence from Morgantown, West Virginia.) But somehow the Deep South assignments had always taken precedence. Now, with the time finally allotted, Mrs. Marion Post Wolcott had lost a lot of the desire to go. She didn't want to leave her husband and her two small stepchildren. She had bought Gail, four and a half, an easel and a set of paints and was trying to work with her on weekends in the backyard. And there isn't much doubt, after browsing the scant correspondence of the period, what Lee Wolcott thought of the idea of his wife going out west alone. He despised it. Actually, that's not a strong enough word.

She departed town in the last week of July in a new Buick convertible which her husband had bought for her right after the wedding. (It was a spring model, meaning it didn't have a heater; it was the same convertible the Kimmels' goat would later eat the top off of.) On August 2 Marion wired from Madison, Wisconsin—she put in overnight with old academic friends of Lee's—that she was en route to St. Paul and Fargo. She worked her way through the Dakotas, then went on to Montana. Roughly at the time she would have been entering Montana, an article appeared in *P.M.'s Weekly* in New York. It was an article about her, and it was written by her old teacher, Ralph Steiner, who was serving a stint as the newspaper's photography critic. The piece was stuck in amid features about Whirlaway taking the Travers Stakes and about the Dodgers fading in the clutch against the Braves. The big story of the day concerned whether Britain might invade Nazi Europe. The two-page spread on the photographer from the FSA presented five of Marion's photographs and carried this text:

> Did you see "I Wanted Wings"? Remember the other girl—not Veronica Lake—who was supposed to be a professional photographer? It's my guess that the writer was thinking of Margaret Bourke-White. And my guess can't be far wrong because there are only a half dozen good women photographers in the country. A newcomer to this honorable company is Marion Post, some of whose pictures—taken for the U.S. Farm Security Administration—appear here.
>
> A rich "art lover" once commissioned Miss Post to take a series of nude studies of herself, and told her that if she had one tooth straightened she'd be beautiful. Her sense of humor got in the way of the nude studies and the tooth-straightening. She is no fancy Powers model—she's a good-looking, hearty girl who looks as if she might have won the Iowa Grange prize as the healthiest girl in the state.

Marion Post, who is thirty [*sic*] and married, started as a progressive-school dancing teacher, photographing her pupils. Her first real job was on the Philadelphia Bulletin, where she was bored to death by fashion photography and Philadelphia. Wanting to photograph things that matter she got a job with the U.S. Farm Security Administration.

She has a tough job: She tours the country alone for six months at a stretch, she meets only strangers and sleeps and eats wherever she finds herself. But she loves it.

Thirteen days after that appeared, Lee Wolcott arrived in the West to find his wife. He had arranged a trip to San Francisco to meet with executives of the Weyerhaeuser Company about making waterproof boxes for the government. His real goal was to get in bed with Marion, seize her as his own. But vice versa, too, it should be said.

In a letter dated August 21, Marion informed Stryker that Lee was coming. She was then at a ranch near Birney, Montana. Before telling him, however, the good-looking hearty girl who might have won the Iowa Grange prize described her feelings about the West:

Having gotten an eyefull, camerafull and carfull of wheat, flatlands and sun, I spent a brief weekend in Glacier Park "recuperating." The weather and the cloud effects were so dramatic and such a startling change and the mountains so terrific that I just kept taking pictures of the different "expressions" and changes in the landscape as I would with people.

I worked very early in the morning and very late a couple of evenings too, trying to get the weird strange quality and feeling that a human sometimes has in seeing mountains and being "on top of the world" and not exactly part of it anymore. I was so dizzy and lightheaded and headachey most of the time that I am not to be held completely responsible for the results. I'd get excited and go tearing along and get so out of breath—even when I knew better. I just forgot. I didn't think that you'd object to a little of that kind of America-the-Beautiful for your files.

Then she gave the news about Lee.

County judge on Main Street in front of mortuary,
Leadville, Colorado, 1941

Freight train, grain elevators, wheat, Great Plains, Carter,
Montana, 1941

My dearly beloved husband has gotten so many grey hairs and is so lonely that he is coming out here! Arriving Labor Day, or perhaps Tues. I expect a wire from him this coming week, with more details. But I *suspect* that I might like to take a few days leave while he's here—perhaps go to Yellowstone or Jackson Hole country, I don't know. Anyway, wherever we are, I'd sort of like to see him without three cameras hanging around my neck, & one in each hand, & film coming out of my ears, for a couple of days at least. He can only stay a week. I wrote him that I expected to be heading into Wyoming & Colorado very shortly. I've missed him terribly, so am delighted he could get away at all, even for such a short time. His letters seem to have conveyed the same idea—that he has missed me intensely, so maybe this will help.

The reunion was in Cheyenne. They pushed around the Rockies together for about a week. The lovestruck husband kept trying to aim the car eastward, toward Virginia. They got to Aspen, which they decided to call their honeymoon, and booked into the Hotel Jerome. It had goose-down coverlets. It was the first week of September and already snowing. The honeymooners got under the covers on that Friday night and didn't come out again for twenty-four hours. On the way out of town two days later, with Lee driving, Marion framed the Aspen post office with sleet on her lens. There was an Elks lodge shingle in the shot, and an old car tilted to the curb, and a white porcelain water bubbler. It was just a grab pic out a window, but it would turn out to be one of the best of the trip, one of the better ones of a career.

Crossing Independence Pass on September 8, they hit another terrible storm. They could barely see five feet in front of them. They pulled off and huddled together in Marion's heaterless car, hoping that help would come along. Finally two men showed up with a snowplow, and Marion and Lee followed them down the mountainside. Lee emptied his pockets of change and gave it to the men.

The next day, from the Cosmopolitan Hotel in Denver ("Rotary-Optimist-Breakfast Club-Movie Screen Club"), Marion wrote to Stryker. Her husband had just departed on a plane from Stapleton Field.

Lee finally met me for a few days. . . . He insisted on just traveling with me, instead of my taking leave & vacationing—so as not to delay my trip any, & keep me away longer than necessary. But he could stay such a short time anyway that it was hardly worthwhile trying to relax & enjoy a restful vacation—So we worked hard—he helped locate towns & places & did most of the driving—But in just those few days I realized more than ever how much more interesting & alive this kind of job can be when there are two people (if compatible, etc.) doing it. What a difference it makes!

As always, the spy loose in the land had sopped up the local intelligence: "The 'run' of cattle & sheep is still so light that the Denver stockyards are relatively empty now too—even early in the morning the first of the week. October & November are best, I was told out here. But I did get a few good pictures, I think."

She headed back up toward Cheyenne, turned east, drove into Nebraska. At Scottsbluff, she lodged at the New Emery Hotel, "European" in style. Two days later she was at a place called Two Rivers, where she was supposed to shoot some Hampshire hogs and litters, "but the damn little suckling pigs didn't want to suck this afternoon, so I'll try again tomorrow. Any *other* day they wouldn't *stop* sucking if you wanted them to!" She seemed in fine form. Her letter of that Thursday night went on and on. She started it in ink, ran out on the first page. "No more ink for you," she ya-yahed in the boss's face, then said:

I was too early for the potatoes in the No. Platte Valley around Scottsbluff, etc., & too late for them around Kearney & Gibbon (enroute Omaha). The sugar beets will also not be pulled for about another month. The unusually early frost (see clipping) got most of the tomato crop, & killed the potato vines, arresting further growth of the 'spuds,' & making it bad for pictures.

Two pages later:

Now, let me see—where was I before that—Oh yes! Wonderful Wyoming! Which you can have if you want it—I don't. In the Big Horn mountains, around Sheridan—or between Laramie & Cheyenne—or maybe around Cody—but such a monotonous god forsaken empty state otherwise—I didn't even see a sheep in the Big Horn mountains.

Workhorses on an FSA project, Scottsbluff, Nebraska, 1941

In Omaha, she found a room at Mrs. Grace B. Butts's boarding house, 3515 Dodge. The chief, perhaps irritated at her pace, wrote to her there in longhand (perhaps he wrote the letter from home, not waiting to get it typed at the office), outlining things he wanted her to get as she came through the Midwest: "*Very important*—a few more pictures of corn on the cob.... *Roadside stands selling fruit & vegetables*.... Wichita, Kansas. Oil—most important. Airplane assembly." He said he expected her to cover the oil industry in Kansas: "... oil derricks, tanks, drilling equipment, *oil men* (*portraits*)." And he told her to write captions of earlier work as she went. "Don't come into Washington with all of that bunch of contact prints to caption."

This letter from Stryker has never gotten into the FSA files. After she read it, Marion scribbled her resentment in the margins, then mailed the letter to her husband in Washington. Her marginalia consisted of such things as "I doubt that I'll bother with this at all.... It will probably be impossible to get.... I'm not going out of my way for it.... To hell with that state this trip." This last was put in response to Stryker's wish that she come home through the West Virginia mountains.

Lee's response to the letter was immediate: "Sweetheart, That no account S.O.B. didn't even ask about your health, how you feel, or anything. He should be fired immediately." He went on: "It's very difficult to realize that you will be home in a week. You are so far away, have so much to do that it doesn't seem that a week will, can, bring you to me. Please don't see too much to photograph. Go to movies in the afternoon and drive here in the evenings, as you suggest, so you won't see too much." At the end he said, "Sweetheart, I love you more and more—if that's possible. I can't wait to see you. Gotta get to work. Leon."

On September 30, from midcontinent, she wired Washington: "CAN BE REACHED THROUGH WESTERN UNION WATERTOWN IOWA. HAVE MAILED MORE CAPTION PRINTS TODAY. GOT OIL PICTURES BUT IMPOSSIBLE GET AIRPLANE ASSEMBLY WICHITA." Three years earlier, almost exactly to the day, Marion Post had cabled her boss from the bottom of West Virginia that she had found wonderful material and that all she needed, if she could only have it, was just one good day. Those were her first clicks, these were her last, and perhaps as many as 100,000 clicks had occurred in between, though not every click had gotten into the file.

She drove through lower Indiana and Ohio, saw the Morgantown area of West Virginia again. There's no record whether she got out of the car to take any pictures. Back in the office in early October, she did her captions, sorted through negatives, wrote the reports, mailed letters, collected comp time, gabbed at the water bubbler. Her heart must have been in so very little of it. There are no letters or any other archival materials from this period.

But there is an interesting paper trail having to do with her husband. Lee insisted something be done, and as quickly as possible: a postcrediting of all of Marion's work to reflect her new name. He had talked to his wife about this when they were out west, and to Marion it didn't seem very important at the time whether she should be permanently identified on the back of a photograph as Marion Post or Marion Post Wolcott. But it was of terrible importance to Lee. Stryker was incredulous when he heard about it. He said he probably could arrange for "Photo by Marion Post Wolcott" to be stamped on the several hundred pictures that had gotten into the file since June 6, 1941, but he'd be damned if there would be time to go back and do all the rest. He'd be damned then, said Lee, whose name sat above Stryker's on the Agriculture Department's flow chart of authority. Lee told Stryker that he personally was going to see it to that government clerks dug back into the FSA files, through the tens of thousands of photographs by some dozen and a half photographers, to make the necessary changes. It was a clerical nightmare, a bureaucratic nightmare, but Wolcott's will prevailed. Eventually he sent the following memorandum down to the FSA photo unit: "Memorandum to Division Chiefs and Regional Directors Regarding Female Employees: Please call to the attention of employees of your office U.S.D.A. regulation paragraph 3221 which provides that when a female employee in government service marries, her legal surname *must* be used by her instead of her maiden name." In later years, certain feminists would view this as a husband's symbolic appropriation of his wife's work. It isn't clear whether Marion herself ever regarded it that way.

The wife of the man who had sent down that memorandum stayed on the payroll until after Christmas. December 7 had brought the nation its day of infamy. Washington was a city now filling to the gills with government girls. This government girl was going in another direction. In one of her letters to Stryker from out west, Marion had said, "It's sort of awful to be separated from someone you love very much, for a long period, & at a great distance, & keep reading in the paper that we may be getting closer, very rapidly, to the kind of world system that may drastically, & perhaps tragically & seriously, change our whole lives. There seems so little time left to even try to really live, relatively normally. I get frightened at times."

Her letter of notification didn't waste typewriter ribbon:

Dear Mr. Stryker:

I hearby tender my resignation as Principal Photographer in the Historical Section, Division of Information, Farm Security Administration, effective at the close of the business day February 21.

Sincerely yours,

Marion Post Wolcott.

She wrote that the day before. A shooter was three months pregnant. A shooter was tired to her bones. A shooter was about to go into almost fifty years of photographic hiding, but who could have said so at the time?

FRAME FIVE

SILENCES

Rimbaud has gone to Abyssinia to make his fortune in the slave trade. Wittgenstein, after a period as a village school-teacher, has chosen menial work as a hospital orderly. Duchamp has turned to chess. Accompanying these exemplary renunciations of a vocation, each man has declared that he regards his previous achievements in poetry, philosophy, or art as trifling, of no importance. But the choice of permanent silence doesn't negate their work. On the contrary, it imparts retroactively an added power and authority to what was broken off....

—SUSAN SONTAG
"The Aesthetics of Silence"

AFTER

Q. Did you have any sense of your mother as an important American photographer when you grew up?

A. Nothing. Absolutely nothing of that.

　　　—M I C H A E L W O L C O T T , the youngest child

Perhaps he had a concern underneath, which he didn't express, that it might interfere with the marriage or the care of the children. He didn't object if I took the kids down to the creek and photographed them, or when I would photograph on the farm or other nearby farms. And I think he didn't object to my photographing other people's children because I usually did it on our farm. He realized that I had to have *some* free time and I think he was pleased when other people liked the photographs. There wasn't any objection to that. There wasn't any encouragement either. Now, of course, he is very supportive. He has turned around completely.

　　　　　　　—M A R I O N P O S T W O L C O T T ,
　　　　　　　　from an interview in the early 1980s
　　　　　　　　with FSA historian F. Jack Hurley

I don't think it was only the lack of encouragement. . . . And
of course he wouldn't have been silent about it all the time. My
father's will is just something you can feel in a room. He was
afraid for her to leave the family and go out and be a photographer again—afraid on many levels, I think. But I have some
compassion about it now. I think I can understand a lot of
it now.

—GAIL JOHNSTON,
the eldest Wolcott child

In photography, perhaps because of the speed with which the
medium itself has changed, only a very few workers have been
able to maintain the vitality and plasticity of their conception
for a full working lifetime. The genuinely creative period of
most photographers of exceptional talent has rarely exceeded
ten or fifteen years.

—JOHN SZARKOWSKI,
Looking at Photographs

SNAPSHOTS OF THE LONG after-years. They are crammed, these five decades of mystery and shadow and movement, with uncounted exits and reentries, switchbacks, way stops, temporary domiciles. Although in the beginning there had been a geographic stability, relatively speaking:

A woman is holding an infant. She has on an old shirt that could be her husband's and her long hair is attractively mussed, as in a 1916 summertime Jersey backyard photograph. The woman in the picture looks like she's in her early thirties. You can't see all of her face, but it's obvious from the way she's holding her cradled infant she's happy. On the back of the picture, barely legible, are these words: "MPW *w.* Linda—not long back from the hospital? 4–6 wks?"

At first they were hoping to get a place in the Berkshires and had even looked at a chicken farm up there. But chickens aren't very romantic. In 1932, a radical socialist and university economist named Scott Nearing had left New York City with his wife for an organic, subsistence, romantic farming life in the Green Mountains of Vermont. The Nearings said they were leaving the city to throw off "the yoke of a competitive, acquisitive, predatory culture." That wouldn't exactly describe the recently married Marion and Lee Wolcott, but there must have been something of that impulse in their joined hearts.

What they settled on, although it turned out to be only the first of three moves in that area, was a beef-and-cattle operation on 180 acres outside Lovettsville, Virginia. They unlocked the door and sashayed across sometime in early 1943. (Prior to this, they had continued living on Lee's small rural holding in Oakton, Virginia, much closer to the city.) They knew next to nothing about real farming, but they could borrow books, they had their energies. In Marion's case they were renewed energies from a career lately abandoned and also from the difficulties of childbirth.

The farm was on Route 693 in upper Loudoun County, just off the macadam, about four miles south of the Potomac River, which serves as the natural boundary between Maryland and Virginia. This is Civil War country, whale-humped and blue-green and beautiful. Harpers Ferry, West Virginia, is just a couple of knobs over. Even today these wide Catoctin Mountain valleys, less than ninety minutes from the eight-lane beltways of Metropolitan Washington, remain remarkably placid. During the War Between the States, as Loudoun Countians still tend to call it, there was a local priest who refused to perform any marriages on that ground: The Commonwealth of Virginia belonged to the Confederacy—and pre-

Linda and Marion Post Wolcott,

Oakton, Virginia, fall 1942

(photographer unknown)

sumably hell. The priest would put couples in his boat and row them out
to the middle of the river, where they could then be joined in matri-
mony—in the free state of Maryland.

Richard Creek curled out back. The Wolcotts' fireplace, nearly big
enough to walk into without lowering your head, had a smithy's iron railing for hanging cauldrons. No one knew exactly how old the house was,
but a tinner named D. N. Rathie had carved his initials in one of the chim-
neys in 1725. The house was a monstrous old thing, made of wood and
brick and locally quarried stone—pebbledash, as it's called in these envi-
rons. It had seven fireplaces and thirteen rooms and was built in three
sections with three levels of rambling porch: You had to go out on one
porch and come in another door if you wanted to get to the next section.
It had a widely known nickname: "woman killer."

There was an ice-cold spring purling over stones at the foot of the back
steps. There were hedges and crumbling stone walls, there were neighbors
rattling by with their horse-drawn dump rakes. The newcomers to the
valley remodeled and repainted and busted through walls and didn't even
live in half of their creaky dream.

They named it Grass Roots Farm.

Among other problems, Marion and Lee discovered the house was much too close to the road so that in summertime everything got coated with dust from the flying gravel. And in the winter the snow tended to bank up against the doors in huge drifts, making the family feel even more isolated than it was.

They had an old car, in addition to the Buick convertible Lee had bought Marion after the wedding, and every morning Marion would drive her husband into the town of Waterford—it was three-and-a-half switch-backed miles of either the dust or the snowdrifts—to catch his ride to the city and the paper war against Hitler. Lee was eager to quit Washington altogether, but at the moment it was a financial and patriotic imperative that he keep on in government. After she had dropped her husband off, Marion raced back home where baby Linda lay sleeping in her crib. Dec-ades hence she would look back and be stunned she could have done such a thing.

Marion: "I learned to rake hay, which I loved to do. You could look back behind you and see the pretty rows you were making. Lee and I would discuss a farm program for that week, and I'd oversee it. I canned, I darned socks, I talked to my nearest neighbor, Betty Campbell. We planted hedges and boxwoods. I supervised the farm hand and made a report to Lee on Friday night. I didn't really have that much to do with the farming, to tell the truth. In the good weather I'd study the newspaper for auctions, see which ones were close. Even to go to farm auctions on a Saturday with your family, you had to figure how many coupons it would take. Gas rationing was on. And we didn't have any money anyway."

Were they content? It certainly seems so. Were there growing pressures and strains? By the wagonful, the isolation and cultural sterility being perhaps the worst of it for Marion, although a difficult child being right up there, too. The difficult child was their eldest, Gail, who knew her real mother had gone to heaven and that Marion was an imposter and her father's lover to boot. Sometimes in her small mindless fury, Gail would scream and beat her fists against her stepmother's curled back. Marion would bend her back and shield her head with her arms so as to blunt the blows. After five or ten minutes the storm would pass.

A letter came in the mail; it is lost now. Marion: "I may have been pregnant with Linda, I don't remember. I don't remember if Lee had re-tired from the government yet to go to work fulltime on the farm, but anyway here comes this letter to me from Nancy Newhall, the wife of Beaumont Newhall, director of photography at the Museum of Modern Art in New York. Maybe it was late 1942 or 1943, I don't remember. And she says something like, 'Marion, is it true you've given up your important work for a life out among the chickens, and if so, I hope you know it'll be a great loss and we'll all be disappointed.' Well, do you know I never answered it. I just let that letter sit around on a dresser for the longest time."

Another child arrived. They named him Michael. He was sweet and hardly seemed to cry at all. There were now four children under the Wolcott roof. The two older ones—Gail and John—were Lee's from the tragic short-lived marriage to Margaret; the two younger—Linda and Mike—were Lee and Marion's own.

V-J Day came and went. The head of the household was a full-time farmer. He consulted the county extension agent, and he borrowed more books from the USDA's national library in nearby Maryland, and he worked dawn to dark. The former city boy from Red Bank, New Jersey, could put in a row of fence posts before breakfast. Lee Wolcott was becoming expert on blackleg and the horn fly and cattle tick fever.

A collie came into the family; she was named Dixie Belhaven Princess.

It isn't true to say the artist never took a photograph. There is a moody one, for instance, of Linda, maybe three or four, bathing in the creek and looking back over her shoulder at her mom. No amateur in the world could have achieved the texture and sense of light and shadow that exist in this photograph.

When she photographed her neighbors' kids, she'd charge a minimal amount. It was loose change for the Saturday farm auctions.

The artist in suspension took another fine photograph—of her grinning husband on his tractor in a short-peaked leather cap, his youngest, Mikey, sitting between his legs. Little Michael had developed a serious health problem by then, and it became another anxiety in the family. Medicines had to be carefully administered.

Willy and Tony Kraber, her old friends from Group Theatre days, came to visit. Willy: "I took the train down from Pittsburgh with my son Fritzie, where we'd been visiting for the holidays. We had met Lee by this time and liked him, though we didn't know him in any real sense. There was just something very fraught about that weekend. Just a lot of tension in the house. I put it down to the house itself, the size of it, the unmanageability of it, how Marion could never seem to get a handle on how to keep

Linda Wolcott,
Loudoun County,
Virginia, c. 1946

anything clean. But what it really must have been, I see now, was Lee. He wanted her to run it, and to keep the children, as he demanded. And she just couldn't. It was over her head. Partly out of response to what I saw, I arranged to take Gail later that year to Martha's Vineyard, where we'd rented a place for the summer. I could see how bad the situation was and I just wanted to try and help out."

. Three female Loudoun County voices. The first, the lengthiest voice (the other two will follow shortly), belongs to Betty Campbell, the Wolcotts' closest neighbor from the first half-dozen years. All three of these Virginia women, now upper-aged themselves, still live in one or another part of Loudoun County.

Betty Campbell:

"We were about a mile and a half down the road on the left from them. It was beautiful there. All the barns were fieldstone and wood. People baled their hay in rolls. . . . I remember Marion's manicotti. She wasn't a great cook, that wasn't her interest, but she could do the manicotti. She wasn't a great dresser, either, but she had a way of putting on an exotic skirt or scarf at a party. Sort of gypsylike. It worked on her. . . .

"I remember the night their last, Michael, was born. I made elderberry pie and took it over to them and then we got her in the car and took Marion out for a ride on bumpy roads. She was so nervous that night, but I settled her down with the elderberry pie. . . . I knew nothing about her earlier life. I had no idea she did all that traveling around by herself back then. Oh, maybe once or twice she said something like, 'I used to take pictures for the government, Betty, and that's how I met Lee.' But she never explained it beyond that. It just didn't come up. I'm not saying she was hiding it. It was just as if it had never happened. Lee never mentioned it either. It was only years later I began to hear about what a great photographer she was. You could have knocked me over. Maybe she didn't think I'd get it.

"We were different people, Marion and I, but I felt very close to her and wanted to be her friend. I was a country woman married to a country man. Oh, that's another thing: My husband Tom was a real honest-to-god dirt farmer, and what used to gall him no end was that Lee would come over and argue with him about how to farm. Lee got his farming lore from books, but he was prone to argue with my husband anyway. Tom liked him, and so did I, but that just got us, the way he'd come over and argue about the right way to do it. . . . I don't think I ever really heard Lee and Marion in an argument of their own. But I remember his stern voice

Michael and Lee Wolcott,
Loudoun County, Virginia,
c. 1949

with her now and then. He'd say something like, 'Now you listen to me!'
He could be terribly stern with the children, too, especially the older two.
I know he made Gail's life miserable for a time. Marion intimated that to
me. She didn't condemn him or anything like that. Lee cared for his family a lot, that's one sense you always had about him. He loved Marion
deeply, I'm not suggesting otherwise. I guess it was just his way. . . . Toys.
I shouldn't say this, but I remember that any kind of toy they bought for
the kids, it had to have some kind of educational aspect to it. It couldn't
just be a toy. That was Lee. . . .

"I can tell you at least one thing about Marion and photography. We
wanted her to come over and take a picture of our kids on the Massey-
Harris combine. I guess I *must* have known something about her earlier
life, come to think about it. Maybe it was the equipment she had, not that
I ever saw it that much. But it wasn't amateur's equipment. Anyway, we
asked her to come over and shoot the kids on the combine and she kept
saying, 'Okay, I'll do it, Betty, but wait till the clouds are right.' She always
wanted to wait till there were puffy clouds. Finally they must have been
right because she came over and took it. She didn't seem to be particularly
enthused. She just did it because we asked. It was a good picture, too. It
got in the Loudoun *Times-Mirror.* In fact, I still have it on my wall. . . . It
seems such a shame, this business about Marion and the stopping. Why
didn't she go on? It seems to me that if she really wanted to go on, she
would have gone on. I don't think she truly wanted it after she had kids.
On the other hand, I guess I've always secretly wondered if there wasn't a
little part of him that wanted to put her down. Maybe he didn't want her
to come up to him."

ONE DAY IN 1948, roughly five years after they'd been living on the
first Loudoun County farm, Marion wrote a letter to Roy Stryker. Stryker
himself had left the federal government in 1943 and was now working for
Standard Oil of New Jersey out of an office in Rockefeller Center in Manhattan. He was running another documentary photography project that
would end up being famous in its own right, though not to the extent of
the FSA. Standard Oil wanted to record the role of oil in modern civilization—essentially a P.R. move—and the pictures, like the FSA pictures,
would be available free of charge to schools, publishers, libraries, the general public. Some of the old gang from FSA and OWI had followed Roy
to the new job and were now bringing him back shots of wells, barges,

refineries, transcontinental trucks—and, always if you worked for Stryker, pictures of people. Marion had heard about the project, and her letter
had traces of yearning in it. Anxiety was there, too. The old letters from
the Depression road always had their anxiety and yearning, but at the
same time a ribaldry.

Mrs. Leon Wolcott
Rt. 3, Lovettsville, Va.

April, 1948

Dear Roy,

    I don't have time for a very newsy letter, but wanted to say hello,
& ask you to be good enough to have your secretary send me a couple
of addresses—(card enclosed)—Jean & Russell Lee's—the Ros-
kam's—& also a good camera repairman, for my Ikoflex—(NOT
that I'll ever take any pictures with it, but it still helps to feel that I
might or could if I wanted to!)

    At the moment we are under a lot of strain & pressure, having
bought a small dairy farm (135 acres & 45 head) about 6 miles from
this place, in January. We are still hoping to sell this, & move over
there eventually, but I'm afraid that this house is not to be sold very
easily. Labor, both household & farm help, is still very scarce & poor
& unreliable, making life difficult & keeping us tied down.

    The kids are fine, but I wish we had better schools. Our youngest
son is two and a half now, & adorable, & I'm glad I haven't missed the
everyday waking & living hours with him—as one does with a regular fulltime job.

    I wish you could come down for a visit sometime—& if you
should visit Washington at any time, please be sure to call us. I'd love
to see you.

    Give my love to all—Arthur R., the Johns, & everyone—& best to
Alice—too.

Faithfully,
Marion

Stryker's reply seemed warm enough on the face of it. He described
what various shooters were doing—the Rothsteins had had a baby boy,

Dorothea Lange was recovering from illness, Russell Lee was in Chicago, John Vachon was free-lancing, John Collier had moved to Taos. Roy said he didn't know whether to vote for Henry Wallace for President, he had no use for Truman, "and I could never face my grandchildren if I ever had to admit that I voted for any of the Republicans that are anywhere on the horizon." Then he said:

> Here is a little advance notice of a wild idea which Stryker is carrying around in his head and please—it's off the record. Ever since I left Farm Security I have been a little disturbed by people who know how we conducted that operation better than we do ourselves. You know, the kind of people who wrote articles and books about Stieglitz. They worry me because they make the job we did so complex. If you will remember, there was just a bunch of people who had a budget, were excited about the country and its people, and took pictures, wrote captions, put them in the file, got them used and had a lot of fun doing it.

He went on to say he wanted to do an FSA book and hoped it could become a reality. Finally he said:

> By the way, if you do get your camera fixed up and can do farm stories, it might be that Aron Mathiew of Farm Quarterly could give you some story assignments—the pay isn't high but it would be good. If you do decide to write him, tell him you are one of my old gang from Washington. You might look at some old copies of the Quarterly to see the type of pictures they use.

Later Marion would wonder if she hadn't received the Stryker brush-off. Perhaps she might have gotten hold of Mr. Aron Mathiew of *Farm Quarterly* had there not been the stress of two relocations in the next four years.

The first relocation, to Purcellville, came at the end of the forties. Lee saw more opportunities for income growth by putting the Lovettsville place up for sale, and as usual he turned out to be correct. The farm sold for $15,000, a gigantic sum to a cash-poor family.

Willy Kraber: "I came on another visit. It must have been the second place, the one in Purcellville. It seems she met me up in Harpers Ferry and then drove me back to this new place they'd bought. What I essentially remember about that weekend is the mud. Mud everywhere. You squished around in it every time you stepped out the damn door. The cows were close to the house and they were full of mud, too. That mud just seemed to epitomize everything about Marion's life. Then we were in the kitchen alone—I guess I'd been there several days—and Marion said, sort of exploding, 'Willy, this is what I mean. The farm women around here would just leave the bottle of ketchup on the table and the dirty spoons on the counter. But it's *demanded* of me that I have this table cleaned after *every* meal, and fresh flowers put out to boot.' Of course, what you have to remember about this is that Marion was always a great complainer. About anything. I'm convinced she would have complained no matter whom she married or where she went in life. But still, that stress was there. I remember it."

In Purcellville, Lee and his second-born, John, drove a little gray Ford Ferguson tractor and a big John Deere A two-cylinder. They had fifty cows and milked forty—Holsteins, Guernseys, and several Jerseys. When the hired hand couldn't get there, Lee and his eldest got up at all the terrible hours to do the milking themselves. There were lots of barn cats at the Purcellville farm; some of them didn't get named. Lee bought Gail, a teenager now, a Jersey heifer calf. They named her Hotshot. Hotshot won Reserve Champion at the Loudoun County 4-H Fair. But the public schools proved bad in Purcellville, and the isolation seemed even worse than in Lovettsville, and anyway the head of the family got restless again, and so about a year and a half later came the family's third move, this time to a farm outside Waterford, the county's most appealing town. All these farm properties were no more than ten miles apart, though they seemed farther than that. Lee, ever astute with a deal, held on to the dairy operation at Purcellville while selling off the rest of the property separately. Later, when he liquidated the dairy operation, he figured he'd made at least an extra ten thousand in cash.

The Waterford house—the Wolcotts would always speak of it this way in the afteryears, just as they would refer to the earlier two as the Purcellville house and the Lovettsville house—stood high on a knoll, a mile and a half from the town limits. It had a long skinny living room with a great fireplace at one end. Waterford had been settled by eighteenth-century Quakers from Pennsylvania, and they had been followed to Virginia by Scotch-Irish craftsmen who did beautiful interior woodwork in the old valley houses. Marion and Lee and the kids pulled off the newspapers that had been varnished onto the walls and found gorgeous pine underneath. During the week they worked at farm chores; on weekends they'd work on the house. The kids pitched right in. They all got the flu together, they all got the mumps together—even Lee, who hadn't been laid up in years. When the snows came, Gail and John and Linda and Mike went sledding down the big hill out front and then hooked the ropes of their sleds onto the drawbar of the tractor while their dad, waving, earflaps of his old snow cap pulled low, towed them back up. Marion got some of this on film with her repaired Ikoflex.

She got the idea of doing a children's book of farm photographs—you know, keep it in the hobby vein, send it in on spec to some New York publisher. The idea never materialized. Lee was concerned about the time it would take—this was his stated objection. Lee himself was on the local selective service board in these years, but that didn't demand a huge amount of his time.

One day Marion told Lee she was thinking of joining the League of Women Voters. An older Waterford friend, Mary Stabler, was trying to start a League chapter among Loudoun County farm wives, and Marion's main interest didn't seem to be politics as much as trying to help get the organization off the ground. But she also was enthused about the socializing possibilities. Lee kept saying he didn't think it was a good idea for her to get involved. They argued about it back and forth and in the end Marion joined—but then went to only a few meetings. It was just too much of an issue. She had won but hated what the winning entailed. It's true her husband hadn't "forbidden" her to join. She wouldn't have stood for that. Lee had just applied once again, as was his wont, his hugely forceful way of speaking and acting and willing.

A second female Loudoun County voice. It belongs to Anne Parsons, a housewife and mother in those years, a successful real estate agent in later years: "I purchased their Lovettsville house in nineteen forty-nine. We became friends. I was a good deal younger than Marion and Lee, but I had married early and our kids were the approximate age of their younger kids. My parents, Fred and Mary Stabler, were their friends, too. It was kind of a unique social situation, really. Marion used to confide in my mother. My mother was about fifteen years older than Marion. Anyway, Mother would tell me that Marion used to talk to her about Lee, sometimes pretty bitterly. She didn't condemn him, or talk about leaving him,

at least that I know of, but she used to complain about how everything
had to be his way. She could complain with a smile on her face, but it was
a lot of complaining. . . .

"By the time they moved over to Waterford, their third house, they had
a little more money, I suppose. Lee liked having parties, and Marion was
good at entertaining, but I think she had to be pretty creative with the
small money Lee gave her. Arthur Godfrey and his wife, Mary, lived outside Waterford. Arthur was still a big radio star in those years. He'd fly his
plane in from New York on weekends. . . .

"When I stop and think of Lee Wolcott, I see someone intense, churn-
ing, vital, handsome, intellectual, very talented. Also someone who had a
wandering eye for other women. I suspect they were faithful, though. I
see Marion as someone seeming unsure of herself, and as far as I was
concerned, had no reason."

At least once in the Virginia years, Marion consulted a lawyer about
leaving her husband. She never followed through, and a central part of it,
she later told one of her children, was her fear she'd be left with nothing.

Occasionally the woman who seemed unsure of herself could be quite
flinty. Once, when her frustration had spilled over, Marion pulled her eldest child down the stairs by the back of the hair, flailing at her with a
hairbrush. Gail was a teenager then, in increasing conflict with her parents, but especially her father, and that day she had just taken her stepmother to the limit.

When Gail, highly intelligent, not fifteen, fell headlong for a local boy
named Barty Johnston, Gail's dad did everything he could to stop the
romance, which he felt—perhaps correctly—was headed for disaster.
After ninth grade, Gail was sent to a Quaker boarding school near Philadelphia. Nearly forty years later, after a series of marriages and divorces
(two marriages to and two divorces from the same man), Gail Wolcott Voit
would reunite with and marry her old teenage Waterford love, Barty.

Once in a while Marion opened the mailbox and found a note or card
from somebody she'd worked with at the FSA. This would kindle distant
urges. What was she to do with such urges? Her life was so different now.
The spaces between these notes and cards from old associates seemed to
grow wider, as did the spaces between her round-the-farm picture-taking.

Once she opened the mailbox and found an overture from the people
running *LOOK* magazine. Several FSAers had gone to *LOOK*. She didn't
show the letter to her husband. She didn't throw it away, either.

The last Loudoun County female voice, Anne Carter Smith. In all the after years, she made it a point to try to keep in contact with the far-flung Wolcotts: "Lee is your explanation for all this changing and moving around. That's what I think anyway. He's just got to go somewhere else, try something else, and she goes along. It's probably not any more mysterious than that. I love them both dearly, but I'm not going to sit here and tell you I didn't see the tension in their marriage. Marion knew how to swear, I remember that. Lee called me 'Annie.' I always had a sweet relationship with him. I'm very fond of him. If you're asking me to remember Marion, I can see a woman in not exactly fashionable clothes bending down and taking a casual picture, probably of children. She has a happy look on her face. I do remember that happy look. That's all I'll say."

The Jeffersonian farmer of northern Virginia negotiated the purchase of two town properties. One was an old tin-and-plumbing concern in Waterford he picked up for $2,500; the other was a large building in Leesburg he got for $22,000 and then quickly turned into a rental space for a Western Auto franchise. Lee let the black barber, who'd previously used a corner of the space, stay on for a pittance.

In the winter of 1952, the barn at the Waterford farm burned. Lee, ever the wizard with a new idea, had obtained at minimal cost hundreds of pounds of sweepings from the floor of a local pasta factory—elbow macaroni and so forth—that he and the kids then proceeded to enrich the silage with so that their milk cows could eat more nutritionally. A semi-trailer had brought out to the farm scores of bags full of pasta sweepings, and after several months, when the empty bags had begun to collect in the barn, Lee asked his eldest, John, to start a fire far from the house and outbuildings and burn the discarded bags. John and his best friend, Ronnie Campbell (Betty and Tom Campbell's son), lit the fire about fifty feet from the milking barn, which would have been fine, except the wind suddenly came up. An unseen spark flew toward the barn. John was in ninth grade then. He and the Campbell boy were leaning on their pitchforks, watching the fire, talking about Houdini, when Mike Wolcott, the youngest, ran up and said, "The barn's on fire."

Lee and the two older boys thought sure they'd succeeded in getting the thing put out by themselves. But that night, when the family was in the house, the barn started to burn again. Marion was the one who discovered this second blaze. Lee quickly called the volunteer fire department, and the men with the antique pumper got there as soon as they could, but things were bad now. It was so cold that evening you could look up and see flames licking one part of the rafters, while icicles hung from other parts.

The next day Lee told the local paper the cause of the fire was unknown. This wasn't the truth, but it was in a good cause: He was trying to protect his son, who felt something close to hysteria about the incident. When John got on the school bus a day later, he told his classmates that the thing had been all his fault. "But the paper said cause unknown," several of his friends said. Perhaps this is how the rumor got lit, that John's father had burned down the barn to collect the insurance money, that maybe the fire started by accident the first time, but that Lee had applied some good old self-induced lightning to the second blaze. When the insurance adjustor came out and looked things over, he said that the site John had picked to burn the empty pasta bags looked like a perfectly reasonable distance to him. The second fire was judged to have started from some smoldering embers. John Wolcott has always believed this to be the case, and probably he's right, even though the rumor about the insurance money still hangs.

The following year came the accident. It happened one cold spring morning in 1953. Lee was killing honeysuckle weeds out by a fence row about 150 yards from the house. Suddenly Billy the hired hand was screaming. A man was on the ground, rolling, an envelope of bright color in the still day.

Lee: "I was working with a gasoline-powered brush burner, a cone-shaped thing, with the fuel tank strapped to my back. It had started to die out and I knelt down to pump it up again. When it exploded the fuel drenched my legs. The burns were third degree."

Marion: "Pieces of raw hot metal came up and hit him just above the eye. The heavy jacket he had on saved him. That and his shoes. They were L. L. Bean hunting shoes with rubber tops. I was wild. I got the truck and put him inside it and started driving toward Leesburg while the hired girl held a rag to his face. The doctor met us at the hospital."

Lee: "Cadaver. That's the one word I heard the doctor say. He was studying the skin on my legs."

He was in the hospital for five months and then in bed at home for several more months. Lee's farming life was effectively finished, though he has never particularly wished to understand it that way.

Willy Kraber: "She was thinking of leaving him before the accident.

Then she nursed him back to health. And then she was with him forever. I'm sure about that."

(And yet, at least once more in succeeding years, according to one of the four Wolcott children, Marion would again seek out a lawyer about getting a divorce. Again, she wouldn't follow through.)

Here is something ambiguous: During her husband's hospitalization, Marion made a secret appointment to see Roy Stryker. Stryker had moved on from Standard Oil to a similar photography project at the University of Pittsburgh and then on to a third project at the Jones and Laughlin Steel Corporation. Marion met him in Washington and managed to keep it from Lee. She told herself the lunch would only distract her husband, disturb his recovery, and certainly there was truth in this. She put on her best dress and drove to the city. Stryker was in town for several days.

"Roy, I want to shoot again," Marion said. "It's not the money, though of course we could use the money. I just want something to do. Isn't there something you could give me that might not take me too far away from home?"

Stryker seemed to pull back. Later Marion would wonder if there had been something too desperate in her voice at the lunch. Perhaps Roy was still angry at Lee Wolcott's unreasonable post-crediting demands of 1941. The meeting ended with no promises. In fact, Stryker seemed to be spending too much time during the meal telling Marion that her real place, now more than ever, was beside her husband. "A good man needs a good woman when he's recovering, Marion," Stryker said. But in her heart Marion was sure he was telling her something else: He didn't want her. She'd been away too long and couldn't cut it on the road any longer. Probably he had never liked her pictures that much to begin with, at least compared to the work of some of the others—Russ Lee and Rothstein and Vachon and Dorothea and Delano. Marion never heard from Stryker again regarding her plea. What she also never knew was that almost twenty years later, when he wasn't long from death, Stryker sought to keep Marion out of his FSA book, *In This Proud Land.* If it hadn't been for Nancy Wood, the young writer working with Stryker on the project, Marion's pictures probably would have been excluded. According to Wood, Stryker, who was close to eighty then and whose memory was failing, had convinced himself Marion was one of the lesser of his crew—a white-gloved girl who had never had the real guts for the job.

Summer came and the younger Wolcott children took strands of alfalfa to Leesburg Hospital. The patient chewed on them, broke them in half, said, yes, it was time to make hay.

But the agrarian was now talking from his recovery bed about giving up the farm—or at least his wife would remember it this way. Lee himself would insist, when asked about it years later, that he never once spoke of quitting the farm while he was in the hospital—that wouldn't have been in character. Such a thing would imply a depletion of his spirit. It was only after he had gotten going again fully that he and Marion began reevaluating their life in the country—this is his memory. But the way it would stick in Marion's memory was that one morning Lee, who was still bedridden, either in the hospital or at home, sat up and took her by the wrists and said, "We'll sell out, Marion. We'll sell out and go west, babe. We'll have an auction, the tools, the stock, every damn thing, and I'll put you and the kids in the car and send you west and then I'll meet you. This climate is too damp for you. Your asthma will be better in the next place." There was such adventure and enthusiasm in his voice, which is one of the things she'd always loved about Lee.

In any event the farming period seemed done, even though more than a year was to elapse before the actual sell-off. As with any history that has complex parts, it must have been more than the accident alone that pushed the Wolcotts toward the next segment of their lives. In a way it was as if Marion and Lee both instinctively recognized they were through with farming and with rural Virginia by the early fifties, and the explosion of the brush burner that day just certified it.

After the auction—it was held in August of the following year, 1954— Marion and Lee had $115,000 in cash and felt wealthy, although impoverished in deeper ways. The retired agrarian was almost forty-nine, his wife forty-four. They had owned three farms in one county for something over a decade and would never again be this connected to a place. They sold almost everything except the clothes off their backs and Lee's books, which he stored with a merchant in town. That drizzly day of the sale, Marion stood on the fringe of muddy-booted neighbors and cried huge tears as the auctioneer's song took the property down to the bone.

MOVEMENT AND AILMENT enter the story more radically now. Consider: Over the next three decades, from the midfifties to the early eighties, Marion and Lee switched residences and countries about thirty times. And those are just the ones I have been able to track. Sometimes they changed addresses three or more times within the same metropolitan area, in one case, three times within the same complex of apartments. For a while they seemed to be richocheting continents. It's almost as if someone were after them. On the other hand, I should emphasize here that at least half a dozen of their moves abroad were at the behest of the Agency for International Development, for whom Lee had gone to work in 1959, and in that sense could be thought of as something almost beyond their control. But this doesn't answer the larger question of why two middle-aged and then upper-aged people—one in shaky health—seemed to be in need of so much continual pushing on.

"Moves/upheavals/migrations," Marion once said in a note to me, as if the whole thing were beyond her. She had sent me in the mail that day some photographs of Reasie, the long-dead Alabama black woman who had cared for her when she was a child in Bloomfield. The yellow Post-It note attached to the cellophane said, "These pix of Reasie may not look moldy but I found them in a very old moldy box of other very moldy photos I'd dumped on Michael, no doubt during one of our many moves/upheavals/migrations." There was a series of exclamation points and question marks.

I've since seen a snapshot of a pickup truck crammed with two people's belongings. It's their son Michael's truck, and the things in the back—rugs, lamps, bookcases, magazines, bedding, pots and pans—look as if they've just been tossed in on top of one another, as if the decision to make an exit had come about thirty minutes earlier. When Marion got this picture out for me, during one of my visits to Santa Barbara, she said, "This should tell you a lot."

But back to the ribbon of chronology. After the 1954 sell-off, the Wolcotts and their two younger children moved into a cabin in Evergreen, Colorado. (The place was owned by a friend of Lee's first wife whom he had contacted when he knew the family was heading west.) Marion and the two kids left for Colorado almost immediately in a groaning Ford station wagon, while Lee stayed behind to dispose of the last of the real estate. The family camped out in the Colorado cabin until the weather turned cold. (The cabin didn't have heat.) Then they found a house in Colorado Springs. Lee, nominally retired, looked after his investments. Marion took walks in the good mountain air. The kids skated at the outdoor ice rink at the Broadmoor Hotel.

A retired shooter learned that Roy Stryker, not yet retired himself from his various wanderings in the universe, was across the Colorado Rockies, in Grand Junction. "Why don't we go visit him?" she said. Lee wasn't interested. They didn't go. Small a thing as this was, the anger over Lee's refusal stayed with Marion for years.

In the spring of fifty-five, the family went on a six-week motor trip through Mexico, cutting down through the central part of the country, coming back up into California. Since they were taking their two children out of school, Lee and Marion decided they would tutor Linda and Mike themselves. Halfway into the trip Mother Wolcott flew to Mexico City to meet them, and then the number of tourists in the Ford station wagon became five. They sat in plazas on the Gulf of California and hunted sand crabs and dined on Guaymas shrimp and oysters that seemed as big as tennis shoes. A few times they camped out on the beach. They felt like a unit.

Back in the States, Marion wrote to the Krabers. She mailed them several prints and wrote the note on a piece of green cardboard that might have been torn off a shoebox lid.

Dear Willy & Tony—

We sold our farm, house & all belongings last Aug. & moved out here—trying to decide where we might *like* to live, *if* we could earn a living too. Haven't decided yet—pulling up roots is tough—the west *is* big & magnificent. Not quite as friendly—in a transient *and* boom city—as cracked up to be—unless one belongs to a certain business or university group, etc. Mike & Linda are with us. John in boarding school in Pa., Gail in Mary Washington college. Mother in California & her arthritis now very crippling & no job possible. The enforced inactivity most depressing & hard on her. The kids & I drove out there this Xmas—Lee went back East to straighten (?) Gail out on her proposed plan to quit college, get married & get a job as soon as she became 18. Her guy is now in the army & just left last week for Germany. Linda is 12—maturing nicely & a satisfying child—quite grown up now—tall & pretty. Mike is fine too & a good kid. How does Fritz like Harvard?

Before leaving for Mexico, Lee had received a letter from Howard McMurray, one of his friends from graduate school at the University of Wisconsin two decades before. McMurray, who'd briefly been a congressman, was now running the department of government at the University of New Mexico in Albuquerque. He knew about the accident with the brush burner in Virginia. Would Lee be interested in a visiting professorship? When he got back to the States, Lee called from California and told his old colleague yes. In the interim, the family went back to Colorado Springs so Linda and Mike could finish out the school year. Lee had to scramble around and find a short-term rental, but he managed one at a good price.

From 1955 to 1959, the Wolcotts had at least three residences in Albuquerque. The first proved too close to an aircraft-testing facility. They bought a house at 609 Girard, close to the university. It was a low, one-story adobe with pecan floors, handhewn doors, walls eighteen inches thick that tended to keep the house cool in the summer, warm in the winter. The place was on a busy street, with other houses close by, but still there was a kind of hacienda effect. At the university, Lee taught courses in public administration and political parties. Several times he got his name and photograph in the paper—they amounted to small news features—especially when he was being considered for an appointment to a state committee investigating public welfare. ("Nobody seems to know where he's visiting from," a reporter for the Albuquerque *Journal* wrote.) He took that job and did the teaching too. Marion, who didn't get her name in the paper, but whose arthritis and allergies and other respiratory problems seemed briefly to get better in the desert, took courses in remedial reading for teachers and worked in a hospital with tubercular Navajo children. New Mexico, a land where D. H. Lawrence, Paul Strand, and Georgia O'Keeffe—to name three surpassing artists—have seen so much. Under "Wolcott," the 1956 Albuquerque city directory carries only one line about a former documentarian, as though aiding and abetting a mystery: "Marion P. Mrs. tchr Presby. Hosp. Center."

"I tried to be as creative with that as I could," said Marion. "I set up a trading post for them. I taught them crafts, I got them easels. I was trying to use some of my old progressive education skills from so many years earlier. The idea was that if they turned in their multiplication tables, they could then get chits at the trading post. Oh, I took a few pictures of them now and then. I didn't have much desire."

When Gail (she had left college in Virginia and come out to New Mexico to enroll at the university) announced toward the end of her sophomore year that she was getting married to an athlete, her stepmother

assumed the burden of handling the arrangements, and this helped draw
her and Gail closer together. The groom-to-be had showed up twice at the
Wolcott doorstep before he could summon the nerve to ask Lee for his
daughter's hand. Gail wanted a girlfriend from the university to be her
maid of honor, but Gail's father insisted the maid of honor would be her
half sister, Linda. Gail and Linda had always squabbled, but the father in
this family said that a sister is a sister for life—while most girlfriends pass.
He was right, of course. After the marriage, the newlyweds lived briefly
in an apartment adjoining the main house, and Marion always seemed to
be fixing a stew and bringing it across the patio to Gail and Keith, always
seemed to be telling Lee not to worry, things were going to work out fine
for his daughter and new son-in-law. Within a month Gail was pregnant.
And things didn't work out fine.

The Agency for International Development, part of the Department of
State, came recruiting at the university. Years later, in an interview with
an oral historian for the Foreign Service Family Oral History Project,
Marion described, or sort of described, what happened: "We lived in Virginia and went to Colorado Springs and put the children in school there.
And then we just took off and went to Albuquerque and we were there
six years [sic] while Lee taught. So the recruiter came to the university and
they needed someone in that field. So Lee said, 'All right, I'll be interviewed anyhow.'"

Marion and Linda had whiskey and gin planned for the AID interviewer, but when the fellow inquired without any humor if she or Lee
drank, they adroitly switched the refreshments to tea. After Lee landed
the job, the Wolcotts sold the Girard house and moved in the interim to a
rental on Tulane.

Over the next ten years the two sojourners lived mainly abroad. These
were pretty good years. They were posted, in rough chronology, to Teheran, Iran (1959–1961); Lahore, Pakistan (1961–1963); Teheran (1964–
1965); Washington, D.C. (1965–1966); Cairo (1966–1967); New Delhi
(1967–1968). In Iran, Lee's title was American Adviser to the Prime Minister for Iranian Bureaucratic Reform, and every Tuesday the onetime bureaucrat from Henry Wallace's Agriculture Department met with the
shah's principal deputy. Lee was an important figure and extremely good
at his job. He picked up Farsi in no time. He gave an address in Farsi. His
high position drew the family into local society, not something Marion was
fond of.

Lee Wolcott,
Iran, 1963

Was Lee really CIA? He has said no when the question has come up, at least said no to his children, several of whom have wondered about it in the intervening years. Say this about such speculation: There are photographs of Lee taken by Marion in Iran in which he at least *looks* like the conventional Hollywood version of a spook: trench coat, short haircut, blocky face.

Lee Wolcott: "I assure you I wasn't involved in anything subversive."

Lee Wolcott's spouse: "Just me."

On their first day in Iran, one of Marion's cameras was confiscated. There was a darkroom at the embassy, but one of the Foreign Service nationals on the staff abused the privilege and the darkroom was closed.

It didn't seem such a huge loss to Marion; she'd been away from dark-rooms for a long time. Again, quoting from that same years-later Foreign Service oral history: "Well, I didn't really want to . . . not the darkroom, no. And I was involved in teaching at that time. So between teaching and the obligation of a certain amount of social obligations, plus my children."

Interviewer: "Sounds like you had a plateful."

Interviewee: "I had enough."

She taught fourth grade and remedial reading at an American school in Teheran. She hosted parties in the way of the dutiful State Department wife. Spouses of State Department employees weren't supposed to be run-ning around in the community taking pictures. Really, they weren't sup-posed to be running around doing much of anything. Marion felt herself alienated from most of the embassy wives, who seemed only to want to cocktail and bridge-game their way through an afternoon. In truth, the chauvinistic and paternalistic attitudes of the Ivy-educated Foreign Ser-vice system of that era would have conspired against any kind of yearning, unsure, suspended artist-wife.

"But the ceramics, the old ceramics in Iran, that was one of my pas-sions. . . . And of course the carpets. . . ." Marion said years later in that same oral history interview.

There was much to seize an eye overseas—a house painter (was it Egypt?) who demonstrated his dozens of possible paint schemes by blow-ing whipped-up mouthfuls on the wall. Marion to the Foreign Service oral historian: "He did that about three or four times. I couldn't stand it any longer. I said, 'That's all right. That color is fine.'"

That ironing man (it was either New Delhi or Cairo) who stood stoi-cally at his cloth-covered board, moving his arm back and forth, moisten-ing Lee's shirts with *his* mouthfuls of water.

Little of this got freeze-framed within the geometry of a black photo-graphic box.

She did, however, get Jackie Kennedy touring with the president of Pakistan in an open convertible. Jackie, in a pillbox hat, seemed to be sticking out her tongue. In Iran she got women washing pots, pans, clothes, and children in the "jube," which is a gushing trough running down the middle of the main streets. In Aswan, Egypt, she got women buying kerosene from an Esso tank truck.

In Pakistan, Marion taught the young boys in her kitchen the impor-tance of rinsing vegetables and fruits in iodine and chlorine. She sat in her

Washing children and laundry, cooking
utensils, etc., in "jube." Iran, 1961

small garden and stared at the beautiful mango tree. She worried about
her son Michael's difficult time at school. She tried to help a sweeper who
was pregnant and without means, but the sweeper refused any medical
help and lost her baby. She walked in the markets and she read the Koran
and she studied Tantrism and she collected veils that seemed as delicate as
cobwebs and she took some color slides of a family planning program and
she thought aloud: "How strange this world is—my mother used to work
in family planning clinics. It was worlds ago."

   At the Pakistani clinic, she left some of her pictures with the administrators without bothering to make prints for herself. Most of them were
slides. Years later she noted to the Foreign Service oral historian, as if in
explanation of this seeming listlessness: "And by that time I was also suf-

fering from amoebic dysentery which dogged me the whole time, almost the whole time I was overseas."

The hard truth is that something was mislaid in her. Something was broken off. It was as though she were living her life in an artistic middle zone. But is there another way entirely to look at this? A critic once wrote of the great Paul Strand: "Painfully and slowly he felt his way through the world of sight, measuring progress not by thousands of photographs taken, but by quintessence of experience captured in one print. This tempo is characteristic of one kind of creative temperament, which grows as slowly as a century plant to produce one prodigious flower."

Back in the states, the third Wolcott child, Linda, by now a college senior at Berkeley, decided to marry. (This would have been 1962. Earlier, Linda as well as her stepbrother, John Wolcott, had attended the American University of Beirut, but then went back to the States.) Marion wanted desperately to go home for the wedding. Linda was her first child. Lee also wanted badly to go but said they were just too far away. It might cost as much as $1,000 for Marion herself to go home. This was part of the trade-off they'd made when they agreed to join the State Department. He was right, certainly. Lee said his mother, who was living in retirement in

Clinic, Lahore, Pakistan, 1962

the Bay Area, would handle the arrangements for Linda. A relative or future in-law could give Linda away. They argued back and forth and Marion ended up not going. It was so much larger a blow to her than not being able to go across the Rockies that time to visit Roy Stryker, but it was the same kind of anger.

One day Lee and Marion's youngest child, Michael, suggested that some decision or other should be put to a family vote. Michael had been sent to school in Germany and was now back with his parents in the Middle East. After all, Mike said, the United States is a democracy. "But this family isn't a democracy," the father shot back. "It's a dictatorship." The youngest child, most malleable of the bunch, never quite forgot that.

The adventurers returned to America on home leave. It was now the latter part of 1964. The real rediscovery of Marion's astonishing camera work of the thirties was still more than a decade and a half off. But an enterprising historian working for the Archives of American Art tracked her down in Mill Valley, California. He was trying to do interviews with all the old FSAers. In the postwar books that had come to be written about the Roosevelt years or the Depression or American photography, you could find the odd sentence or two such as this about the mysterious and vanished Marion Post Wolcott: "During the war her husband's travels took her away from her photographic practice." The sentences were usually off, but then the people writing them never had very much to go on. The shooter had just disappeared from American photographic sight. Any photographic sight.

For the first part of their home leave, Marion and Lee stayed in Mill Valley with Lee's mother, Edith, who, like Nan Post, had battled cancer. (Nan had fought cancer twice by this time.) Dorothea Lange's home was just across the bay, but the FSA was such a long time ago that Marion wondered if the now-legendary Lange would even know her name. She thought of going over to introduce herself to Dorothea, but changed her mind.

Anyway, that January 1965 day in Mill Valley, the man from the Archives of American Art probed a little on her early married years on the farm. The woman answering the questions was not quite fifty-five years old. Her husband wasn't present.

Interviewer: Did you ever go back to photography after that period?
MPW: No, not to any extent.

Interviewer: Why?
MPW: I did a little bit, of course. Well, I "inherited" two children, and the war, and living in the country, and subsistence kind of living in the country, and victory gardens, and no help, and that kind of thing. And you just can't do it. And then we went from that to a much larger farming proposition and I had two children of my own, which made four altogether, and we remodeled the houses that we moved into, and the farms. And my husband continued to work in Washington the first, well, four years, and I was sort of the farm manager as well as everyone at that time was working overtime, all government people were working six days a week and coming back in car pools, commuting fifty miles each way, waiting for people and meeting so they didn't get started coming home, and they left very early in the morning before dawn to commute, and came home at seven or later at night. So I was sort of farm manager and during the war I learned to use the farm equipment, too, as well as doing all the housework and taking care of the kids, remodeling the house. And this went on for ten years or more and so I just didn't get a chance to do any.
Interviewer: It didn't give you much time, did it?
MPW: I did photograph the kids, and the farms around me, but I didn't do any professional photography. I never did again. In fact, now when I see these ads for photo competitions and it always says, "Only amateurs can participate," I wonder if I couldn't be an amateur and maybe win a prize, and I don't know what my status is.

The interviewer went on to other things. Perhaps there was something in a long, derisive, run-on answer that made him uncomfortable.

During the year of home leave, Marion made a trip east to see her sister and mother, then stopped in to see the Krabers, who were living on Washington Place in the Village. Willy: "She had some pictures of Iran with her. She was talking about taking them to the Magnum agency. She seemed very unsure of herself, but these pictures meant a lot to her. There weren't very many. They were of markets in Iran, tribes on hillsides, that sort of thing. I probably should have been more encouraging. I probably missed it. At one point she said, 'Oh, Lee's so jealous of any photography I try to do. The truth is, Willy, he just doesn't want me to photograph anything.'"

"Why do you stay with him?" Tony Kraber asked Marion, after the complaints had gone on. He was serious but not deeply serious.

"Because the sex is awfully good," Marion said, grinning, defusing the moment.

Still on home leave, the Wolcotts took a small house in Falls Church, Virginia, just outside Washington. On Saturday, October 30, 1965, Marion opened the Washington *Post* and was going through it idly when her eye caught a three-column headline on the top of page four in the A section: "RUSSELL LEE'S PHOTO EXHIBITION HAS AIR OF HONESTY, NO TRICKERY." It was a preview of a one-man show set to open the following day at the Smithsonian. This was the lead paragraph: "Russell Lee cut his photographic teeth during the grand epoch of documentarians in the mid thirties heyday of the Farm Security Administration. This was the agency that produced such photographic giants as Arthur Rothstein and Dorothea Lange."

There was to be a reception after the opening, hosted by the great American documentary filmmaker Pare Lorentz. Some of the old shooters from Stryker's project, the secretarial staff and lab people, even Roy himself, were scheduled to be on hand. Marion put the paper down and said to herself: *I think I'll go. No,* she said. The next morning she got up and said to herself: *Well, I think I'll go anyway.* Lee wasn't in the house that weekend. (He may have been traveling briefly, stateside, for AID.) She rummaged in the closet for something decent to wear. She got the car and drove to town and went up to the door of the Smithsonian castle.

"I'll need your invitation, ma'am," the guard said. But she didn't have an invitation. Sorry, the guard said. Well, could she go in for just a minute? Sorry, ma'am. But, listen, she used to work with some of these people in there. Can't let you in without your invitation, ma'am. She scribbled a note. The note said something to this effect: "Dear Russ. I read about you yesterday in the paper and drove in here today. We happen to be living in this area temporarily. I just wanted to say I'm so happy for you. The guard won't let me in. Can you come out for a minute?"

She waited about an hour on those steps. Russell Lee didn't come out. Convinced this meant only one thing, Marion got into her car and drove off with some of the blindness, fear, confusion, and rage with which a Waterford farm wife once drove her husband to a hospital while the hired girl held the blood-soaking rag to his head. She drove for several hours, then parked the car in the drive and went into her house. Years would pass before Lee Wolcott heard this story.

What really happened with the note is that the guard got distracted and didn't get it into Russell Lee's hand until after Marion had left. Of course, Russell went right out when he saw the note. He looked everywhere for her. Some time later he was able to reach Marion on the phone and say how awful he felt. "Do you think for a second any of us would not have come out?" he told her. Well, not really, she answered.

The two travelers went back overseas, this time to Egypt. Their apartment in Cairo was directly on the Nile, the river so beautiful in the sunset. She didn't reach for the camera very much. Anti-American feeling was rife in Egypt; once Marion got spat on as she walked to the embassy from her and Lee's apartment. They had been in Egypt for about a year when the Six-Day War broke out. On the night before their separate evacuations, husband and wife sat together on a sofa and destroyed slides and negatives. They knew the government would confiscate them anyway and didn't wish to give them the pleasure. Marion and Lee got rid of about 200 images that night, which was not quite everything she had taken—or at least saved—in ten years overseas. It was not a lot, but it was an awful lot in another sense. She and Lee cut the pictures into little pieces, flared them brightly with matches. It was just something to do to ease the tension. The next day she left the country ahead of her husband. She flew to Athens with several cameras hanging from her neck. Lee was later evacuated to the Hotel Palestine in Alexandria. Their reunion was nearly as passionate as those spring courtship nights in 1941.

Marion, to the Foreign Service oral historian: "I think I was too numb and too sad and too worried . . . to really care about taking photographs. It had been such a traumatic night and I was so worried about Lee and about being separated and not knowing really what was going to happen to him. . . . And we really didn't know whether we would see each other again. And we were still in love and still cared about each other, so it was painful. . . ."

After Egypt came India. Marion, to the Foreign Service historian: "Lee was offered a post in Seoul. So he said, 'Pack up, we're going to Seoul.' So I packed everything. . . . So he came in and said, 'Forget it, we're not going

to Seoul.' And I said, 'So what now? Where else?' ... Then the next post
he was offered was India. And I said, 'Well, I don't know whether I really
want to go with you to India or not.' That was the first time in our marriage, I think, that I had said what I wanted to do." She wasn't sure she
wanted to go to India, she said, because Indira Gandhi, the prime minister, had taken up so quickly against Israel in the Six-Day War.

Lee's title in New Delhi was Social Science Advisor, Family Planning.
The government paid him $20,956 a year.

Again, what one saw but didn't photograph in India: immense black
buffaloes wallowing streamside. Naked men on their haunches, thin as
pipe cleaners, stroking their thighs white with shaving brushes. It's true
Marion tried to document a little at the birth control clinic. But the locals
there were suspicious of her. It was intimidating. It fell off. Explaining this
inertia to the oral historian: "I took a few photographs then, and I didn't
have fast enough film, fast enough lens really at that time, but I could have
done better now. But I did get a few photographs."

After India, which seemed especially fatiguing to Marion, came retire-
ment: home. Where on earth would that be? Initially the couple decided
to return to Falls Church, Virginia, outside Washington. For unclear reasons the decision turned out to be wrong, so they left and went to the
opposite coast. (Probably they wanted to get closer to their kids.) For
$61,000 they bought a house in Montecito, California, just below Santa
Barbara. It had a swimming pool with imported tile, but somehow the
property wasn't right. So they sold it, took the profit, moved into something smaller several miles away. It still wasn't right. They found another.

Sometimes Marion's insomnia stabbed her awake for a week running.

On January 2, 1970, Nan Post died in a Connecticut nursing home. The
four-graph obit in the Lakeville *Journal* ("Planned Parenthood Pioneer
Dies") described her as the "widow of Dr. Walter Post and former co-
worker of Margaret Sanger." Nan had lived in a series of Connecticut
nursing homes, each one seeming worse than the last. She had glaucoma
and needed a new hip and was swollen with arthritis. At the end, her
powdery coils of white hair had gone streaky. So had her mind: She would
congratulate visitors to her bedside for having won air medals overseas.
But even then there was something striking and a little extravagant about
her—her huge opal pinky ring, for instance.

For a time, while she was in California, Nan had worked as a house
mother at Whittier College. Then she'd come east and had moved in with

her daughter Helen and her husband, Rudi, and their two children in
Sharon, Connecticut, deeply resenting the fact that she couldn't support
herself. Finally she'd been put into a home where she continually did
battle with officious administrators who thought they could stick up their
idols of Jesus and his mother in the hallway alcoves. Nan Post was eighty-
six when she died, a lifelong figure, especially for her second daughter, of
pain and inspiration and impecuniousness and the undiluted but never-
gained dream. Way back there, after Cousin Ed and the scandal at 17 Park
Place, there had been another love for Nan, a Catholic, who tried to get
her to marry him in the church. Initially Nan had said yes. The Catholic
said she could continue believing in her crazy birth control ideas, as long
as she didn't try to proselytize them. Nan pulled out. That man could go
to hell. He was quite wealthy and could have fixed her for life and he
dropped dead about two weeks after the date of the intended wedding.

Nan's daughter Marion took a job at the Santa Barbara art museum—
a graying, asthmatic woman behind a gift-shop counter. No one knew
about her photographic past. She liked the job quite a lot, being steps away
from all that art.

The photography critic Gene Thornton would soon write of the FSA
in the *New York Times:* "It is one of the oddities of our times that photographs like these are still not considered an important part of art history.
The standard histories of American art from the ashcan school to abstrac-
tion concentrate on painting and are more likely to notice the museum
and gallery photography of Stieglitz and his successors than the documentary photography of the FSA photographers and their successors among
the photojournalists. I will hazard a guess, however, that in one hundred
years, or perhaps even fifty, the documentary photography of Arthur
Rothstein and his colleagues will seem far more important as art than all
the American painting of the past fifty years."

In the way a muscle will spasm unexpectedly, or perhaps in the way an
old vessel may react to new wine, a sixty-odd-year-old found herself attracted to the life in a student village at the University of California at
Santa Barbara. She wandered around amid the counterculture with a
35mm, working in Cibachrome, fooling around, getting graffiti and street
fairs. She took a picture of a wildly colored VW repair garage named
Doug's Bugs. She got the hallucinogenic-looking Sweet Potato Café and
the Sun & Earth Organic Kitchen. Perhaps she felt a little like that green-
eyed girl in Vienna, the old radical socialist, who'd been handed Trude

Fleischmann's baby Rollei. Marion's morale seemed to flare briefly, not unlike some flaring colored slides in Cairo on the night before an evacuation.

What else did she do with her life? Well, she worked on a state senator's campaign. She read her grandkids the Beatrix Potter Peter Rabbit stories and taught them artistic ways of making ice cream sundaes. She designed ornaments out of fallen tree pods. She repotted, she transplanted, she got down on all fours and looked for snails and slugs in her garden. She wrote self-deprecating notes to friends because the humor and the rueful irony had never really deserted her: "I'm waiting for my memory to suddenly become activated by a jolt of ? or a B-12 shot." To another friend she wrote: "I love (& non allergic) iris (Jap. & others), cymbidium, pansies, larkspur, violets, African daisies, ranunculus, anemones nemesia, snapdragons, delphinium, daffodils, tulips, day lilies, columbine, & cats, dogs, deer, rabbits, & some people!"

They moved up the California coast, to Mendocino, into a woody, rambling house on the outskirts of what looked like a rock-bound Maine village. It was the midseventies now. Mendocino was saltbox houses, winter storms blowing in from Alaska, buoys singing out beyond the breaker line, carnations blooming in a hundred window boxes, deer and raccoons showing up in your yard for food at fog-shrouded sunset. Their first place in Mendocino (inevitably there would be a second) was on five acres, 700 feet back from cliffs that dove straight to the Pacific. There was wildness in the weather and in the landscape. The couple could see migrating whales from their breakfast room. Marion put on her red parka and put her hand in her husband's and walked in the high yellow grasses below her house, picking blackberries, listening for the music of shore birds. Her hair was wire-gray, her face had grown lined and leathery, her fine old bones seemed to have pushed themselves inward so that she looked almost concave. But still she was a beautiful woman. She liked wearing men's unironed checkered shirts.

One day she took from a closet a 16 × 20 vintage FSA print. It was made from the original archived negative, and it was a picture of a sulky race at a fairgrounds in Mercer County, Kentucky, summer of 1940. An itinerant photographer had caught it all—the powdery dust, the centrifugal force of the goggled riders leaning into the last turn, the straw-hatted fairgoers hanging at the rail. The person who had taken the picture so long ago was trying now to trim the edges of it on an art cutter. But she couldn't get the picture aligned. She messed up and tried again. The edges still weren't square. She tried again. She swore at the thing, crumpled it up, threw it in the trash, retrieved it, crumpled it up again. "Who gives a shit for a picture of a goddamn sulky race?" she yelled to herself. "I'll bet it's worth nothing."

On a spring day in 1975, two esteemed West Coast photographers, Jack Welpott and Judy Dater, plus a New York gallery owner named Lee Witkin, drove up from San Francisco to visit Marion. Witkin, who was opening a new gallery on East 57th Street in Manhattan and trying to put together an FSA show for the following year, told Marion that her work amounted to buried American treasure. Welpott, who had known of her work for years and had showed samples of it in his photography classes and had no idea she was now living just up the coast, would later write a wonderful piece stemming from this visit: "Marion Post Wolcott. 'My God, isn't she off somewhere in India or Egypt searching for the divine light of Shiva or something? Marion Post Wolcott in California, I don't believe it.' ... She certainly was a mystery figure in the FSA scheme of things." Welpott talked in his piece of "the rhythm of textures and surfaces so exquisitely rendered," of the "transcendent moment in the unfolding of life."

All three visitors that day urged Marion to reestablish her bond with photography. Lee Wolcott listened and said it was a good idea. He said he'd like to get involved, too. In fact, not long afterward, they began building a darkroom in the Mendocino house. They taught themselves how to make fine prints. Marion borrowed negatives from the Library of Congress. She started shooting, this time in earnest. Her spirits lifted. Her children remarked on this. Mysteriously, it fell off.

Marion: "I doubt any of this rediscovery would have happened in my lifetime if Witkin and Jack Welpott and Judy Dater hadn't made that trip that day to Mendocino to see me. Lee Witkin is really the one who dragged me out of the closet. It's also true that by that point there was no argument from Lee."

Lee: "Because now there was time. It's that simple."

A feminist graduate student from Buffalo working on a history dissertation came to see her. In the opening pages of her thesis, Julia Boddy wrote: "When I first asked about Wolcott, no one could tell me whether or not she was still alive. Discovering whether she was alive and, if so, where she was living, took weeks. There seemed to be an atmosphere of privatization that shrouded her existence, both past and present. I discovered that these basic facts about her existence were carefully guarded, as if she were unable to determine for herself whether or not she might want to respond to a letter from a person who admired her work.... A few weeks after asking the first questions, I was summoned to the head curator's office. Behind closed doors, he told me that Wolcott was living in California and gave me her address.... When I arrived there, I had been able to learn very little about her. She knew me only through the letters I had written her. When I began to talk to her, she let me know that she was more interested in her recent work and future prospects than in the past. I wondered what to expect from the reserved though vigorous woman, who talked with me accompanied by her watchful husband...."

During a vacation in Hawaii, the shooter again picked up the camera. She photographed some overweight women lounging poolside, coated in their baker's glaze of oils. There's nothing technically wrong with any of these pictures. In the late seventies a few of them wound up being exhibited in a one-person Wolcott show at the Witkin Gallery in New York. But a critic for the *Village Voice,* who happened to know the early work well, dismissed these Hawaii shots: "Little more than bright bold decorations.... To take someone like Post Wolcott, who has never been adequately shown, and make her look better forgotten ... is inexcusable. Post Wolcott is also partly to blame for not taking her work more seriously."

Galleries had begun to show a little of her work, usually as parts of larger shows. Also in this period, books about the FSA had been coming out, most notably Hank O'Neal's *A Vision Shared,* F. Jack Hurley's *Portrait of a Decade,* and Nancy Wood and Roy Stryker's *In This Proud Land.* Marion found herself in them to lesser or greater extents, and certainly it was flattering and pleasing to her. In 1973, the same year Stryker's book had appeared, *Documentary Expression and Thirties America* was published. It was regarded as a major study of the thirties. Marion got two citations, both of a passing nature.

A general awakening to the culture of the thirties seemed to be taking place in the mid- and late seventies. Photography itself in these years was being reconsidered as a medium. After a one-person Wolcott show in Berkeley in 1978, a critic for a publication called *Artweek* wrote: "While Marion Post Wolcott's pictures do not convey the pathos of a Dorothea Lange or the elegant formalism of a Walker Evans, they do present an important and intelligent viewpoint on the Depression." That must have felt balmy. A few months later, across the country, in Syracuse, another exhibit presented the early work with several of the Hawaiian and Santa Barbara student subculture shots. A critic for *Afterimage* wrote: ". . . there is a sense of poignancy in the new work. It is as if the sharp edge has been lost." And as if to pile cruelty on insult, the early work, even by academics, was often misunderstood and not recognized for what it was. Marion Post Wolcott—wasn't she the one who shot the FSA cheesecake? Those hay-fields and dreamy creek banks?

In 1979, just as the Wolcotts began to wonder if maybe they shouldn't move on from Mendocino, Marion's sister died in the East. Helen was the last blood link to that far-off continent called Jersey. A person can say the name "Helen Post" today and the art world will know it even less than it does Marion's name. And yet five thousand of Helen Post Modley's impressive documentary photographs of Indians are now being catalogued and processed at the Amon Carter Museum in Fort Worth, Texas. Helen's adopted son, Peter Modley, has written of his mother's uncelebrated and often pained life, and it could almost be a summation of Marion's life, too:

> The concrete accomplishments resulting from this work included some gallery hangings in New York City, the use of some of her pictures by the Bureau of Indian Affairs, and the illustration of two books. . . . However, the majority of the collection was never published, and only a few prints sold from a handful of exhibitions between 1940 and 1978. . . . Between 1945 and 1947, Helen and Rudi adopted two children, Peter and Marion, moved from New York City to rural Connecticut, and planned a spectacular house. . . . For the next twenty years Helen dedicated herself to being a mother and managing a country property. She raised two children and developed an interest in breeding German Shepherds with temperaments which made them good guide dogs for the blind. The family album, the children's schools, and various friends benefited from her high quality photography, but she undertook no professional assignments. . . . In the early 1970s Helen attempted to get back into her career. Because of nagging doubts about her ability to produce photographs of the same quality as her earlier work, she never followed through on a half-planned project to revisit her Indian subjects and photograph them or their descendants. Instead, she turned to

schemes to publish or display her existing work, none of which met with great success.

Two gifted and competitive sisters doing government-sponsored camera work in prewar America. Two sisters marrying extremely strong men who did stints in government. Two sisters letting go of their gift, one way or another, one force or another, one reason or another.

Through the years, Helen had stayed in close contact with her old Viennese teacher, Trude Fleischmann, who'd come to America during the war (partly at the urging of the two sisters) and later established a portrait studio at 127 West 56th Street in New York City. Eventually Sis and Trude lost touch: another link destroyed, or at least given up. Helen chose to hold on.

Toward the end of her life, just as Marion was being refound as an American photographer, Helen, unfound, had come back all the way with her little sister. After she made a trip to Syracuse to see an exhibit of her little sister's work, Helen generously wrote: "The show was fabulous, the whole space for it was the best location and just as we entered the first gallery to the right MARION WOLCOTT caught my eye. We were the first to arrive that morning, and spent all the time we needed to read and look and also to watch some more people. It is a very well used place." And from another letter, after the two had spent part of a day together: "Again, it was a fantastic few hours and thanks for yesterday, we know more about each other and must not let it escape us. I don't deserve the credit you expressed, I gladly accept your warmth & love and am especially proud of you. All you have been through now has an open channel and currents slowing with you, keep swimming—you are at a realization or the brink of it. Do what you feel. Alle Liebe. Helen."

In the final year of her life, Helen lost her sanity. She died of a stroke in a nursing home in Washington. But despite this report, a younger sister across the country would always carry a feeling inside her that Helen had somehow taken her own life.

The year Helen Post died, which is the same year the impulse arose to go to the next place, a feminist author from Australia, Germaine Greer, published a book about women painters called *The Obstacle Race*. "All women are tortured by contradictory pressures, but none more so than the female artist," Greer wrote in her final paragraphs. "Understanding how women artists sometimes led men, were plundered and overtaken, is an important part of recovering our history."

By 1980 Lee and Marion Wolcott were living in San Francisco. Part of the explanation for the uprooting can probably be attributed to the bad rains of Mendocino. Part of it seems to have been a desire to get closer to a real art community. San Francisco was the home of a Depression high school dropout and ex-housewife and world-class unprolific author named Tillie Olsen. Olsen had just written a quirky, beautiful book called *Silences*. From the opening: "What is it that happens with the creator, to the creative process, in that time? What *are* creation's needs for full functioning? ... I have had special need to learn all I could of this over the years, myself so nearly remaining mute and having to let writing die over and over again in me.... These are not *natural* silences—what Keats called *agonie ennuyeuse* (the tedious agony).... The silences I speak of here are unnatural: the unnatural thwarting of what struggles to come into being, but cannot. In the old, the obvious parallels: when the seed strikes stone; the soil will not sustain; the spring is false; the time is drought or blight or infestation; the frost comes premature." Olsen wondered on page after page about "the source or nature of this inexplicable draining self-doubt, loss of aspiration, of confidence."

Was there no artist's rage left inside, nothing unspoken and unattainable, no stay against all these sleepless nights? And yet ... what people seemed to be seeing in this woman, now a temporary San Franciscan, was a beautiful person.

Esquire magazine ran some photos of the Depression in a back-of-the-book piece called "Prevailing Images." They picked one of Marion's juke joint shots in Mississippi and put this caption on it: "Even in Mississippi they always thought tomorrow would come. One of them said, 'I always knew that if I didn't stumble, I could make myself win.'" Across the page was a picture of a small-town beauty parlor. It isn't Marion's, but these are the words printed underneath: "The women have moved great mountains, and yet many cannot understand their own strength. And some still doubt the beauty that walks within them."

In the East a pioneering Yale psychologist named Daniel Levinson was just beginning to study the lives of forty-five anonymous American women. He had already published a landmark book called *The Seasons of a Man's Life*. He was discovering women with two voices in them: "A perpetual state of conflict," he would later note.

American Photography magazine came to call.

Interviewer: In some ways you've been an orphan among the FSA
                 group. Less is known of you or your work than the others,
                 even now in the rediscovery period.

MPW: I never had time for that sort of thing, and I was usually
                 too far away.

Interviewer: In essence you raised kids, remodeled houses, helped farm,
                 taught school, and acted the role of the proper and useful
                 foreign service wife?

MPW: Indeed. At certain times I would take photographs, but I
                 didn't have any searing sense of loss because my life was too
                 full to take on major photographic projects. I always felt it
                 was there to return to.

Their handsome new condo was at 2265 Broadway in Pacific Heights, across from the Convent of the Sacred Heart. You could cut through the parish school grounds and stand on the edge of the slope and see Alcatraz Island, see the bay flecked with sailboats, see all the low, whitewashed pastel houses reaching down to the water as if you were in a Mediterranean village. Marion and her granddaughter Carey, Linda's child, stole flowers from people's yards, and ran away, and giggled at their thefts.

The Broadway apartment didn't do, though. Parking was bad. There were to be at least three relocations in San Francisco.

Marion's bronchitis worsened. She came down with pneumonia in the city's perpetual damp. She felt acutely ill. After a while it seemed an effort even to think of holding a camera and she wondered if she wasn't going through motions to please others. Just going near any of the chemicals used to develop and print photographs could knock her nearly to the floor. There were days—no, weeks—when she seemed wildly allergic even to handling certain kinds of prints.

F. Van Dern Coke, former director of photography at the San Francisco Museum of Modern Art: "I got to know them pretty well in that period. I had always admired her work, not least because I'm from Kentucky and she had shot there so brilliantly and sensitively. I think San Francisco was a pretty yeasty period for her. I think all of the renewed attention stirred something up in her. Maybe she said something to herself like, 'It's not over yet.' No, I never saw her taking any pictures in San Francisco. I didn't think it was my place to push her toward that. But she and Lee both attended a lot of openings. You'd see them at symposia and whatnot. She's such a charming person, people loved to be around her. For all her ills, she could light up a room. Lee was always there with her and seemed very enthusiastic. I don't recall him seeming threatened or pulling back from it in the least. I remember him being quite encouraging, as a matter of fact. I think part of the reason they left was because of that last place they had. It was a lovely three-story house on a little side street. They each had a darkroom. As I say, it was a wonderful house, but it got hard for her to climb the stairs."

By now Marion's work had gotten into the permanent collections of the Metropolitan Museum of Art, the Smithsonian, the Art Institute of Chicago, the Houston Museum of Fine Arts, the National Gallery of Canada, the International Center of Photography in New York, the George Eastman House in Rochester. But it was still only esthetes who knew her name, who loved her eye, who puzzled about what had happened to her career. Among photo historians and critics—the bulk of whom didn't actually know the Wolcotts—the conventional wisdom was that a husband had done it to his wife, and if this same man was now being very supportive and enthusiastic, it must be because he saw he was on the wrong side of history, couldn't stop the tide. It was all a rear-guard action. Well, that would be one theory.

St. Martin's Press put out its encyclopedic *Contemporary Photographers,* and here is part of what the entry on Marion says: "... gradually relinquished photography to bring up a family ... in a mere half-decade ... created a remarkable and diverse body of work, including some of the most powerful images in the vast FSA collection."

Two old married people went to the Southwest on a visit. Marion caught valley fever, a kind of fungal disease of the lungs. They left the Southwest, returned to San Francisco, put their place on the market, moved back to the same compound of apartments in Santa Barbara where they had lived fifteen years before when they first came back from overseas.

Maybe it was just them, their way, all this movement, these unexplained leave-takings and returnings. There is a John Cheever story, "The Bella Lingua." Somebody is explaining to somebody else that when you're in one place and would give anything to be in another, the remedy isn't as simple as taking a boat. Because you don't really long for another country, one of the characters is saying. "You look for something in yourself that you don't have, or haven't been able to find."

In 1983 the Friends of Photography in Carmel, California, published the first monograph of the work of Marion Post Wolcott, forty-eight pages long, thirty-three luminous prints. The book was put together by a young teacher, historian, and feminist named Sally Stein, who came to know Marion quite well and had traveled on her instincts to Washington to comb the FSA files and see just how wide a lost shooter's range had been. Marion was seventy-three years old when the monograph came out. At first she didn't want such a thing done. It was too late. But then she did an about-face. Yes, a monograph would be fine. These are the first nine words on the inside of the front cover: "This book is dedicated to my husband, Lee Wolcott." The rest of the dedication is to her old teacher, Ralph Steiner, himself a forgotten—or at least greatly neglected—American artist.

Several years later Marion gave a keynote address at a Women in Photography Conference at Syracuse University. Her husband was in a front row, tape-recording, snapshotting, beaming, cocking his thumb at her in approval and pride. Lee had helped work on the speech, given many hours to it, in fact. Marion's legs were shaking when she began, but she gained her confidence, and part of the reason was that when she had looked out, there was Lee. "Women are tough, supportive, sensitive, intelligent, and creative," the keynoter said. "They're survivors. Women have come a long way, but not far enough. Ahead still are formidable hurdles. Speak with your images from your heart and soul. Give of yourselves. Trust your gut reactions. Suck out the juices—the essence of your life experiences. Get on with it; it may not be too late."

Some while after, she was walking with her stepdaughter, Gail. Gail, an independent woman and spirit, had known so many heartaches in her life, always seeming to choose the wrong man. Just lately, though, as she had come over the top of fifty, Gail was feeling much better about herself and also better about her relationship with her father. For years she had been convinced the only way she could love this acutely intelligent and terribly difficult man was by keeping a continent between them. Now, though, daughter and father seemed to be finding the makings of a separate peace with each other. "Mommy, don't you finally think people do the best they can, and, well, for whatever reasons, it was probably that way with Daddy?" she said.

Like a flash from crumpled foil, an elderly woman shot out to her adopted child: "No, sweetie, I don't think he should be let off quite that easy." Right away, though, Marion Post Wolcott softened.

Minister, relatives, and friends of the deceased at a grave,
Breathitt County, Kentucky, 1940

FRAME SIX

THE LOST STONE OF A FRIEND

All our knowledge brings us nearer to our ignorance.

—T. S. ELIOT

IN THE SANTA BARBARA CONDO

A SUNDAY MORNING in July several years ago.

A thin, weary woman, suffering from neuropathy and low blood pressure and chronic respiratory problems and a weak hip and curvature of the spine and bladder disorders and about a half dozen other specified and unspecified ills, gets up from one end of the sofa and goes slowly over to where her octogenarian husband is sitting. She motions for his glasses in the way a mother might motion for something from a recalcitrant child. "How can you see through these things, Lee?" she says in that strained and almost singsongy voice I have come to be oddly charmed by these last three days. There is a kind of disgust in her tone but unmistakable affection, too. She exhales on the lenses, polishes them with the tail of her blouse (she has yanked her shirt from her trousers for the chore), hands the glasses back, then returns to where she was sitting a moment ago when she had interrupted herself.

"Thanks, babe," Lee Wolcott says, smiling back at her.

And I write down in my notebook, trying to make it seem as if I'm really recording something else: *See, of course they love each other, you idiot. It's got to be more complicated than what you came out here believing, that he just crushed her, that he just made her give it up back then, one way or another, subtly or with no subtlety at all, broke her creative spirit because he was too threatened by it. No, no, her choices must have been at work in this all along, too.*

And as I am writing, Marion says to me, returning to something I had asked her at least five minutes ago: "Yes, I worry about them terribly. I sweat about them. I have nightmares about all of them, in fact." She means her children.

"You have nightmares about them?" I say casually, trying to get her to go on.

"Well, yes, sometimes," she says, dropping it there.

And I write this down: *See, it was her maternal instinct, how much she loved her family. The biological pull. Follow that.*

She is no sooner into her seat than she rises again, with obvious difficulty, and goes a bit stiff-leggedly across the room to retrieve a greeting card from a bookshelf. She has the uneven gait and slight list of someone who long ago might have carried heavy equipment as a part of her work. "Here," she says, bringing the card over. "It's from my granddaughter Robin in San Diego. I'd rather get something like this any day from one of my children or grandchildren than be able to take one hundred good photographs, I don't care how wonderful they might be or how important somebody in the art world might think they are or what that would prove about me." It is said a little defensively but with force and conviction, too.

This is the message on the inside of the card:

> Dear Grandmommy:
>   A somewhat sad thing happened to me the other day, but I want to share it with you anyway. I watched a movie that forced me to think about the day when my grandparents were no longer around. I was devastated for the rest of the night, crying myself to sleep. I know it's a long way away from now (yes, it is) but I really came to know how much you mean to me. I want you two to live forever! I want you to be my grandkids' grandparents! I love you so much, Grandmommy. I hope you understand how much. I hope this year leaves you with some wonderful memories. I hope I can be there to share some of them.

Her feet are propped on a low coffee table, ankles crossed. She's in flat sandals and cream-colored pants and brown hose, which I think are support hose. Her necklace is made of turquoise. On Friday, when I got here, she had on a cranberry-colored string of beads lying against a lovely turquoise-colored blouse. I've come to understand there's something loose, flinty, leggy, profane, cussed, witty, flirty, gutsy, and thoroughly modern about this woman, the hell with all her wrinkles, the hell with all her age, the hell with how fragile and uncertain and infirm but most of all weary she seems.

But what is this weariness? A kind of cover for some deep-down unbelievable and never-quite-expressed rage? Well, maybe. And maybe not. And at whom would such a rage be directed primarily, if not her husband? And maybe it isn't rage at all I am sensing. Maybe her weariness is . . . weariness.

Her beauty breaks me from these thoughts. She reminds me in some ways of Katharine Hepburn, although the two don't really look alike. Her lips are glossed with rose lipstick, and there are smart little gold rings in her ears. Her hands are clasped behind her neck, and she's just fluffed up the back of her hair. The sleeves of her blouse are shoved up past her knobby elbows. I think I've come down with a monster crush on her. Probably I got it that first redemptive moment when I stood in the Library of Congress basement holding in my hand a photograph entitled "Snowy Night, Woodstock, Vermont." She's close to eighty, and I'm in my forties, and she's been married to the man on the other end of the sofa for almost half a century and besides that she's a great-grandmother. Not exactly what I'd have in mind were I trying to wreck my own marriage and run off with another woman.

But still.

A minute flicks by. Half a century flicks by. An old and unwell but somehow oddly vital woman in a one-story Santa Barbara condominium is tapping one of her prints against her temple. There is a kind of deep staring-off quality about her, yet she seems to be missing very little. It's as if her skin has a light box under it this morning; there's such a fine, white, soft, almost parchment texture to it. She looks candled, haloed, with— what? Well, indefinable sadnesses, confusions, regrets. As if she doesn't quite understand what could have happened to a part of her life that she now recognizes as crucial, as integral. Or am I imagining it this way because I want it this way? And, if I am not imagining it, if my feelings are even halfway to the mark, could it also be possible that she now sees this missing part as the crucial part because people such as myself are coming to her door, rediscovering her, telling her—in her husband's presence— how incredibly powerful her work is?

For the past three days, the elderly and quite beautiful Mrs. Marion Wolcott and her equally aged and arresting husband and I have been circling the same awkward questions, the same painful issues, never quite coming to rest with any of them, each of us, I think, being a little dishonest with our feelings, a little afraid of coming out and saying bluntly the real thing: *So why did you stop, Marion? How could you have stopped, Marion? What happened here, in this life, in this family, was there a huge injustice done? I want to know the secrets.* That is what I wish to say but can come nowhere close to saying. None of us, I think, has been able to come out and say what is at the center of our being. And yet these issues are before us; we are talking of them, or around them. It's as if something spiritlike has passed into the room.

And Marion says: "You see, I didn't want to give up my work. Not really. I loved learning how people lived. I was learning about the world. I was learning about social issues in the real world. I guess I thought of myself as being able to use photography as a tool for social reform. I guess I thought of myself as something of an artist, yes. And, look, I was pretty good at photography. I was exhilarated by it. It was a kind of living on the edge for me. Oh, I was exhausted, yes. Oh, I was sick of it in a certain sense. I didn't have any love, any affection, and I had been used to that. Practically no sex life whatsoever. I was always so torn when I had to go back out on the road after being in for a while—although I liked it once I got out there again. And, yes, I had fallen pretty passionately in love with a passionate man. Let's face it, Lee and I really didn't know each other when we got married. I thought I was going to be a Washington bureaucrat's wife. Ha."

The man on the sofa: "I just don't think when she left FSA, Marion had any idea of the greatness—of either FSA or her own work. That's something for you to remember. It all happened afterward. She knew she was good, sure. But did she think she was 'great'? I don't think so. If she had known that at the time, that might have changed—"

Marion, interrupting: "You see, I guess I believed back then, or was supposed to believe, that my place was in the home, that I couldn't do both, you know, be a photographer, a would-be artist, and try to raise children. It just wasn't as easy in those days."

A little later I say: "When was the last time you tried to take a serious photograph, Marion, you know, something you felt compelled to shoot, something you knew had magic in it, that you were dying for the world to see?"

She doesn't answer, just shrugs. Lee answers for her. "You shot some pretty things on that drive up the coast a while back, didn't you, sweet-heart?"

"Oh, I was just sort of imitating other people for the hell of it," she says. "They were terrible and you know it." The briefest flash of something.

There is another silence in the room, and again I try to fill it, not with any aplomb. "Is it possible, Marion, you knew all the pieces for a lasting kind of work were in the right places on the chessboard, and that they'd never quite come together in this way again, and that, well, you just stopped, maybe because you didn't think you could be that good again?"

"Well, yes, a little, maybe," she says.

But now returning to an earlier thread, and with more softness than before: "And probably underneath all of this, I think both of us believed that if we were away from each other for long periods and if we had extracurricular affairs—let's put it that way—that the family would break up. And I think we had an agreement about it. I don't know that we ever spelled it out as such, but we did have a sort of pact between us. I'd seen so many of my friends who had poor or weak marriages. And I'd come from so much of that myself, with my own parents and all. I vowed if I ever got married, I'd never get divorced."

Facing the strong-willed man Marion Post married in 1941, I ask, prob-ably reddening a little, because I can't help thinking of an even-longer-ago small-town Jersey doctor and father named Walter Post, "Lee, do you think you understood enough that your wife had a deeply creative tem-perament and needed, in intensive ways, to be able to find outlets for it?"

"In the beginning, not as much as I should have," he says evenly.

There's something almost doctorish about Lee Wolcott. In this sense: *I can fix it.* He can't be over five-foot-six now. He's wearing a blue Angora sweater on top of a green polo shirt, and he's been out walking already this morning—two miles up a hill. Long, uncombed, shock-white hair flops over his large ears. He could pass for some bohemian painter or filmmaker out of the socialist thirties.

And yet ... I've begun to notice how his eyes will suddenly cloud up and moisten over when he is speaking of certain things in his or Marion's past. He blows his nose a lot. Despite my awkwardness and feelings of wariness, I've come to like Marion Post Wolcott's husband a good deal in the past forty-eight hours, to reappraise some of my early prejudices, which in some cases I wasn't even fully aware I had. In fact, I think I'm feeling certain small kinships with him now, which strikes me as almost comic, because I think I had come out here ready to slay him figuratively, avenge something. When I told Lee earlier this morning that I thought he was a gentleman and that he had treated me courteously during my stay, especially in view of some of the things I'd been stumbling to ask, he suddenly said, "You mean you've decided I'm not the villain of the piece?" We'd both laughed at that—and not gone on with it.

When I first got here on Friday, Lee seemed to be trying to control everything, monitor every word out of his wife's mouth—or at least this was the powerful impression I had. Indeed, long before I got here, it seemed to me he was attempting to control everything that might or might not transpire during my visit. Every time I'd called in the past few weeks, trying to arrange a time to fly out and see his wife, Lee had gotten on the phone. Usually he had picked it up first, and if not, he had made sure to get on the extension. Sometimes he would announce himself, other times just listen in until Marion said something to him. I had the feeling of a man's hand resting lightly on my metaphorical throat. *Let me pass on the message, no need for me to get Marion* always seemed to be the message within the message when just Lee and I were on the phone. "Why don't you let her speak for herself?" I had wanted to blurt out but of course hadn't. It is absolutely true he had always summoned his wife from another part of the house as soon as I asked for her. (Often as not she had found her own way to the phone, and then there would be a seriocomic moment of three people trying to speak at once.) Is it possible he was just trying to preserve Marion's strength?

I had arrived much later on Friday than I had intended (freak thunderstorm in Minneapolis that canceled my flight), and when I called from Los Angeles to say I had rented a car and would be driving straight up to Santa Barbara, Lee had said, right over the top of Marion, "Well, I suppose you might as well come on, as long as you're here."

And yet . . . when we went out to lunch in their BMW at a restaurant on Saturday, I noticed how Marion was nagging Lee on his driving, on his momentary loss of direction. And he had taken it, or most of it. She had on an old floppy linen hat and she walked behind him with a cane when we got out of the car, but she was nagging, all right. It didn't quite fit in with my picture of the bullied wife, the crushed spirit.

On the drive to the restaurant, Marion had brought up her peripheral neuropathy, a degenerative disease of the nerves. "It gives me tingling," she said. "Stabbing. Dizziness. Agoraphobia—in mild doses." Lee had looked down, not the safest thing for a driver to do.

At the restaurant, overlooking the Pacific, we had drifted to various subjects, and I kept noting how Marion seemed prone to correct her husband on about anything that came up.

"Probably the only explanation for our moving out into the country for good was a romantic one," Lee said. "The back-to-the-land business. We were going to raise our family in the good pure air of Virginia farmland."

Marion: "I think I knew in some sense that would end in a more formal way my photography."

Lee, frowning: "In fact, Marion found that first farm in Lovettsville for us."

Marion: "Well, not exactly."

Lee, turning: "What do you mean, sweetheart."

Marion, going ahead: "You couldn't buy it because you were working. You had me find it because you didn't have time."

Lee: "Well, yes."

It went on like this. Marion took out of her purse a small faded snapshot of her sister to show me what Helen Post had looked like as a young art student in Austria. The figure in the photograph had on pants and boyish socks and banded moccasins and was sitting on a balcony in the countryside. I studied this sepia image, trying to see Marion in it as well, and then said, without thinking about it, "Boy, she's interesting—and men were attracted to her, I suppose?"

"Yes, and women, too," Marion said.

Lee had shot her a look, she had reddened, had seemed almost disoriented, but then went ahead. "I suppose if she were growing up now she would have been an active lesbian."

She added, slowly: "Helen was the sort who always tried to boss me around when I was growing up. That's why it didn't really"—she tilted her head ever so slightly in the direction of her husband—"work with Lee."

We got off it.

And yet . . . later, back at the house, when Marion and I were looking at some of the lovely detail in one of her old FSA photographs, she said, pointing to an antique piece of office equipment, "I wonder what in the hell that thing is." Lee had heard this, come over, peered at the picture, and then said, "It's a check writer, babe. Don't you remember those?" She had nearly dug me in the ribs. "I told you he'd know," she whispered, almost exultantly, as if no other man on the planet save the one she had married could have come up with the right answer.

And at another point yesterday, when Marion was describing for the two of us what it felt like to pull into one more of those damnable three-dollar tourist courts with their quaint bark-lashed beds, knowing you had to get a wire off to Washington and reload your equipment and on and on, Lee had chimed in with: "And, say, as regards this thing about having to wash out her socks every night, I mean, okay, she's lonely enough out there, she's tired as hell, she's living totally on her own resources, and yet she still has to do this wash so she can look presentable in the morning, I mean, it's a small thing, but this was way before synthetics, you know." He said it as if he wanted me to be sure and make a note of that small fact, get it in, in whatever I wrote.

Late yesterday, having talked to both of them for long periods over two days, I had gone back to my hotel room feeling confused and vaguely depressed. The phone rang. It was Marion. She said Lee was out for a walk, and she wanted to elaborate on some things. It felt funny to me. She did elaborate on some things and then brought up several new things. "I don't sleep so well," she said. "So I go to bed late. Maybe I sounded groggy to you today." I told her she hadn't.

She spoke again about how quickly she had fallen in love with her husband back then. "Couple of times on the farm . . ." she said, letting sentences fade. "In those first few years. There was a lot of . . . struggle. I think about eight or nine years in—no, maybe even earlier than that, but certainly by then, too . . . I think we were . . . questioning, realizing certain things about each other that might not be changed. Not that we didn't care for each other deeply." She seemed to break off this last sentence cold, and for an instant I had the not totally irrational fear that her husband had come back into the house.

We talked on. It continued to feel funny—though not funny enough for me to hang up. Marion wanted me to know—I'm convinced of it—what some people from those FSA years think of her husband: not much. She said: "There was this one reunion of all the FSA crowd—oh, there have been several reunions through the years, one in Florida a couple years ago that we got to, and so forth—but for one reason or another I didn't get to this particular one that I have in mind. Some people will tell you that this has happened several times and that it's always because of Lee, that he's kept me from going, that he doesn't want me to attend. Well, maybe that happened once. A lot of people from back then don't really know much about our lives. Of course, most of those FSA people would be dead now, although a couple are around."

We kept talking. She spoke of her dead sister, Helen. "You see, Helen never really liked Lee. I think she thought Lee was partly responsible ... for what happened." The "what happened" came out almost listlessly. She mentioned an exhibit at a New York gallery and how her sister had pressed her to attend. "I don't remember which one it was. Maybe it was that big one at the Witkin Gallery in the seventies, I forget. But anyway I convinced myself I should have this tumor removed from my leg that very week. Well, you see, once again Helen could only understand that as Lee." I wasn't sure what she meant, though I think she was speaking of the subtle forces of persuasion and manipulation by one's partner.

"You wouldn't have been able to stay with a man who was overtly repressing you, would you?" I said.

"Of course not." There was something so emphatic, almost incredulous, in it.

THAT WAS YESTERDAY. Right now we're looking at pictures.

We've been doing it for nearly an hour, luxuriating in them, holding over this one, passing up that one, just letting talk come, or in some cases not come. An old woman's voice, like an old woman's memory, is going in and out. The prints, dozens of them, unmounted, selenium-toned, archival in quality, no doubt worth thousands of dollars on the current art market, are sitting in a large blue box on a white Formica table before us. She takes each one out, holds it flimsily at the edges: drifts, drowses, tries to recollect.

Ancient shooter, dreaming.

"Now, this was an itinerant peddler in Vermont. He went door to door selling hardware, groceries, things like that. I just liked him, I guess."

She turns it over, picks up the next.

"This woman had TB. [See page 68.] I think she was living in an abandoned store. It was in West Virginia, down near Welch, on that first trip I made for Roy. I can see the road in, I can see her leaning over that railing talking to me. There may have been four or five families living in that store. They were all piled together. She's pretty erotic, isn't she? I probably

Young cotton pickers waiting to be paid in Marcella plantation store, Mileston, Mississippi, 1939

admired that. I knew immediately I wanted to shoot her. There was just
something about her. She was so beaten down by life and yet there was all
this sexuality in her, not just sexuality but sensuality. I talked to her for a
while and then I went on. But I knew I had it."

A second later: "Oh, I used to tell people things I didn't believe at all.
Anything practically. Outrageous things. Flatter them. Flirt with them.
Just to get them to hold still so I could shoot it."

She puts it down, goes to the next.

"These Negro boys. Their bodies are so beautiful, the way they're
draped along this wooden bench. Look at how natural their clothing is. It
just seems to flow off their bodies. This one here is like a dancer. I suppose
that's what I saw, what I wanted to shoot. It was how elegant they were
without really knowing it."

The fingertips of her right hand have begun to touch several of the faces
in the photograph. She is moving in a kind of elegant slow motion—does
she know? Her fingers are grazing the faces. At her elbow is a bottle of
Long's Oyster Shell Calcium pills. Also a box of Betaine Hydrochloride
tablets, whatever they are. Also pills I think she takes for breathing.

"Now, I call this 'The Hepcats' Jalopy.' I've got shorthand names for a
lot of my pictures. I took it in downtown Louisville. I think it's been
printed in a couple of books. I must've liked all that writing on the doors
and hood. 'Ladies Enter Here.' And 'Cicero the Dope.' Ha. I probably was
just walking by when I saw it."

The next. It's that county fair harness race in Kentucky, the one she
crumpled in her Mendocino rage and threw in the wastebasket. I've given
a name to it: "Bending Out."*

She studies the people in the print, all those railbirds rooting home their
nags. "All the kinds of hats," she says, "look at all the different hats." She

---

*It's become one of my favorites, and a signed print of it hangs now in my kitchen,
but I should say that for a long while there were two things about the photograph
that didn't make any sense to me: Why are the horses running the wrong way? And
why aren't they hanging at the inside rail? In America harness and thoroughbred
races proceed counterclockwise. And the shortest distance to a finish line, any turf
rat knows, is via the inside rail. This can't be a warm-up run or a parade around the
track before the real thing: These boys are whipping and driving in their spindly
little carts. Nor is the picture reversed, which was my first thought.

I went to the Library of Congress and studied the dozen or so other sulky-race squints at a soldier with his coat off who seems to be leaning on a cane. "Was he wounded?" She lets go of the picture and mimes the position of the soldier's hand. "Yes, that's how you would lean on a cane."

Lee comes over. He places his hands on the back of her chair, leans down, as though perhaps to kiss his wife. He's just put Beethoven on the stereo. In profile this morning, Lee looks like an aged and fierce and proud and scrinched-up hawk. This man and wife seem very much in love. I am the intruder in their lives.

"What are they doing in this one, babe? Trading horses?"

"Yes, it was court day."

He stays for several more. The next one in the box is the hand—the *hand*—reaching through the wire-meshed Mississippi pay window.

"There's his brown-bag lunch," Lee says, pointing to the paymaster.

"I'll bet he's got a donut in it," says Marion. The line cracks her up.

"He's about to take another drag on his Lucky, isn't he?" says Lee.

"I suspect an Old Gold," says Marion.

"Look at that crisp little sheet where the bastards are checking off names," says Lee. "How much do you suppose was in the envelopes?"

"Look at the satin on the back of the Number two," says Marion. "He's fixing his tie."

---

shots Marion made at the Mercer County Fairgrounds in Harrodsburg that August day in 1940. In one frame she'd caught a wider view of the wooden grandstand, with its lettered advertisements for Bluegrass Pharmacal (on Greenville Street), for Chancellor's Men's Shop, for McNamer Bakery, for Smalley's Tourist Home. Below the signs, in a grandstand box, there was a substantial-looking man. Beneath him was a banner asking the electorate to vote: "Happy Chandler, U.S. Senate." He was a great Kentuckian. Later he'd become commissioner of baseball.

No clues to riddles, though. One day I called up Frank T. Phelps, venerable Kentucky racing scribe. I described the picture, told him about the woman who'd taken it long ago. "Interesting story," he said. "Those little country tracks liked doing things their own way. Maybe they just decided to alternate it that day, run it back toward the grandstand. I never heard of a harness race going clockwise. I'd guess the reason they're not on the inside rail is because they weren't running it on a banked surface. This was just a little old fairground track. On a flat surface any horse tends to drift out. That's what the rider is for, to keep him from swinging off the rail. Probably didn't make much difference to the outcome anyway."

I told him it didn't make a difference to my love of the picture anyway. I said I'd send him a copy of it, and I did.

Sulky races, Mercer County, Kentucky, 1940

*Country peddler who goes from door to door selling hard-
ware and groceries, Woodstock, Vermont, 1940*

"The Hepcats' Jalopy." Transportation for hepcats,
Louisville, Kentucky, 1940

"You know it wasn't enough," says Lee. He means the money in the envelope.

"It was good there was light coming from here," Marion says, tracing a line with her fingers. "You know, to outline the hand."

"It's a wonderful picture," says Lee.

She goes to the next: "Picnic. Winter visitors picnicking on running board of car on beach, Sarasota, Florida, 1941." The Museum of Modern Art has a print in its permanent collection, along with seven other Wolcotts. What I love about this picture, in addition to everything else, is that Marion got a reflection of the deck chair in the car's glossy fender. There's a kind of surreal quality about the photograph: pale people against a black car on white sand.

"So which one do you suppose that poor guy's married to?" says Lee.

"I don't know, but aren't you just sure all three of those women have beat him down?" says Marion.

"You're in fine fettle this morning," he says.

"Drunk," she says. "Well, the Valium I took."

He wanders off; he'll be back in a while.

I say, "How did you manage to shoot so much? You must have been jumping from the car with the engine running half the time?"

"That's what I want to know—and why? It's almost as if I was note-taking in some instances. I suppose I was. What the land looked like, the way the river went. I guess I was just making a record, for my head, in case I wanted to come back someday. I mean, some of it wouldn't be very interesting at all, except historically perhaps."

She's been looking off from the picture in her hand. Now she comes back. It's a Western shot, panoramic, beautiful. I've never seen it. The caption on the back is her handwriting, all right, shaky, but the same loops and slants to the left, same as fifty years ago.

But the date is wrong. I say, "I don't think you were in Montana in nineteen thirty-nine, Marion. You just went out west once in your FSA career, in forty-one, right after you married Lee, remember?"

"Oh, shit. You're right. Where's the g.d. eraser? I don't know about time. Oh, I've just lived too longggggg."

The next print is of the shooter herself, coming through a barbed-wire fence in Vermont. She's wearing an old camel coat and a funny-looking woolen stocking cap. Her grin is almost snaggletoothed. A bang of hair is

"Picnic." Winter visitors on running board of car on beach, Sarasota, Florida, 1941

falling down in her eyes. She's cradling her Speed Graphic and another piece of equipment. Who could resist this woman?

"That smaller camera is a Rollei, a two-and-a-quarter by two-and-a-quarter Rollei. Well, I think it's a Rollei. I've been wondering if I took the picture, set it up on a tripod or something and then went back around and came through the fence. A little of my own publicity. Mmmm, I don't think so, though, because for one thing, I never used a thirty-five millimeter on a tripod. Maybe I had a friend take it. Maybe somebody was with me. Maybe I put it on a rock or something and used that—what's that little time gadget called? Time release. Yes. Maybe I used a time release. Or did they even have them then?"

She gets up, goes out into the kitchen, pulls out a drawer, gets several bags of snacks. The bags, previously opened, very wrinkly, are tied at the neck with rubber bands. She undoes the bands, pours out a mixture of the food into a ceramic dish, stirs it around with one hand. She then comes back to her seat, positions the bowl between us, ties up the bags, puts them beneath her chair. I am trying not to laugh: this wheezy old California bag lady with her moldy rubber-banded pretzels and blue tortilla chips.

She wipes her hands on a cloth, returns to the box.

"I've always been fond of this one. She was the wife of a muskrat trapper. In bayou country, in Louisiana. Look at how she's holding up those two muskrats, as if they were prize turkeys or something. They probably were to her. We had to go over in a boat that night. The regional supervisor took me, and I stayed to dinner. I had a little wine before dinner. I think I was enjoying myself. They were already drinking red wine by the time I got there. They'd finished their work. I didn't know what they were going to have for dinner, but obviously it was muskrat, cooked in wine, red wine, and garlic, lots of garlic. The FSA supervisor down there, George Wolf, he knew them, and took me over. It was wonderful eating, believe me. I suppose I also wanted to stay around in hopes of getting more stuff. That was always in the back of your mind, of course. I'm glad I didn't have to go alone that night. I might have had trouble getting away."

"But weren't they all trying to pick you up—even those gas jockeys wiping their faces on their sleeves when they came out to pump?" I ask.

She considers this. Her right hand is pulling at the back of her hair, almost yanking at it, as if she'd like to take it out in clumps. "Not so much, actually. You generally knew what to say. They were curious about me, all right. They'd bribe the bellboys to find out what room you were in. Sales-

*Cutting crested wheat grass with an old binder pulled by
a four-horse team, Judith Basin, Montana, 1941*

men would see me coming through the lobby and follow me up the stairs."

Pause. "I had a close call in Kentucky once. A guy got in my bed. 'Who's going to know?' he said. 'Everybody's going to know,' I said, 'because I'm going to start screaming bloody murder if you don't get out of here.' He got out. I think he was some county agricultural agent or other who'd been showing me around that day. I probably put a chair against the door or something."

"But, really, who could resist you?"

She emits a grunt.

THEIR DAUGHTER LINDA is coming down the walk with her boyfriend, Bob. They have been out on a Sunday drive. The parents get up and embrace their child hugely, as if they haven't seen her for weeks when actually they see her almost every day. Linda, in her forties, is an attorney who is also an extremely caring and protective daughter. She is slender, raven-haired, striking. I am getting a focused picture of Marion Post of half a lifetime ago. At length I manage to bring up the subject Linda's mother and father and I have encircled for the better part of three days. Linda is nervous. She knows what this is about. *I* am nervous.

"Daddy wasn't pushing her out the door, that's for sure," she says. "There was some resistance there, I could sense it, yes, I suppose it would have been a little threatening to his ego."

Linda's boyfriend, addressing Marion: "So it was a conflict for you?" He, too, is a lawyer. What is this, "Divorce Court," and the witnesses are now testifying under oath because of my subpoenas? I wish I were back at my hotel. I wish I were back in Washington looking at drawers of lovely old FSA pictures. This seems mean. Whose business is it? I should have let the whole thing lie. I've pushed it too far. They should kick me out of here.

"Yes . . . occasionally, Bob," Marion says.

Linda: "I knew she was a photographer. An artist. I didn't know her reputation was going to evolve as it has. I always felt she had a . . . a kind of a compulsion to do this." She turns to her mother, talking quietly. "You know, Mommy, I have really all my life felt a great deal of comfort, of empathy, with your pictures. Not just daughter to mother, but woman to woman. I mean, watching you always with a camera around your neck when we were growing up. I can remember you saying so many times to Daddy, 'Pull over, pull over, I see something.'"

Wife of muskrat trapper, bayou country, 1941

After Linda and Bob are gone, and when Marion is in another part of the house, Lee says to me, his eye contact very steady: "What was lost, Paul?" He is back on the sofa again, stretched out, an attorney taking up for himself, but in another sense just asking the question, like Aristotle.

"Well, I've heard it said that maybe Marion would eventually have left documentary work and gone into landscape photography," I say, "so in that sense maybe another Ansel Adams or Edward Weston was lost—but then we have an Adams and a Weston, don't we, Lee?"

I say this all in one breath, my eye contact not steady at all.

"Yes, we have Adams and Weston."

"We'll never know, will we?" I say.

"We'll never know," he says.

ENDINGS

FIVE MONTHS PASSED. And then on a December day, my eye contact still unsteady, I got on a plane and went back to Santa Barbara and to the house on Pedregosa Street and spent another long, lovely, lingering afternoon with Marion and Lee. As always they were gracious people, though of course some of the old barriers and controls and cautions were up, especially in Lee. Why shouldn't they have been up? I certainly didn't know everything about Marion's life or work by then (nor do I have any notion I know everything about her life and work now), but at least I knew enough to go back and try to ask them both several questions I had been too afraid to ask in that first three-day visit.

I went back with the feeling I would never be able to repay an old, beautiful woman in kind, but only somewhere else in life. I went back not with any sense of romantic doom—not Marion's, not my own concerning a book I could not write when I most wanted to write it. As it turned out, I was to keep on traveling to old Wolcott photographic haunts long after this visit, was to keep on discovering new things about her life, was to continue trying in my disheveled ways to solve the unsolvable riddle. But by my second visit to their home, which came shortly before Christmas that year, I could already feel the buoyance that continues in me to this moment.

The first time I had gone to California, I was operating on such a distorted conviction: that the only real art was what Marion had finished, had left behind, early in 1942. The original question in my mind had been: What possibly could be powerful enough to erase the compulsion to create once you're on this level? And the answer, I saw now, was that there can be hundreds of things.

I had been so damn worried about myself in the beginning. I was so scared that if I ceased working on something that was supposed to be my "major professional success" that my writing life—really, I should call it no more than my journalistic life—would be over for good. That I'd never again be able to finish, let alone undertake, anything remotely in a creative vein. And what Marion's life had begun to reveal to me even before I went back to visit her that second time—and reveal it to me in almost existential ways, the ways of being—is that such thinking is bunk.

Marion lasted with Lee, and vice versa, and there is a kind of art in that. It's not art that will ever hang in museums. It's closer to the art of a rickets child named Jerry Little coming down his scabbed hill in North Carolina to get a look at a government lady photog's box.

What I couldn't see before, or at least was unable to focus on with any clarity, is that Marion has a fine extended family—yes, much-married and much-divorced—but all of whose members have loved her deeply. That, too, is art, and not in the least a narcissistic one. I have almost never received a letter from Marion where she isn't telling me what various of her kids and grandkids are doing. Just lately I have begun to think of the basic unfairness of overweighting her FSA life. It was only three years.

To hell with Ernest Hemingway and his pat sentiment that if we win here, we win everywhere, and if we lose here, we lose everywhere. What has become much more meaningful to me is a line from an old French movie, *A Man and a Woman*. I remember a question being posed in that beautiful sixties film, as two lovers walk hand in hand on the French coast: If your house were on fire and if you had the chance to rush in and save either the one true piece of lasting artwork you own, or your dog, which would you choose? And the answer, of course, is your dog. Because between art and life, what is finally far better is life.

Before going back to see Marion and Lee for the second time, I spoke by phone with John Wolcott, an ionospheric physicist in New Mexico. He is also the stepson who never knew as he grew up that Marion wasn't his real mother. Gail, the eldest, knew almost from the first. Here is part of what John told me about Marion:

"She never let on the whole time that I wasn't her real child. . . . What I'm saying is that she was determined to be our real mother to the best of her ability. I think that says a lot about what you're searching for. I can hardly imagine a better mother. My perception of their lives together is that she was desperately in love with my father. That's from everything I know, and I have no reason to lie. And something else: My father has had to try to grow in all this. It cannot be easy. He's a terribly strong man, a terribly proud man. I think for him to be able to step back now and let his wife be in the front row, get attention, after all those years on the farm and everywhere else, the Foreign Service and their other travels, when he was so dominant, when he was so totally in charge of everything—well, I think for him to be able to attempt to do that, at least a little now, shows a real growth, real strength. And I assure you, he is very proud of her work."

On the flight across the country, I wrote this, among other things, in my notebook: *The light failed. But maybe the life won. And yet I wonder what goes through her mind when she's in a bookstore and comes on a book of Ansel Adams' or maybe Henri Cartier-Bresson's. The hurt must be awesome. I don't know, maybe she wasn't ruthless enough as an artist. Is this to be despised? She chose not to put her work above everything else—or at least a part of her chose to do that. . . . When you add up all the reasons, there's still her sadness, the loss. But it's okay now, no, it's a lot more than okay, because it's who she is, it's her humanity, it's both their humanities, and there is a hard-won beauty in it, all right.*

"He's always bragging on me," an old shooter said almost as soon as I got inside the door. I had driven straight up again from Los Angeles. The Pacific, on my left as I sped, was blue as Appalachian crockery. I passed a migrant town called Camarillo where the winter produce was coming up fine. In Washington it was forty degrees and raining. When I got into the city limits of Santa Barbara, I stopped at a store to buy the object of my affections a single long-stemmed rose. When I gave it to her, Marion rose to get the vase, had filled the vase with water, but then sort of got lost in the rest of it. It wasn't for a long time afterward that I learned that roses are the one flower that really affected her allergies and asthma.

Lee was in the other room when I arrived. He was loading the dishwasher. He had done the grocery shopping that day. He had an apron tied around his waist.

On the white table was a half-filled bowl of floating pink blossoms.

There was also a camera on the table. "Oh, that," she said. "It's an old German view camera. This complete stranger from San Luis Obispo called me up and raved and said, 'Look, we can't just let this wither. You have to take this camera I'm going to send you, and you have to go out. It's very small and easy. All you need is your eye and you've always had that.'"

She finished a story. "As I say, he's always bragging on me. We went to a camera store the other day. I was getting him a camera for Christmas. The guy said he needed some identification. And I said, 'My husband has a driver's license and can it serve for both of us?' And Lee piped up and said, 'Identification? Why, she's Marion Post Wolcott, she's an important American photographer.' And, you know, I just got so furious at him."

Lee came in from the kitchen. I cleared my throat. "Lee, if Marion had come to you back then and said directly that she had to leave you and the family to pursue her work, that it meant her survival in some sense, would you have said no?"

"I was so deeply in love with her, that I can't imagine my saying no," he said.

"He would not have forbidden it, no—" Marion said.

"—I don't think I would have liked it," he cut in.

"You're damn right you wouldn't have liked it. And you would have been very persuasive," she said.

"But how could you have liked it, you weren't an eighties man back then, Lee?" I said.

"Oh, in some ways I was an eighties man in the nineteen forties," he said, laughing.

"You were no eighties man," she said quickly, "and I was no eighties woman, either." She was looking directly at him. "You would not have handled your children in the way you did then. Your whole willful, forceful personality."

"If you would not have forbidden it, Lee," I said, "do you regret that you could not encourage her more?"

"No," he said flatly. "And I want Marion to hear this. Babe? The answer is no. That just wouldn't have been me. And I say that loving you with everything that's in me."

"Marion," I said, again feeling invasive, feeling awkward, "what about *your* choices? What if Lee had been an entirely different Lee? What I mean is, are you angry at yourself? I didn't have the courage, exactly, to ask you this last time."

She answered slowly. "I admit to that. By the time I would have thought

it was okay to go out, I guess I didn't have the confidence. I was afraid. I
didn't know I could do as good a job as I once had. I was afraid I wouldn't
be able to carry off an assignment. I mean, all of us who were in FSA had
standing offers at *LOOK* or *LIFE*. I think I was deeply afraid. I think I
was afraid I couldn't really be free of my family. You know, once you have
children, I wonder if you can ever really be free again. Maybe some people
can. And yet I wanted to try to go out. I wanted to be an artist again. . . .
Now whether or not I actually would have gone out, had somebody come
along and offered me a job, I just don't know. . . . I'm sorry, I was . . . I was
just afraid."

Her old voice, probably like her fine old bones, cracked on this, though
just a little and the recovery was swift.

Later that day we spent time looking through some of her pictures
again, but not the FSA ones. She took out one I had never seen before. It
was in black and white and blown up large. It was in a large box of snapshots and 8 × 10s. "He ordered me!" she whispered, coming close. "He
instructed me last night to get out a bunch of pictures for you that had
nothing to do with FSA." She handed the photograph to me. It had very
little magic, and I think she knew, and couldn't say.

"This picture is so special to me. Lee and I were on a trip. We parked
our VW camper up there on that little hill and made love outdoors."

Lee went to the other room and came back with a letter. "I've just sent
this off," he said, handing it to me. The letter was addressed to a respected
FSA scholar, F. Jack Hurley, who'd also been engaged in writing about
Marion. He'd come to California and interviewed both Wolcotts. Although he was primarily interested in her work and how it fit into the
FSA scheme of things, he couldn't write about Marion's work without
getting into difficult parts of biography, namely, the decades of artistic silence. The professor had agreed to show the Wolcotts what he wrote and
get their basic assent to the manuscript. After Lee had read an early draft,
he wrote a scorching letter (never mailed), arguing aspects of the text point
by point. One of his chief points was that it had been Marion's idea, far
more than his, to move to a farm shortly after their marriage and that all
the subsequent stopping had really arisen because of this unforeseen isolation. Lee had brought the letter to Marion, and when she read it, she
refused to sign it. She said, "Lee, what you've written isn't true, and if you
go ahead and send this letter, I'll have to send my own contradicting you."
It was a tough moment. That night Marion had crossed the house to Lee's

room, had gotten into bed with him, had snuggled up close. "Honey, I
love you deeply," she'd said. Lee was turned in the other direction and
made no sound. One of his children has since told me that you'll do almost
anything to avoid Lee's silence at moments like that. "He will turn absolutely cold and shut himself off from you," this Wolcott child told me, who
asked me just to put it down like that: "Wolcott child."

Anyway, Marion talked that night to the back of her turned husband.
"What you've written isn't the truth as I know it, sweetie. Please try to
think about what I'm saying."

Lee drafted a second and toned-down version—though still hot-
collared in parts—and this one Marion agreed to sign. She felt she had
won something, even if the something wasn't near enough. She took what
she got.

I now sat reading the second draft of the letter, which Lee had brought
to me from the other room. "Maybe you can make use of this," he said. He
had just run a copy off on his word processor.

> ... When Marion left FSA in 1942 it was understood by both of us
> that she would, sometime after the birth of the child with which she
> was then pregnant, return to work. Had she done so, our lives would
> have been very different. I, too, would have continued to work (we
> would commute together), we would not have bought the Lovetts-
> ville farm. I might have joined UNRRA and we would then have
> moved to New York City. Or, I might have—could have—joined a
> Ford Foundation project in Resource Conservation which was then
> headquartered in Washington. Where we might have gone from
> there can only be speculation, but, obviously, our careers would have
> been very different—for better or worse! But it did not happen that
> way for the simple reason that competent help was unavailable to
> care for baby Linda, three-year-old John and five-year-old Gail. It
> was not because I had opposed Marion's return to professional pho-
> tography. I did not! It was because the situation demanded that Mar-
> ion take over the care of the three children. We were at war.
> Everyone, aside from the draftees, who wanted a job could get one
> at higher pay than most had been accustomed. We tried several
> women while we were both still working and were thoroughly dis-
> pleased with their performances. The "situation" was in control....
> Never, and I mean NEVER, did Marion indicate any desire to return

to photography as a professional. NEVER!! I cannot believe that Marion ever "swallowed her pride and her professionalism." I do not believe that Marion then realized she was a "great" or even a "significant" photographer. . . . So her photography did become more a hobby than a profession. But as "a necessity if the marriage were to survive" is, in my judgment, groundless. And that "Lee seemed to become uncomfortable when the subject of her earlier work came up" is also without foundation.

The scholar? He ended up making changes in his text, moving it more in the direction the signatories of the letter wanted. The changes he made were against his better judgments, and he felt angry at both Wolcotts afterward, but he had experienced once again the amazing force of someone's will.

Marion and Lee and I continued talking, and then after a while Lee left the house for a meeting. For some time he'd been on the board at their complex of condominiums, where his presence was always forcefully felt among his neighbors.

"You know, at one time I thought you didn't love him," I said to Marion when he was gone.

"I love him very much," she said quietly.

She mentioned a letter I had written to her a month or so earlier. We had exchanged half a dozen written communications since we had seen each other last. In one of them she had written, "Let's see—1st I would like to have been a good musician, 2nd a painter, 3rd a filmmaker, maybe a dancer, and a writer somewhere along the line—but a creative writer, prob'ly not—a learned, profound, disciplined scholarly scientist or economist—Never. Another life, another *world??*" Now, though, she was saying to me in the old singsongy and the oddly charming voice: "You put at the end of your last letter, 'Please stay alive, Marion.' Well, that came to me at just the right time. I was struggling with the death of a neighbor. She had a terrible struggle. She lived right over there. We've been helping her son and daughter sort through her belongings, dispose of them. She died of cancer, and just before she died I had a dream about her. She was my closest friend in this complex. She was reaching out her hand and saying, 'Marion, I'm leaving. Come with me.' And I hesitated in the dream and said, 'No, not yet, I can't.' And then, right after that, after my neighbor was dead, I got your letter. And you said, 'Please stay alive, Marion.' Because, you see, Paul, I don't know whether I *want* to stay alive, whether I *should* stay alive."

"But you've got to stay alive, Marion," I say. "For Lee. For your children. For your grandchildren. No, no, for yourself, that's what I really mean."

"Well, I don't know. I think sometimes he'd be better off without me. I hold him back. And . . . and he can forget better."

But this seemed to trip something in her. "What is it about an orange? Oh, yes, I know. He told me something last night I had never heard before. Last night Lee and I were peeling an orange and he said, 'You know, babe, when I was a kid, the only time all year we ever got an orange was at Christmas in our stocking. That would just be something magical.' I mean, right there, that tells you something about what kind of life he came from, doesn't it?"

At the door I asked her once again to stay alive, not to give up. "You know, in a funny way, you saved my life, Marion. I had such a narrow view of things."

"Okay," she said in that funny turned-up mouth squint of hers. "I'll try to stay alive if you will."

And we shook on it. And then we hugged on it.

AND SO WHAT IS ONE LEFT WITH? Maybe not more than this:

Artie Shaw quit blowing the horn, said he had blown enough. And Van Gogh produced 200 works in two years, an almost hysterical output; then he shot himself. And Sandy Koufax, another kind of artist, walked off the mound when the heater seemed still a thing of wonder; there are old Dodgers fans weeping over that one yet. And Gerard Manley Hopkins could produce only nineteen poems in his last nine years—"time's eunuch," he said of himself, "never to beget." And Hammett quit writing mysteries and never explained. And Bobby Fischer, no matter what else he was, was an international grand master at fifteen, a world champion at twenty-nine—and never played another tournament game of chess. And the score of Bach's *St. Matthew Passion* got employed as wallpaper. And Falconetti, a French stage actress, was unforgettable in the only film of her career, *The Passion of Joan of Arc.* And a mind-stricken Randall Jarrell, terrified he'd never regain his poetic powers, went around the house writing on hidden scraps of paper, "Believe, my heart, Believe!" And another great American poet, Robinson Jeffers, told the photographer Edward Weston, who had Parkinson's disease, "You're safe to do what you have to do." And Rimbaud, the boy poet who only changed the face of French literature? Well, he started at fifteen and he was through at twenty. In a famous letter, that mysterious little genius said that the only real subject for poetry is a self-exploration through "a systematic derangement of all the senses." Is that why he stopped? Rimbaud also wrote: "You who maintain that some animals sob sorrowfully, that the dead have dreams, try to tell the story of my downfall and my slumber. I no longer know how to speak."

In *A Room of One's Own,* Virginia Woolf writes of some shrouded women: "Genius of a sort must have existed among them, as it existed among the working classes, but certainly it never got itself onto paper. When, however, one reads of a woman possessed by the devils, or a wise woman selling herbs, or even a remarkable man who had a remarkable mother, then I think we are on the track of a lost novelist, a suppressed poet, or some Emily Brontë who dashed her brains out on the moor, crazed with the torture her gift had put her to."

What I'm trying to say, I think, is that the creative compulsion remains among the most mysterious in the dark folds of the human psyche. If we are lucky, no science will ever get to the bottom of it. Sometimes the gift explodes and sometimes it seems to dry up in the sun. All sorts of known and unknown conflicts can separate an artist from his or her work—and where the creative act comes from in the first place is anybody's great riddle.

And I'm also trying to say that history is redundant with our miserable failure to recognize and encourage and give enough support to art.

There probably can never be a fully satisfying answer in any particular case as to why a creative compulsion died, but when it occurs it almost seems as if something elemental in the universe has been lost. And yet perhaps, with the telescope turned around, one can work hard at trying to be grateful for what is, instead of lamenting for what isn't, for what might have been. What *is,* insofar as Marion Post Wolcott is concerned, are some pictures to last a lifetime, and then some. I've always known that.

What happened, I think, is this, and even as I edge toward trying to say it, summarize it, I feel a kind of self-contempt just for trying:

A rare exhausted artist, who had deep maternal yearnings and selfless impulses, married a passionate and capable and proud and astute and attractive and dominant and scared and chauvinistic man—all too much on the quick. There was a war on; the world seemed a very terrifying place to be. Why was Lee Wolcott scared? Well, for one. thing his wife was so damn beautiful. He was afraid if he let her get out of his sight he'd lose her. He had already lost a wife to something he couldn't control. There was nothing malevolent in this. It was his large insecurities, which he has always tried to hide. Scared people work hard at control. A lot of negative, repressive, authoritarian behavior must come straight out of fear. But in saying that, I should also say *I* probably would have been just as insecure, just as threatened, in fact probably the more so had I married such a stunning woman in those scared chauvinistic times.

You might say a man removed his artist-bride to a farm as one way, subliminal or other, of trying to keep the world and other artists away from her.

But I also believe some significant arrogance and hubris apply here. Lee Wolcott has almost always been the smartest guy in the room. He has always thought his way the better way, and often enough it was, especially when you were talking dollars and cents and other kinds of practicalities.

Okay. He was the wrong man for her art, but he was the right man for a lot of other things, not least the ability to provide. As someone has since suggested to me in pretty strong language, the pressures to provide for four children and a wife have sent lesser men into alcoholism, early death, and escape to Australia.

Circumstances arose. Psychologies intervened. Choices got made, not always consciously. A gifted camera artist didn't get back to her work. It's a complex story in which blame, if blame is the word, is on every side. Too much time went by, and then it was too late. The artist badly needed encouragement and support from her husband, needed him to take her by the wrists and shove her out the nearest door, and she didn't get anything close to this. Her confidence, always shaky to begin with, left her. In time she grew to feel rage about this, and yet somehow the anger and bitterness didn't consume her, didn't twist itself into a permanent ugliness. All of it happened incrementally, by sixes and sevens, like a million beads of water blemishing a stone. Which is how most things happen in our lives.

Did the artist allow it to happen in some sense? I think that could be said. It's part of the anger. Did she even wish it to happen in some sense? This might also be said. She was marrying someone who she knew— subliminally or otherwise—was going to keep her from taking risks that perhaps she didn't want to take any longer.

It was and was not *him*. It was and was not *her*. It was and was not both their histories. It was the times in which they lived. What happened between a man and woman of that time in America was interactive, to use the word of therapists. But I am not a therapist. So let me say here and be done with it that the story of Lee and Marion Wolcott seems no more, no less, than the eternal riddle of families as they seek to love and hurt and nourish one another.

I've come to see that for Lee to have tried to be anyone else than the person he was would have been swimming against too many cultural and personal tides. Which isn't to condone or to excuse; but to understand, or try to.

Once the urge came back, the artist was so conflicted about wanting to do it, and being afraid to do it, that she hid from both the world and the work. It was easier that way. It was easier for both of them to keep on the move, as naturally restless as one of them has always been. Additionally, the artist understood in unspoken ways that to try and resume—even if it could have been managed, given the shakiness of her confidence and the very real problems of child care, deteriorating health, and geographic isolation—would ultimately have meant the death of her marriage. And this was a line she couldn't cross, for many interwoven reasons. I think there was just too much psychic pain in her Jersey past to bear the thought, at least for long.

Moreover, I think Marion took a hard look backward at her own mother's life and saw the costs with which one sometimes purchases one's supposed freedom and independence. In Nan Post's case, the grass did not in fact turn out to be greener.

And anyway this woman, unlike the earlier woman, was in love with her spouse, has always been in love with him. The awful thing about love is you can't help yourself. Even or especially when it's bad love, and this wasn't bad love. Not most of the time, not by my definitions.

So a creator was entrapped. An artist didn't get a room of her own. That's part of the story. A woman who was and was not an early feminist married the "wrong" guy, yes, and then stayed with him for complex reasons, some of which I believe preceded Lee by decades; some of which I feel certain must travel all the way back to a frightened, fragile Bloomfield child who used to run home from school with her head down to avoid facing her peers.

In one sense you might say that the powerful, scared, strong-willed, dominating, and ever-handsome Lee Wolcott is guilty of little more than trying to keep a family intact. In one sense.

Would the costs have been greater for the artist the other way around—had she married, say, some neurotic, brilliant, self-absorbed fellow artist? It is idle to speculate. And yet one wants to speculate.

Does part of her anger have to do with the idea that she let down the legacy of Nan—a woman who was willing to risk everything? I've wondered that. If so, it is a thought not worthy of Marion. Because the plain truth is that Marion was never half as selfish as her mother.

I remember the time I said to one of the Wolcott children I thought Lee had been the wrong man for Marion's art. The child quickly corrected me. "He was the wrong man for her soul. And I say that to you knowing how much they loved each other."

The first time I began to sense all the impossibly jagged and contradictory parts of this, the word "cowardice" occurred to me. It about made me wince. Cowardice? Marion? Yes. For the longest while I could never seem to reconcile the woman who was so demonstrably brave on the prewar thirties road with the woman who had seemed to buckle. That's what threw it all off in my mind. For an arrogant while, I had about dismissed both of them as cowards—Lee, for thinking he couldn't survive sharing his wife with the world; Marion, for fearing she couldn't demand what she deserved and needed.

So I was right. It was her cowardice.

But I was wrong. It was her courage. It was her wisdom.

I mentioned "cowardice" one night to my own wife. "That's ridiculous," Ceil said. "Turn it around. Why is it cowardice? She was wise enough to know no one ever gets it all. She was getting good things with Lee and she was losing things with Lee and she decided to stick. She saw the lessons in her mother's life. She was wiser than her mother, not to say far more giving."

Why, yes, of course. Far from being cowardly, what I've come to see in my late awakenings is that Marion's life is testimony to an immense bravery and generosity, far greater than what she demonstrated in those three short years on the two-lanes of the Depression South. A woman saw her dilemmas, surveyed her options, then refused to subject her children to the kind of traumas she once suffered. Is there greater love? This willingness to give up a crucial part of herself for the sake of Gail and John and

Linda and Michael must always have been there inside of Marion. It's a very large part of what ultimately happened. Yet in all my talks with Marion, she never once assigned any blame to that.

For too long I was blind to a simple, profound truth: Raising good children can be a supremely creative act, too.

Marion and Lee Wolcott, by Jack Welpott, 1984

EPILOGUE

During this past year, between sessions with you (& the carry over after you've left) and what with Lee! and my children, I've been through a mini-psychoanalysis—and not always liking it, feeling it's too late, & not wanting to open up old wounds, failures and trauma. Better left buried. Now so little time left & so much to do. And—maybe—hopefully, to enjoy & NOT do—to learn, to feel & see & distill. AND—God damn it—to FILE, to sign, to discard, so I can find what I'm looking for occasionally!

—MARION POST WOLCOTT
from a letter to the author, 1988

I SAW THEM MANY TIMES in the next few years. We grew a lot more comfortable in each other's presence, and I kept discovering things I didn't know, had never considered, about Marion and her never-to-be-underestimated husband. Sometimes, as the shroud came off, the revelations were comic, though more often they were fragmentary. I once was visiting at their home when Marion brought out an ornate and curious-shaped wooden box with gold hinges. It was from India. She was rummaging around inside it for a snapshot when she picked up a small dark plastic instrument. It almost looked like something you'd roll film on.

"What the hell is this thing?" she said.

"It's a marijuana roller, babe, remember?" Lee said.

"Oh, yes," she said. "Lee and I got into grass for a while there in Mendocino."

Another time Marion and I were sitting at the dining room table. Lee was somewhere in the back of the house. Stoking my nerve, I whispered, "You were in the Party, weren't you?"

"Yes," she whispered back, starting to get up and go into the kitchen.

"When? From Group Theatre?"

"I'm not telling you."

"I figured you had to be, you know. You kept dropping hints."

"It's not that I've ever been afraid of saying it in terms of myself," she said. "It's just that I've always worried about how it might reverberate for my kids or grandkids. These are still scary times we live in. Anybody who lived through McCarthyism ..." She didn't finish. I didn't bring it up again, though on another occasion she told me—or at least hinted very strongly—that Nan had briefly been in the Party, too. And I was also able to get a pretty strong indication of that from another source.

On the day I asked her about the Communist Party, Marion took out a yellow Post-It notepad and wrote: "Rage ... will ... manipulation ... his anger." The words startled me. They started out on the notepad very small but got larger as she went. She tore off the sheet and wadded it and threw it in the wastebasket behind her. Soon after, Lee appeared with some sandwiches.

"Food, ugh," Marion said.

And yet ... I remember sitting another day at that same table off the kitchen and watching Lee "spot" some of her pictures. He had magnifying glasses strapped to his head, like a jeweler. In his sure hand was a tiny brush and at his elbow was clear fluid in a plastic bowl. He spent hours that afternoon carefully removing imperfections from some newly printed Wolcott FSA pictures. He was a man dedicated to his task.

"You're putting it on too thick, sweetheart," she lightly nagged.

"Do you want to do it, babe?" There was no edge in these words at all.

It made me happy that the lens on the Wolcott rediscovery camera seemed to be getting wider and wider. A film crew from "The Today Show" came to Santa Barbara and followed the two Wolcotts around their home. "It was impossible to do this and be the kind of mother I wished to be," Marion told the female interviewer, who was very gentle and yet wanted somehow to get at the nagging question of the stopping. "I don't feel I made the wrong choices," the interviewee said. Later in the interview she told a story about how Cornell Capa of the International Center of Photography came to meet her and asked what the secret of her youth was. She said it was "love, good sex, and yogurt."

A women's group in Los Angeles presented Marion its annual Vesta Award. F. Jack Hurley's handsome book about her work came out from a university press. The Art Institute of Chicago gave her an impressive show. ("Post Wolcott had an unerring eye for the individual experience that could symbolize the larger storm," the Chicago *Tribune* said.) Marion starred in a photography symposium at Stanford University. Curators at the International Center of Photography wrote to her to say that, yes, chances looked good for a Wolcott show in New York sometime in 1990. The show opened in the spring of '90 and to generally good notices and crowds. *The New Yorker* ran a thumb-cut drawing of the lost photographer, wearing an old plaid shirt, chin propped on her hands, hair tousled. It was from Mendocino days.

And yet . . . a year earlier, when the National Gallery of Art in Washington put on a huge cross-country exhibition titled "On the Art of Fixing a Shadow: 150 Years of Photography," Marion Post Wolcott wasn't in it, not even her name.

All during this time, Marion kept sending me hilarious letters, though there was something hurting in every one of them. In one letter she included a clipping about a man who said he had "to keep on writing, otherwise I'm afraid it will go away." In the margins she had written: "Isn't this what we were talking about—the need for continuity, a block of time—without constant distractions & other demands?" In a different color ink, she had added on: "And conflicts."

In another letter she wrote: "There are mockingbirds, finches, woodpeckers, shrieking crows, towhees & all-season sparrows to waken me too early, but painlessly, or with less pain." A few pages later, she said: "Cracking up—sometimes grim, trying to stick the various parts of this old body back together again, or locating new parts. My hip is worse but asthma better. . . . If I have any small thing in my hand—earrings, earplug, whatever, I'm just as liable to automatically toss it into my mouth & swallow. Have to watch it!!" Toward the end, she described a reception she and Lee had attended: "Lee, under protest, wore his dark silk suit with tux shirt w. gold & turquoise studs that I'd had made for him in Iran, & his tux black bow tie. He even bought a new pair of black shoes—on sale. Can you believe it? He straightened up, & did look elegant & played the part of course—and loved it!"

Another letter in which she described herself as ". . . desolate, troubled, anxious & sad." A few pages later, talking of her piled-high bedroom, she said, "I've decided I must have been part Anasazi—1100–1300 A.D. & sometimes lived in a pit house underground."

In another she had said, "Damn—don't like old age—teeth falling apart again, maybe another root canal—When you discover how to get more sleep, energy, zip, piss-and-vinegar, let *me* know—It's been hot here, & smoke from forest fires—Fondly—Marion."

She described the fog rolling in off the ocean: "It's an eerie grey, glowing a little on the edges as it flows across the low sunlite. Smooth—not like lumps & humps of clouds. And not like the wisps that claw at the land & bank in strips along the horizon above & beyond the ocean in Mendocino."

In one letter she included some clippings from the local newspaper; most of them were about religion, though one concerned an Indian movie, *Powaqqatsi,* she urged me to see. One of the religion clips bore the headline PLATES PASSED FOR PAPAL VISIT, over the top of which she had scribbled, "Incredible/Disgusting." Another bore the headline BISHOPS DIVIDED OVER CONDOM ISSUE, over the top of which she had scribbled, "Right on—good that a few don't knuckle under & can see some light in the darkness!"

From another letter, regarding an argument with Lee about a certain sexual revelation from her youth: "What era? What century? Could the almost 5 yr. difference in our ages account for the difference in our perception, imagery, of life in the 20's & early 30's? True, he was a newspaper business man—my friends & acquaintances in the arts & education—& on the fringe of N.Y.C. bohemia. . . . I'm sure you're learning who we are and

I presume deciding what makes us tick & tock, & wondering, maybe, how two people still loving each other after a 47 yr. marriage can be so vulnerable—insecure? threatened?"

From another letter, regarding her daughter Linda and a man Linda was embarking on a professional relationship with: "God I hope [he] doesn't let her down. I'll cut off his balls if he does."

Same letter, trying to solve the unsolvable: "A question I still have—why didn't I disregard opposition & difficulties & *somehow* insist, just *go* myself, if not with G., to a therapist?"

Two pages over: "Gold is down. Coffee is downer. Decaf is OUT—L-Tryptophan KILLS you."

Last page: "Lee is 84 today—amazingly fit, no aches or pains, sleeps more, an enviable 'napper' which refreshes, reads a lot, writes, occasional meetings at museum. . . . I want Supreme Order of the Chrysanthemum & *at least* 2 million dollars so we can have a last fling."

In every dispatch she let me know what her kids and grandkids but most especially what Lee was up to, and there was always small marvel in it. Lee was working out in a gym at their condo unit; he was studying Epictetus in an adult education class; he was picketing on the side of a pro-choice group at the Santa Barbara Cottage Hospital. To the bottom of one of these letters, Lee himself wrote: "Hi. Hope you're ok. I keep on as chief of staff here."

An earlier letter from Marion (almost none of them has a date, so as I inspect them now I'm feeling shaky about time) started off: "Hi—I looked in the mirror this morning & said—'I should be on the endangered species list'—Lee, 'You already are, I'm sure.' Or how about I look like one of those birds they rescued/revived from the Valdez oil spill slick. That too. No doubt I'm NOT aging gracefully—Nor would oil of olay & collagen do it." I was laughing, but then I wasn't laughing.

I'm *So* tired so much of the time, & feel trapped, locked in, immobile, too dependent, unable to make logical *wise* decisions, important ones, & not willing to let others make them for me. Resisting. And there seem to be too many of them all at once. I'm trying to deal with (& schedule) too many different things—Health—several aspects—arthritis & legs, scans (spinal) & x rays say no surgery will help now & too risky—started acupuncture for pain, etc.—but had to quit for operation on toe. Then 3 operations to excise cancer, deeper & more extensive than expected, on & in NOSE—which has healed over but soon (in week or two) must have a "dermabrasion job" done on it, which should eventually smooth out a little, the gullies & soil erosion! It now, across the top below the bridge, & 1 side, looks like a skateboarder's track, & 1 nostril still mashed & crooked—"will improve in 3 or 4 mo.!" The Karl Malden look. My next session—a long one—with my new dentist—is long overdue—postponed by NOSE—5 teeth to be pulled, on same day, then in about 5 weeks a new lower bridge & upper partial plus 2 teeth crowned—totaling $10,000-ish. It's becoming too expensive to maintain this bitch in the style to which she's become accustomed.

I managed to coordinate one of my Santa Barbara visits with an opening of Marion's work. When I called from Washington to ask if it was okay if I came out again, I said, "How have you been feeling?"

"I'm sort of afraid to tell you," she said.

"I'm saying this humorously, you know, but you'd better not be thinking about dying on me."

"But I do. I can't help it. I keep planning it, especially in the middle of the night."

She changed the subject to her husband. He had lately experienced some TIA's—Transient Ischemic Attacks. They are tiny, almost invisible, strokes. They didn't seem to be slowing him up any, she said. But then, too, there was a prostrate problem she was concerned about.

When I came up the sidewalk she was standing outside her front door, looking up into a tree. She spotted me from about twenty yards off but didn't move her gaze from the tree. She reached out for my arm. "Shhh," she whispered. "She's making a nest. Can you see her? Look, no, not over there, silly. Over here. See, she's making a nest for her babies."

Lee had had an upset stomach that particular morning. "It's the poison I've been slipping the old boy," she said with a delicious grin.

We had lunch and sat around and talked and then I followed them downtown to the museum. The back of her head looked so small in the passenger seat of their new car. Once he was in the parking lot, Lee seemed impatient to get into the museum—why were the two of us being so poky? The show's official opening wasn't until the following day; this was a preview. He was very anxious to see how his wife's pictures had been spaced, what the lighting was like. He'd been paying attention to these details for several weeks, nagging the curators into giving their very best effort. He had on a kelly-green sweater, Marion was in a blue sweat suit with elastic ankle cuffs. Over the top of the sweatsuit she wore a light-weight mountain parka, as if she were going up Mount Shasta later in the day. She made her way along behind us with a black-knobbed cane.

She went on her own when we got inside. Lee and I inspected the pictures (he was reasonably content with how they'd hung the show), and then the two of us stood talking in a hallway at a docent's desk. He was leaning forward, resting his elbows on a wooden partition. His hands were clasped, and for the first time I noticed how blunt and scarred his fingers were, especially the nails. They were the blunt hands and rough nails of an old farmer, long off the farm. Suddenly I realized how much I cared for him.

For reasons I don't entirely understand, I took a card out of a book I was carrying under my arm. Typed on the card was this quote from William James: "As for me, my bed is made: I am against bigness and greatness in all their forms, and with the invisible molecular moral forces that work from individual to individual, stealing in through the crannies of the world like so many soft rootlets, or like the capillary oozing of water, and yet rending the hardest monuments of man's pride, if you give them time."

I read it aloud to Lee as we stood at the docent's desk and as people passed among his wife's photographs.

"I should accept that," he said. "You see, I'd like to write a history of the twentieth century. I'd like to write it right now. Do you think it's too late for me to try? When you think about it, Paul, I've seen almost the entire century. I was born in o-five. The airplane is two years old. Einstein's relativity comes later that year. The automobile is barely born, it's there of course. There aren't any roads to speak of. People used to jack their cars up in the garage for the winter—to take the heat off the tires. There wasn't a paved street in my hometown of Red Bank. I can remember women's high-top button shoes halfway up their calf, and you needed a buttonhook to get them on right. I can remember when we moved into our new house—I must have been nine—and found we had electric lights. It was so novel. I can still see my father going up to the light fixture and trying to light his cigarette. He thought it was a real fire. All these things, so many changes in one lifetime. I think of what Henry Adams said in that great book, *The Education of Henry Adams.* Have you read it?

I've read it several times and intend to go back to read it again very soon. You know, Adams thought a man shouldn't spend more than six years in an occupation, lest he go stale. I think that must have influenced me a lot. But anyway he said that by his calculations the amount of energy the United States consumes tends to double every decade. Think of that! And didn't I just read somewhere that there are more scientists alive now than have ever lived in the history of the world? That's what I mean. I've seen the entire century double and triple over itself so many times. Do you think I could do it?"

I said I supposed he could do about anything.

We talked about Brown University in the twenties. "I think it cost two hundred dollars a year, a monumental sum for my family. I went in the fall of twenty-three. There was no scarcity of jobs. I'm not sure I learned that much. I had two hundred when I went in, two hundred when I came out. I came out and started working and never really stopped. Work was one thing I always did well in my life."

Marion wandered up. She had just been to the museum's gift shop. "See the show, sweetheart?" Lee said.

"I kind of spied around. There were two people in the elevator. One said he liked those pictures by 'that Wolcott lady,' sort of reminded him of 'folk art.'"

"Folk art," Lee said. "Haven't heard that one before."

"That's about all he said, too. I just stood there, kind of humming to myself, smiling at the floor. The other one, who was even younger, said, 'Mmm, boy, those pictures were taken way before I was born. They remind me of those Uncle Remus days.'"

While she was in the gift shop a young woman had come up and asked her to sign a reproduction print. "I wonder how she knew who I was—I certainly wasn't letting on this was me. And then of course you know what's coming next. She said she was trying to be a photographer, and did I have any ideas how she could get real good at it. Ha."

Lee said, perfectly serious: "Well, the important thing of course is that she has the interest. That's got to be sustained. Maybe she could enroll in some night course or something. Did you suggest that to her?"

Outside, in front of the museum, there was a grassy space, and on it some Indian teenagers had set up conga drums and were having themselves an impromptu and ear-splitting concert in the Saturday sun. Lee and I walked quickly past, but the ancient photog stopped, leaned on her black-knobbed cane, surveyed.

"Babe, do you *mind!*" Lee said. "They'll charge us another hour at the lot."

"Be quiet!" she said. "I'm framing a picture. I may start up my career all over again right this minute."

HER HEALTH CONTINUED TO DECLINE. At Christmastime 1989, Lee sent me a note that said, "Seems we have galloped through another year at very high speed. Our greatest triumph has been survival. Seemingly in good shape and facing a New Year with some confidence."

Then, on a February afternoon in 1990, Lee called and said Marion was in the hospital. She'd been getting very dizzy. "She's always been prone to seasickness," he said, rushing the words, his voice uncharacteristically high. "I've tried it two or three times myself—she's always the first to want to come back to shore when we've gone sailing."

A week later, they had the diagnosis: Marion had malignant tumors in both her brain and her lung. The lung cancer was inoperable, though maybe they could get some of the brain tumor out and give her eight or nine months of decent time.

She lingered in a kind of half-life and then a quarter-life and then almost no life at all through most of the year. The Wolcott children would tell me in phone calls that their father was being extraordinarily caring, and indeed I got to see some of it for myself. Even when the nurse was in the house, Lee didn't like leaving Marion's side for more than about an hour. He tried to do most of the tending, most of the feeding, most of the linen-changing, most of the turning and lifting, even though it was hurting his back. Twice I saw her. The first time, she was out of bed, using an aluminum walker. Things didn't seem so bad, even though it was clear she was dying. A few days earlier she had mailed a self-portrait cartoon to Washington so I would know what the chemotherapy treatments had done to her hair. The cartoon showed somebody with huge ears and little bristles on a cueball noggin. "So you think you *really* want to come for a visit!" she had written underneath. Linda had bought her a new silky Oriental nightgown, and she was wearing it when I walked in. To the top of her absurd gray peach fuzz, she had affixed a small lovely blue ribbon. Her wristwatch was halfway up her waxy arm. What did she weigh—eighty pounds?

"I can't swallow," she said to me. "It's so hard to eat. And stuff I like to eat I don't like anymore." Her arms were out, her voice was desperate.

The last time I saw her, ten days before she died, Marion was a ghost-white figure in a steel hospital bed that had been brought into the house. Mostly, I just sat beside her that November afternoon and evening, holding her fine old hand. "Are you working with your editor?" she whispered. I nodded. If nearly everything else seemed gone, her hearing was still there. She lifted her finger to the opened window. "Those little birds, they're fighting over a nut." After a while I went out into the front room to chat with Lee. It was getting dark, but still he didn't turn on any lights. "How am I going to make it?" he said. I didn't try to answer. We drifted to talk about the years on the Virginia farms. When I went back into Marion's bedroom, she took hold of my hand again. "He's getting his dates mixed up," she said, each word coming out so slow. "How are you going to straighten him out?" I think she had heard almost everything we'd said in the other room.

Marion Post Wolcott died at 4:30 a.m. on November 24, 1990. All her family had got there by the end. In the last few days she'd stopped taking any liquid—Lee and his daughter Linda were using a syringe and trying to force it gently in drop by drop. They were also using a syringe to give her liquid morphine.

The night before Thanksgiving, November 21, which happened to be Lee's eighty-fifth birthday, Marion's youngest child, Michael, arrived from the Bay Area. "I love you," she said to Michael. It was her last complete sentence.

For the next three days, she kept saying the word "No." She said it over and over.

It is overwhelmingly sad to me that she died having never once discussed her dying in any specific way with her husband or her children. Lee would try to bring it up. "Is there anything you want to discuss, sweetheart?"

"Yes," she'd say.

"What?"

"I can't tell you."

About four o'clock in the morning on the twenty-fourth, her stepson, John, was asleep on the sofa between Marion and Lee's rooms. John was brought awake by strange sounds coming from his mother's throat. The stepson went across the dark into his father's room. Lee rose and went to Marion's side and stood over her and heard the awful sounds for himself.

He knew she was going. What was there to do? He stood there for several minutes, returned to his own room at the back of the house, couldn't stay there, went back to Marion. "Her head was to one side," he later told me. "Her eyes were partially closed. She seemed peaceful."

The body was cremated. There were no obituaries in either the *New York Times* or the Los Angeles *Times* or even in my own paper, the Washington *Post,* for which I am ashamed and hold myself responsible. Oddly, a newspaper in England, the *Independent,* wrote a wonderful obituary, and there were several appreciations in the Santa Barbara paper and elsewhere. But it was a death, hidden, that was like a life, hidden.

I saw Lee in California several months later. The house seemed terribly empty. He was going to sell it, he said, move to San Francisco to be with his daughter, Linda, who'd relocated up there from Santa Barbara. He fixed lunch and then we drove downtown to the art museum to see a small memorial they'd hung in his wife's honor. On a gray card, next to a lovely photograph of Marion, was this:

IN REMEMBRANCE 1910-1990

> Marion Post Wolcott—photographer, mentor, philanthropist, wife, mother—contributed both to her art and her community throughout her life. In the late 1930s she joined the Farm Security Administration, along with other noted photographers, and traveled throughout the South, a woman alone, to capture the complexities of life in the Great Depression. She went from speakeasies to shanty dwellings of the poor, to the beach, where a well-heeled family picnicked beside their car, to present with unerring honesty the picture of the times.

"I dream about her, Paul," Lee told me as we stood reading together.
"You do?"
"Sure."
"And she's real?"
"Oh, very real. And very much alive."

FINAL TAKES

Satterfield tobacco warehouse, Liberty Cafe, Durham,
North Carolina, 1939

*Cars parked along the highway near the Duke University
stadium during the football game between Duke University and the University of North Carolina, Durham,
North Carolina, 1939*

Waiting for strikebreakers (scabs) to come out of the
copper mines, Ducktown, Tennessee, 1939

Coal miner waiting for ride. Each miner pays twenty-five
cents a week to owner of car, Caples, West Virginia, 1938

Mexican miner and child, Bertha Hill, Scotts Run, West Virginia, 1938

Swimming in the fountain across from Union Station,
Washington, D.C., 1938

Lineup of migrant vegetable pickers getting paid off in field, near Belle Glade, Florida, 1939

A Spanish muskrat trapper in the doorway of his marsh home, Delacroix Island, St. Bernard Parish, Louisiana, 1941

A Spanish muskrat trapper telling about the trappers' war,
the long fight and difficulties between trappers and the
company men, Delacroix Island, St. Bernard Parish,
Louisiana, 1941

Sunset Village, FSA project for defense workers, Radford,
Virginia, 1941

Grateful acknowledgment is made to the following for permission to reprint preexisting material:

Cambridge University Press: Excerpt from *The Collected Letters of Joseph Conrad, 1898–1902,* Vol. 2. Cambridge University Press, New York, 1986. Reprinted by permission.

Farrar, Straus, and Giroux, Inc.: Excerpt from *Styles of Radical Will* by Susan Sontag. Copyright © 1969 by Susan Sontag. Reprinted by permission.

The New York Times: Excerpt from "Inspired by Despair" by Louis Merrand (January 29, 1987). Copyright © 1987 by The New York Times Company. Reprinted by permission.

W. W. Norton & Company, Inc.: Excerpt from "December 24 and George McBride Is Dead," from *Making Certain It Goes On, The Collected Poems of Richard Hugo.* Copyright © 1984 by The Estate of Richard Hugo. Reprinted by permission.

Pantheon Books: Excerpt from *Bearing Witness* by Michael Lesy. Copyright © 1982 by Michael Lesy. Reprinted by permission of Pantheon Books, a division of Random House, Inc.

Paul Strand Archive: Excerpt from Paul Strand's letter of June 20, 1938, to Roy Stryker. Copyright © Aperture Foundation, Inc., Paul Strand Archive. Reprinted by permission.

A NOTE ABOUT THE AUTHOR

PAUL HENDRICKSON IS A STAFF WRITER ON THE WASHINGTON *POST*. HE WAS BORN IN
CALIFORNIA BUT GREW UP IN THE MIDWEST AND IN A CATHOLIC SEMINARY IN THE
SOUTH, WHERE HE TRAINED SEVEN YEARS FOR THE MISSIONARY PRIESTHOOD. TWO
DECADES LATER THIS BECAME THE SUBJECT OF HIS FIRST BOOK, *SEMINARY: A SEARCH*.
HE HAS WON SEVERAL PENNY-MISSOURI FEATURE WRITING AWARDS; *PLAYBOY*'S NON-
FICTION PRIZE FOR 1982; AND WRITING AND RESEARCH FELLOWSHIPS FROM THE ALI-
CIA PATTERSON AND LYNDHURST FOUNDATIONS. HE LIVES WITH HIS WIFE AND TWO
YOUNG SONS IN TAKOMA PARK, MARYLAND.

A NOTE ON THE TYPE

THIS BOOK WAS SET IN A DIGITIZED VERSION OF GRANJON, A TYPE NAMED IN COMPLI-
MENT TO ROBERT GRANJON, A TYPE CUTTER AND PRINTER ACTIVE, IN ANTWERP,
LYONS, ROME, AND PARIS, FROM 1523 TO 1590. GRANJON, THE BOLDEST AND THE MOST
ORIGINAL DESIGNER OF HIS TIME, WAS ONE OF THE FIRST TO PRACTICE THE TRADE OF
TYPE FOUNDER APART FROM THAT OF PRINTER.
LINOTYPE GRANJON WAS DESIGNED BY GEORGE W. JONES, WHO BASED HIS DRAWINGS
ON A FACE USED BY CLAUDE GARAMOND (C. 1480–1561) IN HIS BEAUTIFUL FRENCH
BOOKS. GRANJON MORE CLOSELY RESEMBLES GARAMOND'S OWN TYPE THAN DOES ANY
OF THE VARIOUS MODERN FACES THAT BEAR HIS NAME.

COMPOSED BY GRAPHIC COMPOSITION, INC., ATHENS, GEORGIA
PRINTED AND BOUND BY HALLIDAY LITHOGRAPHERS, WEST HANOVER, MASSACHUSETTS
DESIGNED BY IRIS WEINSTEIN